DIAGNOSTIC AND PLACEMENT GUIDE

Be A Better
READER

GLOBE FEARON
Pearson Learning Group

Diagnostic and Placement Guide Revised Edition

REVIEWERS

John Edwin Cowen, Ed. D.
Reading Specialist
Peter Sammartino School of Education
Fairleigh Dickinson University

Virginia McCarthy
Assistant Principal, English
John Bowne High School
Flushing, New York

Art and Design: Tricia Battipede, Robert Dobaczewski, Elizabeth Witmer
Editorial: Brian Hawkes, Eleanor Ripp, Jennifer M. Watts
Manufacturing: Michele Uhl
Production: Laura Benford-Sullivan, Jeffrey Engel
Publishing Operations: Jennifer Van Der Heide

Photographs:
Cover: *Background:* ©Robert Karpa/Masterfile. *l.:* Per-Eric Berglund/The Image Bank. *m.l.:* Steve Cole/PhotoDisc, inc. *m.r.:* Jeffrey Coolidge/The Image Bank. *r.:* Coneyl Jay/Stone.

ISBN 0-130-23885-6

Printed in the United States of America

2 3 4 5 6 7 8 9 10   05 04 03

1-800-321-3106
www.pearsonlearning.com

CONTENTS

About the *Be A Better Reader* Program, Starting Out and Levels A–G

Benefits of
Be A Better Reader

- Manageability
- Flexibility
- Student Independence
- Assessment Options

Dr. Nila Banton Smith, author of *Be A Better Reader*, made many contributions to the teaching of reading. She was among the first to recognize the specialized reading skills that students need to read content-area texts. For this reason, *Be A Better Reader* offers high-interest, content-area reading in literature, social studies, science, and math. Within each of these content areas, content-specific reading skills are introduced and reinforced. For more on these content-specific reading skills, see the Skills Chart on pages 13–14.

The eight levels of *Be A Better Reader* (Starting Out and Levels A–G) correspond to reading levels 3–10. Each level introduces key reading, comprehension, and study skills and allows students to practice and apply these skills. Similar in design and format, the texts can be used in a variety of classroom settings and with students working below level, on level, or above level.

Features of the Student Editions

Each thematic unit of *Be A Better Reader* contains
- a literature selection.
- a social studies selection.
- a science selection.
- a mathematics selection.
- several brief skill lessons that reinforce important phonics skills (in Levels A–C), comprehension skills, and study skills.
- a real-life or school-to-work skill.

The program's emphasis on vocabulary is an important key to its success. Students learn vocabulary words before they read. Students are also given different types of context clues to increase their vocabulary power.

The emphasis on content reading is another proven strength of *Be A Better Reader*. Students gain practice in reading social studies, science, and mathematics, and the high-interest selections themselves enhance and reinforce students' learning.

After reading each selection, students have the opportunity to recall and interpret the information they have read. They also focus on applying the skills of each lesson. The Reading-Writing Connection gives students the opportunity to connect the reading skills they learn to writing tasks.

Each unit of *Be A Better Reader* ends with a brief lesson on a real-life or school-to-work skill, including reading schedules and using maps.

Features of the Annotated Teacher's Editions

Each Annotated Teacher's Edition of *Be A Better Reader* includes
- complete lesson plans for every lesson.
- Professional Development articles (including ESL/ELL support).
- reproducible graphic organizers.
- a series of four assessment tests.
- a Pacing Chart.
- a Scope and Sequence of Skills.
- answers to all of the questions in the Student Edition.

Introduction to the *Diagnostic and Placement Guide*

The *Be A Better Reader* series has been a staple of reading instruction for more than 30 years. The series is composed of eight Student Editions (reading levels 3–10). Each Student Edition is accompanied by an Annotated Teacher's Edition.

The *Be A Better Reader Diagnostic and Placement Guide* was created to meet the needs of classroom teachers. It will help you

- **place** students in the appropriate instructional level of *Be A Better Reader*.
- **diagnose** students who require practice in specific reading skills.
- **assess** students' competency when reading in the major content areas.

Contents of the *Diagnostic and Placement Guide*

The *Diagnostic and Placement Guide* contains the following features:

- **Student Placement at the Instructional Level** and **Student Diagnosis** sections explain how to administer the tests, describe the placement philosophy of the *Diagnostic and Placement Guide*, and provide a scoring rubric.
- A **Placement Test** helps you place your students in the appropriate instructional level of *Be A Better Reader*.
- Eight **Diagnostic Tests** correspond to Starting Out and Levels A–G of *Be A Better Reader*.
- **Student Answer Sheets** are provided for students to record their answers.
- **Answer Keys** correlate test questions to the corresponding skills and lessons in *Be A Better Reader*. You can use the Answer Keys to pinpoint your students' skill needs.
- **Skills Chart** lists the skills that are taught in *Be A Better Reader* and the level of the program in which they are covered.
- Ideas for improving reading proficiency allows you to reinforce and enrich your students' reading experience.

Five Uses of the *Diagnostic and Placement Guide*

1. Placement at the Appropriate Instructional Level

The *Diagnostic and Placement Guide* contains a placement test to determine students' instructional level. Placement test results will indicate the appropriate level of *Be A Better Reader* in which to place your students. You can use the Placement Test to assign students directly to the appropriate level of *Be A Better Reader* or to choose the correct Diagnostic Test to administer to your students for further evaluation. (See Student Placement at the Instructional Level on page 7.)

Be A Better Reader

Level Test	Reading Level
Starting Out	3rd Grade
Level A	4th grade
Level B	5th grade
Level C	6th grade
Level D	7th grade
Level E	8th grade
Level F	9th grade
Level G	10th grade

2. Reading Level Diagnosis

The *Diagnostic and Placement Guide* contains a Diagnostic Test to accompany each level of *Be A Better Reader* (Starting Out and Levels A–G). The Diagnostic Tests can be used to confirm Placement Test results. (Students should be placed at their instructional reading level.) The reading levels of the selections and the questions in the Assessment Tests have been matched to the corresponding level in the *Be A Better Reader* series. For this reason, a student's performance on a test is a good guide for placement in the program. (See Student Diagnosis on page 9.)

3. Skill Assessment

Another use for the *Diagnostic and Placement Guide* is to determine reading skills that require further practice, such as finding the main idea, comparing and contrasting, sequencing, and so on. The Answer Key for each Diagnostic Test correlates each tested skill with the lesson or lessons in the corresponding level of *Be A Better Reader* that develop this skill. Students can then be assigned or reassigned to specific lessons for additional skill practice.

4. Assessment of Content-Area Reading

The Diagnostic Tests are well suited to testing reading ability in particular content areas. Each of the tests includes four sections that assess reading skills in the four content areas—literature, social studies, science, and mathematics. You can effectively and efficiently determine a student's competency in reading in these content areas. In addition, the tests include word attack and study skills questions, such as using a dictionary entry and using an almanac. By reviewing test results, you can pinpoint student weaknesses that may need further remediation.

5. Pretesting and Posttesting

Each *Be A Better Reader Annotated Teacher's Edition* also contains a reproducible Assessment Test. With the tests provided in the *Diagnostic and Placement Guide*, you now have two tests for each level of *Be A Better Reader*. You can use the test in this guide as a pretest to place your students in the appropriate level of *Be A Better Reader*. Then, when your students have finished a *Be A Better Reader* level, you can administer the Assessment Test in the *Be A Better Reader Annotated Teacher's Edition* as a posttest for that level.

Student Placement at the Instructional Level

"How should I determine proper placement for my students?" The Placement Test is a tool that will help place your students in the level of *Be A Better Reader* that will maximize their learning potential.

In addition to the Placement Test, it is important to use some or all of the following criteria to help you either place students at the proper level of *Be A Better Reader* or choose the proper *Be A Better Reader* Diagnostic Test:

- your students' report card grades
- results of standardized reading tests your students have taken
- your own personal observations
- comments from your students' previous teachers

Introducing the Placement Test

The Placement Test contains seven parts, each corresponding to a reading level in *Be A Better Reader*. For example, Part 1 is at the fourth-grade reading level (Level A). Part 2 is at the fifth-grade reading level (Level B), and so on. Each part of the Placement Test contains a fiction and a nonfiction reading selection. These selections are accompanied by four questions that test students' understanding of the selection. The questions test the following skills in the order shown:

Question 1: finding the main idea

Question 2: recalling details

Question 3: making inferences

Question 4: understanding vocabulary

Administering the Placement Test

The reproducible Placement Test is one test that spans the fourth- through tenth-grade reading levels. It should take most students one class period to complete. The test was designed to be given in its entirety. However, you do not have to administer all seven parts in one sitting. You may wish to give one part at a time, and then grade the results before administering the next part.

In addition to reproducing the Placement Test for the class, make copies of the Student Answer Sheet on page 139. Students record their answers by filling in the bubbles on the Student Answer Sheet. The Answer Key on page 140 shows the correct bubbles filled in.

Interpreting the Placement Test Results

Use the Answer Key on page 140 to help you score the Placement Test. You will notice that the Answer Key is divided into sections that correspond to the reading levels of *Be A Better Reader*. Pay particular attention to the point at which your students begin to make errors. When students make two or more errors at a reading level, they have reached the point at which they do not understand the reading selections. Students should be placed in the *Be A Better Reader* level preceding the level at which they made two or more errors. (See the table on the right.) You may also want to administer the Diagnostic Test

Be A Better Reader Placement Guide

If a student makes 2 or more errors in:	Place the student in:
Part 1	Starting Out
Part 2	Level A
Part 3	Level B
Part 4	Level C
Part 5	Level D
Part 6	Level E
Part 7	Level F

preceding that level to confirm their placement. The Diagnostic Test is more comprehensive and will allow you to diagnose skill and content-area needs.

You may disagree with the results of the Placement Test. In these cases, consider administering the first 25 questions of the Diagnostic Test that you feel is most appropriate. You can use the results of this section to help you determine if the student has been placed at the proper *Be A Better Reader* level.

The following diagram outlines two suggested placement paths.

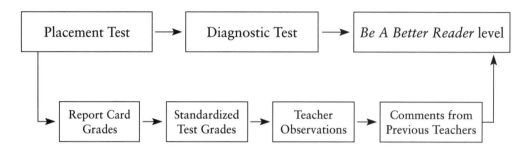

Placement Test Profiles

Here are two different test profiles.

Profile 1: Ms. Jolin has a new student in her seventh-grade class who seems to have difficulty completing his reading assignments. The student's standardized test scores indicate that he is reading at the fifth-grade reading level. The Placement Test results also place the student at the fifth-grade reading level, reinforcing the standardized test results. Ms. Jolin places her student into *Be A Better Reader* Level B, the fifth-grade reading level text.

Profile 2: Mr. Barnes has one student in his ninth-grade class who is struggling with her reading assignments. He has no information to help him assess his student's reading level. He administers the Placement Test. He notices that the student makes no mistakes on Part 1, one mistake on Part 2, one mistake on Part 3, two mistakes on Part 4, and five mistakes on Part 5. Based on these results, Mr. Barnes determines that the student reads below the eighth-grade level, but the student's exact reading level is unclear. He decides to administer the Level C Diagnostic Test to obtain additional information on the student's instructional reading level.

Student Diagnosis

"How can I make sure I've placed my student in the proper level of *Be A Better Reader*?" and "How can I diagnose the skills or content areas my students need to work on?" The Diagnostic Tests will help answer both of these questions.

Introducing the Diagnostic Tests

Each of the eight Diagnostic Tests has the same easy-to-use format.

- Test 1: Literature: The literature section includes a short fiction selection followed by 25 questions. These questions test literature skills, including recognizing plot, character, and setting.

- Test 2: Social Studies: The social studies section includes a short social studies selection followed by 25 questions. These questions test reading skills, such as recognizing cause-and-effect relationships, understanding sequence of events, and making comparisons and contrasts.

- Test 3: Science: The science section includes a short science selection followed by 25 questions. These questions test reading skills, such as understanding classifying, reading a technical explanation, and understanding detailed statements of fact. In addition, this section includes related math questions in the form of word problems.

- Test 4: Word Attack and Study Skills: This section includes 25 questions that test a variety of reading skills, including reading a dictionary entry, using an index, and understanding prefixes and suffixes.

Administering the Diagnostic Tests

Each Level Test contains 100 questions. The variety of questions will help you assess your students' instructional level across the content areas. Giving the entire test will help you place your students appropriately and reliably.

You might feel that a 100-question test is too long to administer in one sitting. If this is the case, administer Parts 1 and 2 in one sitting and Parts 3 and 4 at a later time.

In order to diagnose your students' needs better, the observation of oral reading may be extremely helpful and can ensure proper placement. Included on the rubric on the next page are characteristics your students may display during oral reading.

Interpreting the Diagnostic Test Results

Use the Answer Keys on pages 142–157 to help you score the Diagnostic Tests. There are two ways to interpret the Diagnostic Test results.

- If you are using the Diagnostic Test to confirm your students' placement into a *Be A Better Reader* level, use the scoring rubric on page 11. Students should be placed at their instructional level.

- If you are using the Diagnostic Test to diagnose your students' skill needs, the coded Answer Key will provide you with this information. In addition to having the answers to the questions, the Answer Key provides you with the skills being tested by the questions and tells you where the skills are taught at that level of *Be A Better Reader*. By analyzing where your students have answered questions incorrectly, you can diagnose their skill needs. Once you have diagnosed skill needs, you can group students for instruction on particular skills.

Finding Your Students' Instructional Level

You can use the results of the Diagnostic Tests to place students in the appropriate level of *Be A Better Reader*. The test scores will classify your students into one of the following three levels:

- Independent Level
- Instructional Level
- Frustration Level

The goal is to place students into the *Be A Better Reader* program at their instructional level. At the instructional level, your students will be challenged, but not overwhelmed by the material.

Remember to use the following criteria to assist you whenever possible:

- your students' report card grades
- the results of any standardized reading tests your students have taken
- your own personal observations
- comments from your students' previous teachers

In addition, the observation of students while they are reading orally is strongly encouraged. While not always possible because of time constraints, it can give additional insight into your students' level.

The following rubric indicates characteristics students display at the three levels discussed above:

Oral Reading Rubric

Independent Level	Instructional Level	Frustration Level
Student reads fluently and accurately without teacher cues.	Student is challenged by the reading material, but not frustrated.	Student is frustrated by reading material that is too difficult.
Student reads with excellent comprehension.	Student reads with above average comprehension, but does misinterpret some information.	Student reads with below average comprehension.
Student reads without finger pointing, tension, or uncertainty.	Student reads with very little finger pointing, tension, or uncertainty. Student is challenged, but not overwhelmed.	Student reads with finger pointing, tension, or uncertainty. Student is clearly overwhelmed by the reading material.
Student reads orally with expression and pays close attention to punctuation.	Student reads orally with some difficulty in expression and punctuation, but overcomes difficulty in silent reading.	Student reads orally with no expression and no attention to punctuation.
Student makes one significant miscue per 100 words during oral reading.	Student makes 2-5 miscues per 100 words during oral reading.	Student makes 10 or more miscues per 100 words during oral reading.
Student scores 90% or better in comprehension of reading material.	Student scores 70% to 89% in comprehension of reading material.	Student scores below 69% in comprehension of reading material.
Student summary of reading material shows full understanding.	Student summary of reading material shows basic understanding.	Student summary of reading material is haphazard and incomplete.

Scoring Rubric

The scoring rubric below shows the range of test scores for the *Be A Better Reader* Diagnostic Tests that are representative of each of the levels described on page 10. As such, they serve as a guide in the placement process.

Reading Level	Range of Scores in Percents										
	50	55	60	65	70	75	80	85	90	95	100
Independent Level									▓	▓	▓
Instructional Level					▓	▓	▓	▓			
Frustration Level	▓	▓	▓	▓							

Remember that any scoring rubric is a general guideline. You may disagree with the results of the test because of your firsthand knowledge of a student's ability. Using the scoring rubric in conjunction with your knowledge of a student will help ensure proper student placement.

Case Studies

Independent Level: Manuel T., a sixth grader, scores 95% on the Level C Diagnostic Test. While reading passages in the Level C Diagnostic Test, he is apt to say, "This is easy," or "I like stories like this." Based on these observations, he is an Independent Reader and should be tested on subsequent levels until the Instructional Level is attained.

Instructional Level: Matt K. is in sixth grade and scores 75% on the Level C Diagnostic Test. However, he completes the passages and, in an oral retelling, is able to recount the main ideas in logical order. Based on these observations, Matt is at the Instructional Level. He should work in the Level C text.

Frustration Level: Jennifer D., a sixth grader, scores 60% on the Level C Diagnostic Test. During silent reading in the Level C Diagnostic Test, Jennifer often seems bored with the passages she reads. These observations suggest she is at the Frustration Level in C and should be tested on previous levels until the Instructional Level is attained. Then, Jennifer can be placed in that level working alone or with a group.

Diagnostic Test Profiles

Profile 1: Mrs. Rodriguez has one student in her eighth-grade class who is a struggling reader. She knows that *Be A Better Reader* can help this student raise her reading level, but she is unsure which book is appropriate for her needs. She administers the Placement Test, which places the student at the sixth-grade reading level. She then administers the Level C Diagnostic Test to the student in order to confirm the Placement Test results. The Diagnostic Test places the student at the Instructional Level, confirming the Placement Test results. Mrs. Rodriguez places the student into *Be A Better Reader* Level C.

Profile 2: Mr. Laddin has one student in his tenth-grade social studies class who is having difficulty understanding his reading assignments. Mr. Laddin feels that the student is reading on-level but is having trouble with some specific social studies reading skills. Mr. Laddin decides to administer the social studies portion of the Level F Diagnostic Test of *Be A Better Reader* to his student. Then he refers to the item analysis given in the answer key. He finds that his student is having difficulty with cause-and-effect relationships and sequencing. He refers to the skill list on pages 13–14 and assigns his student to the appropriate lessons in *Be A Better Reader* Level F.

Additional Reading Instruction Tips

Reading proficiency improves most dramatically with frequent practice and with support from everyone: peers, teachers, parents, and the community. Here are a few suggestions for activities that can accelerate student progress.

Student Activities

- Students conduct book-talk groups to bring exciting books to the attention of their classmates.
- Students write letters to other students, a teacher, a parent, or another adult responding to their reading.
- Students create a Notable Books bulletin board that includes brief reviews of high-interest books.
- Students create Readers Theater presentations of favorite books.

Teacher Activities

- Institute quiet reading times at the beginning or end of the day or at other times during the day when appropriate.
- Read dramatic, high-interest books aloud to students, stopping periodically to ask a question that encourages students to reflect on the work, such as, "When do you think that Matt knew he wouldn't make the team?"
- Read young-adult novels with students.
- Play audio or video recordings of high-interest books.
- Encourage people from the community to spend about an hour or two per week reading with students.

Parent Activities

- Talk with students about books they are reading.
- Read aloud high-interest material together from books, magazines, or newspapers.
- Encourage students to challenge themselves by reading a wide range of materials.

Skills Chart for *Be A Better Reader*

Reading research has shown that different types of content require specialized reading skills. The *Be A Better Reader* series was created with these specialized skills in mind. The following chart lists some of the skills needed to read in literature, social studies, science, and math, as well some important study skills, and correlates these skills to lessons in the *Be A Better Reader* series. This skills list is not all-inclusive. For a more detailed skills list, refer to the Annotated Teacher's Edition of the level that you are using. Once you have identified your students' skill deficiencies, you can use this chart to direct them to specific lessons in the level of *Be A Better Reader* they are using.

Be A Better Reader Student Edition Levels

LITERATURE	Starting Out	A	B	C	D	E	F	G
Recognizing plot	Lesson 10	Lesson 1	Lesson 50	Lesson 1	Lesson 9	Lesson 1	Lesson 10	Lesson 10
Recognizing character	Lesson 1	Lesson 43	Lessons 20, 30	Lesson 48	Lessons 1, 16	Lessons 18, 35	Lessons 1, 31	Lesson 1
Recognizing conflict	Lesson 39	Lesson 24	Lesson 11	Lesson 41	Lesson 43	Lesson 43	Lesson 16	
Recognizing setting	Lesson 20	Lessons 13, 55	Lesson 1	Lessons 20, 33	Lesson 35	Lessons 1, 27	Lesson 39	Lessons 19, 42
Recognizing theme	Lesson 30	Lesson 33	Lesson 41	Lesson 11	Lesson 26	Lesson 9	Lesson 23	Lesson 27
SOCIAL STUDIES	Starting Out	A	B	C	D	E	F	G
Reading visuals		Lessons 4, 14	Lessons 2, 42	Lessons 34, 42	Lessons 17, 46	Lessons 2, 36	Lessons 17, 32	Lessons 2, 11
Recognizing cause-and-effect relationships	Lesson 31	Lesson 2	Lesson 12	Lesson 12	Lesson 10	Lesson 28	Lesson 11	Lesson 36
Understanding sequence of events	Lesson 11	Lesson 7	Lesson 10	Lesson 42		Lesson 2	Lesson 32	
Making comparisons and contrasts		Lesson 25	Lesson 51	Lesson 2	Lesson 27	Lesson 10	Lesson 24	
Understanding detailed statements of fact	Lesson 21	Lessons 2, 44	Lessons 17, 21, 31	Lesson 49	Lessons 2, 39	Lessons 19, 44	Lesson 2	Lessons 25, 33
Thinking and reading critically	Lessons 2, 40	Lessons 34, 44	Lesson 51	Lesson 21	Lesson 44	Lesson 37	Lesson 40	Lessons 20, 33
SCIENCE	Starting Out	A	B	C	D	E	F	G
Understanding classification		Lesson 3	Lessons 3, 32	Lesson 3	Lesson 11		Lesson 25	
Reading an explanation of a technical process		Lesson 35			Lesson 37			Lesson 37
Recognizing cause and effect	Lesson 22	Lesson 26	Lessons 22, 35	Lesson 18	Lessons 11, 45	Lesson 3		Lesson 3
Following directions for an experiment		Lesson 57	Lesson 13	Lesson 43		Lesson 29	Lesson 33	Lesson 44

SCIENCE	Starting Out	A	B	C	D	E	F	G
Understanding detailed statements of fact		Lesson 45	Lesson 22	Lessons 35, 50	Lessons 3, 28	Lessons 3, 38	Lesson 18	
Recognizing descriptive problem-solving situations			Lesson 52					
Understanding abbreviations, symbols, and equations							Lesson 41	
Reading text with diagrams		Lessons 15, 26, 35, 57	Lesson 43	Lesson 13	Lesson 45	Lesson 20	Lessons 12, 18	Lesson 29

MATH	Starting Out	A	B	C	D	E	F	G
Reading word problems	Lessons 4, 33	Lesson 4	Lessons 23, 33	Lesson 23	Lessons 12, 19	Lessons 2, 4	Lessons 4, 13	Lesson 30
Reading mathematical terms, symbols, and equations	Lesson 42	Lesson 16	Lesson 44	Lesson 4	Lessons 29, 46	Lesson 39	Lesson 42	Lessons 4, 13
Reading graphs and other mathematical visuals		Lessons 27, 46	Lesson 53	Lesson 44	Lesson 38	Lesson 46	Lesson 34	
Reading explanation for processes or principals, such as fractions, decimals, and percents	Lessons 13, 23	Lessons 36, 58	Lessons 4, 14	Lessons 36, 50, 51	Lesson 4	Lessons 21, 30	Lessons 19, 26	Lessons 38, 45

STUDY SKILLS	Starting Out	A	B	C	D	E	F	G
Selecting and evaluating information		Lessons 32, 39, 42, 49	Lessons 6, 18	Lessons 27, 52, 50	Lesson 3	Lessons 3, 6, 10, 17, 40, 42	Lessons 36, 43	Lessons 5, 25, 33, 47
Organizing information		Lessons 28, 31, 32, 42, 50	Lessons 3, 32, 38, 39	Lessons 3, 30, 31, 39	Lessons 11, 14, 23, 28, 31, 32	Lessons 16, 25, 38	Lessons 18, 21, 25, 29	Lesson 14
Locating information		Lessons 41, 52, 53, 62	Lessons 7, 18, 30, 37, 46, 55	Lessons 7, 8, 18, 37	Lessons 6, 18, 27	Lessons 7, 41	Lesson 7	Lessons 7, 8, 48
Reading visuals	Lessons 18, 28, 37	Lesson 54	Lessons 2, 40, 42, 44, 53	Lessons 13, 34, 42	Lessons 36, 45	Lessons 2, 20, 32, 38, 46	Lessons 12, 17	
Following directions		Lessons 7, 23	Lessons 10, 13	Lessons 19, 43		Lesson 29	Lesson 33	
Previewing		Lessons 40, 51	Lesson 58			Lesson 44		
Reading special materials	Lessons 9, 19, 29, 36, 38, 46, 47	Lessons 23, 32, 42, 53, 62, 63	Lessons 7, 18, 19, 29, 30, 37, 46, 48, 49, 55, 60	Lessons 8, 9, 10, 18, 27, 32, 40	Lessons 6, 7, 8, 15, 24, 34, 41, 42, 48	Lessons 7, 9, 26, 35, 41, 44, 48	Lessons 7, 8, 9, 15, 22, 30, 48, 49	Lessons 7, 18, 26, 34, 41, 49

Other Basic Skills Programs

Offering a variety of basic skills programs for grades 6–12, the Globe Fearon imprint has the answer for increasing student competency in reading, writing, vocabulary, and critical thinking. Our educational programs build a solid foundation and genuine enthusiasm for future learning, while preparing students for success on today's proficiency tests. Use the chart below as a quick reference to locate the product(s) meeting the needs of your classroom.

PROGRAMS	READING LEVEL								ALTERNATIVE ASSESSMENT	ESL/ELL
	3	4	5	6	7	8	9	10		
READING										
Be A Better Reader	✓	✓	✓	✓	✓	✓	✓	✓		✓
Reading Comprehension Workshop	✓	✓	✓	✓	✓	✓	✓		✓	✓
Caught Reading	✓	✓								✓
Reading Explorations	✓	✓	✓							✓
WRITING										
Success in Writing:									✓	✓
Grammar Skills			✓							✓
Writing to Persuade			✓							✓
Writing to Explain			✓							✓
Writing to Describe			✓							✓
Writing to Tell a Story			✓							✓
Writing Across the Curriculum:										✓
Writing in Social Studies			✓	✓						✓
Writing in Math			✓	✓						✓
Writing in Science			✓	✓						✓
Writing in Literature			✓	✓						✓
Writing for Proficiency		✓	✓	✓	✓	✓			✓	✓
Stories and Plays Without Endings			✓	✓					✓	✓
Writer's Toolkit CD–ROM									✓	✓
BASIC ENGLISH GRAMMAR										
World of Vocabulary	✓	✓	✓	✓	✓	✓	✓	✓		✓
Spell It Out			✓	✓	✓	✓				✓
Pacemaker Basic English	✓	✓								✓
STUDY AND TEST TAKING										
Survival Guide for Students				✓	✓				✓	✓

Read the following selection. Then choose the best answer for each question.
Mark your answers on the answer sheet.

Broken Voyage

1. The Robertson family had been at sea in their sailboat for a week. It would take them more than a month to reach their destination. Mr. and Mrs. Robertson enjoyed spending time with their three children—Neil, Douglas, and Sandy.

2. One morning, the Robertsons sat down to eat breakfast. Suddenly, something hit the side of the sailboat. At first, no one knew what was happening. Then Mr. Robertson saw a whale heading straight for the sailboat. The second hit was much worse than the first. Mr. Robertson saw a huge hole in the side of the sailboat. Water was rushing in.

3. The Robertsons had to abandon, or leave, the sailboat. The entire family had to squeeze into a tiny rowboat. Before getting into the rowboat, Mr. Robertson grabbed as much food and water as he could.

4. As the sun went down, the Robertsons wondered about their chances of staying alive. They had no radio. They were hundreds of miles from a shipping lane and 3,000 miles from their next port. They would not be missed for at least five weeks.

5. The five members of the family were crowded together in the little rowboat for three weeks. Everyone knew that a sudden movement might cause the boat to tip over. No one moved without warning the others.

6. Their two greatest problems were thirst and hunger. Because most of the food Mr. Robertson had saved was soon gone, they were always hungry. Also, their skin was raw from the burning sun and the stinging salt water.

7. But as long as the rowboat could carry them, they could stay alive on the dangerous sea. During storms, they caught rainwater with a rubber sheet. They filled all the cans they had with water. But each person drank only a little water each day. They did not know when another rain might come. By the time their food was gone, they had learned to catch fish with hooks made out of wire.

8. Finally, after 22 days in the rowboat, a passing ship rescued the Robertsons. It was amazing that they had survived for three weeks on the ocean in a tiny rowboat.

1. What is the main idea of the selection?
   a. The Robertsons had been at sea in their sailboat for a week.
   b. Whales have always disliked people.
   c. The Robertsons survived on the ocean in a tiny rowboat.
   d. The Robertsons learned to catch fish with hooks of wire.

2. What happened to the Robertsons' sailboat?
   a. A wave caused the sailboat to sink.
   b. The sailboat was struck by lightning.
   c. The motor ran out of gas.
   d. A whale hit the sailboat and caused it to sink.

3. Why do you think the Robertsons drank only rainwater?
   a. Seawater tastes too good.
   b. Seawater is dirty.
   c. The salt in seawater can make people sick.
   d. They ran out of bottled water.

4. In paragraph 3, the word *abandon* means
   a. leave.　　　c. swim.
   b. sink.　　　d. free up.

Read the following selection. Then choose the best answer for each question.
Mark your answers on the answer sheet.

Antelopes

1. Antelopes are deerlike animals that live on the grassy plains of eastern and southern Africa and in parts of Asia. Like deer, antelopes are herbivorous animals. They eat only grass, leaves, and fruit. All antelopes have two-toed hoofs and hollow horns. Some antelopes have spiral horns. Others have straight horns. Antelope horns are different from deer antlers. A deer sheds its antlers every year and grows new ones. Antelopes have permanent horns.

2. There are more than 150 different kinds of antelopes. Most live in Africa. Antelopes range in size from the large eland to the tiny dik-dik. The eland may stand up to 6 feet (1.8 meters) tall at the shoulder. It may weigh up to 1,500 pounds (680 kilograms). The dik-dik is about 2 feet (61 centimeters) long, which is about the size of a jack rabbit.

3. All antelopes run fast. They use speed to get away from their enemies. They can usually outrun wild dogs, cheetahs, leopards, and lions.

4. Gazelles and impalas are two of the fastest and most light-footed antelopes. Gazelles are 2 to 3 feet (60 to 90 centimeters) tall at the shoulder. They can run as fast as 60 miles (96 kilometers) per hour for short distances. Impalas are about 3 feet (90 centimeters) tall at the shoulder. They can cover 30 feet (9 meters) in one leap.

5. Today, certain types of antelopes are in danger of being wiped out. Cows graze on more and more land that was once used by wild animals. Also, hunters kill antelopes for meat. However, laws are being passed to make sure that antelopes survive.

5. What is the main idea of paragraph 2?
   a. There are many different kinds of antelopes.
   b. Antelope horns are different from deer antlers.
   c. The dik-dik is the size of a jack rabbit.
   d. Many antelopes live in Africa.

6. How do antelopes escape their enemies?
   a. They outrun them.
   b. They climb trees.
   c. They scare them away with their horns.
   d. They hide in bushes.

7. What kind of laws do you think could help protect antelopes?
   a. Laws that allow land to be farmed.
   b. Laws that stop hunters from killing wild animals.
   c. Laws that encourage tourism.
   d. Laws that allow cows to graze on more land.

8. In paragraph 1, the word *permanent* means
   a. short lived.
   b. kind of hair treatment.
   c. sharp.
   d. long lasting.

GO ON

Read the following selection. Then choose the best answer for each question. Mark your answers on the answer sheet.

Slow-to-Let-Go

1. The year was 1845. The long line of Lakota hunters moved noiselessly through the prairie grass. In the front were the best hunters. In the rear was a ten-year-old boy named Slow-to-Let-Go.

2. A herd of grazing buffaloes moved slowly down the plain toward the hunters. The hunters spread out and quietly inched toward the buffaloes. When they had almost reached the herd, the hunters froze, arrows ready. They waited, hidden by the tall grass.

3. A gust of wind brought the animals' scent to the hunters. The boy watched closely through the crooked branches of a bush. Big and shaggy-haired, the buffaloes passed next to some of the lead hunters. They would soon be nearing Slow-to-Let-Go.

4. Suddenly, the quiet of the prairie was broken by the roar of pounding hoofs. The animals had caught the scent of the hunters and had started to run. The hunters jumped from cover, fitted their arrows, and let them fly. The buffaloes were running hard now. The ground shook beneath their hoofs as the animals rumbled toward Slow-to-Let-Go.

5. Slow-to-Let-Go fitted an arrow into his bow. He picked out a red-eyed bull running straight at him. He aimed just above and behind the animal's front shoulder. The arrow shot from his bow and pierced the galloping animal. Although the arrow stabbed the buffalo like a bolt of lightning, the animal kept running, pushed on by the others, who were thundering close behind.

6. Slow-to-Let-Go grabbed another arrow and ran after the bull. The herd swung away, but his buffalo slowed. The herd had left the injured buffalo behind. Slow-to-Let-Go ran hard, seeking a second shot. Suddenly, the great animal stopped. Its legs folded, and the heavy beast fell to the ground, rolled twice, then lay still.

7. It was dead. Slow-to-Let-Go had killed his first buffalo—with only one shot.

9. What is the main idea of the selection?
   a. Slow-to-Let-Go killed his first buffalo when he was 10 years old.
   b. Slow-to-Let-Go was a great Lakota warrior.
   c. Slow-to-Let-Go picked out a red-eyed bull running straight at him.
   d. Lakota hunters moved quietly through the prairie grass.

10. Why did the buffaloes start to run?
   a. They saw a bear.
   b. They were running toward water.
   c. They smelled the hunters.
   d. They saw the hunters.

11. Based on the story, you can infer that
   a. Lakota hunters rarely killed buffalo.
   b. killing the buffalo was an important event in Slow-to-Let-Go's life.
   c. Slow-to-Let-Go would become a great Lakota leader.
   d. Slow-to-Let-Go did not want to kill the buffalo.

12. In paragraph 5, the word *pierced* means
   a. froze.   c. holes in one's ears.
   b. stabbed.   d. pounded.

GO ON

Read the following selection. Then choose the best answer for each question.
Mark your answers on the answer sheet.

Mexico's Natural Resources

1. Mexico is the northernmost country of Latin America. It lies directly south of the United States. Mountains and plateaus cover about two-thirds of Mexico's land. Forests, deserts, and valleys are also found in the country. Mexico is rich in fertile soil and deposits of minerals, or substances in the earth that are not animal or vegetable. These natural resources are used in manufacturing, farming, mining, and other industries. The products that come from these natural resources are made in Mexico's largest cities and major manufacturing centers and then are exported for use in other countries.

2. Many kinds of crops are grown in Mexico. This is possible because of the different kinds of soil and because rainfall varies so greatly across the country. The best lands for crops are found in the central part of the country, where the soil is rich and where there is sufficient, or enough, rainfall. This central region is called the Central Plateau of Mexico.

3. Rich soil is also found in rainy, hot, southern Mexico and along the eastern coastal plains. More farmland is used for corn than for any other crop. Other leading crops include beans, wheat, cotton, sugarcane, and coffee.

4. As early as the 1500s, Mexico's rich silver deposits attracted Spanish explorers. Since then, Mexico has become one of the world's leading silver producers. Silver mining is one of Mexico's chief industries today. Mexico mines about 1,200 tons (1,080 metric tons) of silver a year. Other important industries include zinc, lead, gold, and sulfur. Large deposits of iron ore and coal support Mexico's growing steel industry.

5. In the late 1970s, vast deposits of petroleum were discovered along Mexico's east coast and in the Gulf of Mexico. These deposits greatly increased the importance of Mexico's petroleum industry. Oil is Mexico's leading export.

6. Mexico's rich soil allows farmers to grow a variety of crops. Mexico also has many different mineral deposits. Both the rich soil and the mineral deposits are important to the future of Mexico's economy.

13. What is the main idea of paragraph 2?
    a. The best farmlands are found in the central part of the country.
    b. This central region is called the Central Plateau of Mexico.
    c. Rainfall varies greatly across the country.
    d. Many kinds of crops are grown in Mexico.

14. How many tons of silver are mined in Mexico each year?
    a. 12,000 tons
    b. 1,200 tons
    c. 1,500 tons
    d. 1,970 tons

15. Why do you think oil is important to Mexico's economy?
    a. There are a lot of cars in Mexico.
    b. Oil is Mexico's leading export.
    c. Most countries have large deposits of oil.
    d. Oil is Mexico's leading import.

16. In paragraph 4, the word *chief* means
    a. leader.   c. most wealthy.
    b. smallest.   d. most important.

    19

Read the following selection. Then choose the best answer for each question.
Mark your answers on the answer sheet.

The Flight of Daedalus

1. Long, long ago there lived a proud and terrible king named Minos. Minos ruled the kingdom of Crete with a fist of iron. Daedalus, another proud man, also lived on the island of Crete. Daedalus was a sculptor and a builder.

2. One day, Minos became angry with Daedalus, and he ordered his soldiers to prevent Daedalus and his son, Icarus, from leaving Crete. The two men tried many times, but they could not escape the island.

3. As he watched sea gulls soaring in the sky one day, Daedalus had an idea. "Minos may rule the land and sea, but he cannot control the air!" Daedalus sent his son Icarus to gather the feathers that dropped from the sea gulls.

4. Soon Daedalus had built wings for Icarus and for himself. He sewed some feathers onto the wings and attached others with wax. "Don't fly too close to the water," Daedalus warned Icarus, "because the fog will weigh you down. And don't fly too close to the sun because its warmth will melt the wax on your wings." Icarus listened impatiently to his father's warnings.

5. One fair morning, Daedalus and Icarus headed out over the ocean with their new wings. Icarus understood the thrill of being a bird. How wonderful to be soaring above the waves! Then he looked at the clouds above. How exciting it would be to fly above them! In his excitement, Icarus ignored his father's warnings.

6. Icarus flew even higher. Then, suddenly, his wings began to droop and his feathers began to fall like snowflakes. The sun's heat was melting the wax! Icarus's wings could no longer support him. Instead of gliding gracefully, he plunged into the sea and was lost.

7. In deep grief, Daedalus flew to the temple of the sun god Apollo. There he hung up his wings as an offering to the god.

8. Daedalus had beaten his enemy, Minos, but at the terrible cost of his son's life. Perhaps the gods were punishing Daedalus for daring to do something that humans were not meant to do: fly with the wings of a bird.

17. What is the main idea of the selection?
    a. Minos was a proud and terrible king.
    b. Daedalus was a sculptor and a builder.
    c. Icarus flew too close to the sun.
    d. Daedalus was punished by the gods for daring to fly.

18. Why did Daedalus make wings for Icarus and for himself?
    a. He loved watching sea gulls and wanted to fly.
    b. He wanted to escape from Crete.
    c. He didn't have a boat and wanted to take a trip.
    d. He liked to build things.

19. Why do you think Icarus flew so close to the sun?
    a. He wanted to see if his father was telling him the truth about the wings.
    b. He was chasing a sea gull and didn't notice how high he had flown.
    c. He loved flying so much that he ignored his father's warnings.
    d. He wanted to fly until he could touch the snowflakes.

20. In paragraph 6, the word *plunged* means
    a. fell rapidly.   c. soared.
    b. rose.   d. glided gracefully.

20

Read the following selection. Then choose the best answer for each question.
Mark your answers on the answer sheet.

Flying to Fame

1. Amelia Earhart and Sally Ride, pioneers of flight, pushed back the boundaries of the world and the universe. They proved that women, as well as men, have the courage to make history.

2. In 1932, Amelia Earhart set off on a dangerous flight. She pulled on her leather flying gear, adjusted her goggles, and climbed into her propeller plane. Alone, she took off from Newfoundland, Canada, to cross the Atlantic Ocean. The world cheered when Earhart landed safely in Ireland. Earhart had become the first woman to fly solo across the Atlantic Ocean.

3. In 1935, Earhart became the first person to fly nonstop alone from Honolulu, Hawaii, to the United States mainland. Later, she became the first person to fly nonstop from Los Angeles, California, to Mexico City, Mexico. She also flew from Mexico City, Mexico, to Newark, New Jersey.

4. Earhart's daring flights made her a hero to people in the United States. At the time, her accomplishments seemed especially amazing because of her gender. But Earhart believed that women "must earn true respect and equal rights from men by accepting responsibility."

5. In 1983, another woman made history. Sally Ride donned her spacesuit, pulled on her bubble helmet, and climbed aboard the *Challenger* space shuttle with three other astronauts. When they blasted off, Ride became the first American woman in space.

6. Ride never planned a career in flying. "Then one day," Ride said, "I read that NASA was accepting applications." After her training, Sally Ride was chosen to be the first woman to fly in the *Challenger* space shuttle.

7. As one of the first women astronauts, Sally Ride broke barriers for her gender. Treated with respect by fellow crew members, Ride was simply another good astronaut. She had confidence in the experience and technology of NASA and in her own abilities and training.

8. Amelia Earhart took off across the ocean to achieve a dream. Sally Ride blasted off into space. Amelia Earhart and Sally Ride both made history as brave women and as pioneers of flight.

21. What is the main idea of paragraph 2?
    a. The world cheered when Earhart landed safely in Ireland.
    b. Alone, Earhart took off from New Foundland, Canada.
    c. Earhart pulled on her leather flying gear and climbed into her plane.
    d. Earhart had become the first woman to fly solo across the Atlantic Ocean.

22. How did Amelia Earhart and Sally Ride make history?
    a. Earhart was the first pilot; Ride was the first astronaut.
    b. Earhart was the first woman to fly alone across the Atlantic; Ride was the first American woman astronaut.
    c. Earhart and Ride were both astronauts who flew on space shuttles.
    d. Earhart and Ride were both pilots who flew propeller planes.

23. How were Amelia Earhart and Sally Ride similar?
    a. Both were pioneers of flight.
    b. Both wanted to fly around the world.
    c. Both wanted to fly from the time they were children.
    d. Both flew from New Foundland to Mexico City.

24. In paragraph 1, the word *pioneers* means
    a. astronauts.   c. leaders.
    b. pilots.   d. settlers on the prairie.

Read the following selection. Then choose the best answer for each question.
Mark your answers on the answer sheet.

The Trojan Horse

1. The Greeks and the Trojans had been fighting for ten long years. The Trojans had kidnapped Helen, the wife of the King of Sparta, in Greece. Odysseus and his Greek troops had tried numerous times to conquer Troy, the city where the Trojans had imprisoned Helen. However, Troy was a well-fortified city, and the Trojans had been able to hold their own against the Greeks.

2. Odysseus knew that there had to be a way to bring the terrible war to an end. Suddenly he was struck by an idea—a gift! They would win Troy with a gift.

3. Odysseus instructed his men to build a gigantic wooden horse. The belly of the horse was to be hollow. The Greek warriors would conceal themselves in the belly of the horse. Then, the Greeks would pretend to sail home, as if they had been defeated. The horse would be left behind as a gift to the Trojans. When the Trojans let down their guard, the Greek warriors would climb out of the horse and conquer Troy.

4. Once the Greeks finished constructing the horse, some of the warriors hid in the belly.

The rest of the Greek warriors made a big show of leaving sadly, as if in defeat. The Trojans were elated, and they jubilantly swarmed out of Troy. When they came to the shore, they were surprised to find this majestic horse. A captured Greek messenger explained that the horse was left behind as a peace offering.

5. The Trojans pulled the horse through the gates of their fortified city. For them, the horse was a symbol of a hard-fought victory. For hours, the citizens of Troy celebrated their victory. Finally, exhausted, they found their way home and went to bed.

6. At this point, the belly of the horse opened, and the Greek warriors noiselessly climbed out. They crept to the gates of Troy and opened the gates wide. Outside stood the rest of the Greek army, who had sailed back to the shores of Troy in the dark of the night.

7. When the Trojans awoke, it was already too late. The Greeks won the battle, rescued Helen, and returned her to her husband. Odysseus's ingenious plan had worked. The Trojans had been defeated by his clever idea.

25. What is the main idea of the selection?
    a. Odysseus conquered Troy by using a wooden horse to deceive the Trojans.
    b. The Trojans pulled the horse through the gates of their fortified city.
    c. The Greeks and the Trojans had been fighting for ten long years.
    d. The horse was left behind as a gift to the Trojans.

26. Who told the Trojans that the horse was left behind as a peace offering?
    a. Helen
    b. Odysseus
    c. a Greek messenger
    d. a Greek warrior

27. Why was the wooden horse so important?
    a. It allowed the Greek warriors to enter the city of Troy.
    b. The Trojans were afraid of wooden horses.
    c. The Greeks believed in leaving peace offerings for their enemies.
    d. It allowed the Trojans to celebrate their victory over the Greeks.

28. In paragraph 7, the word *ingenious* means
    a. genuine.   c. difficult.
    b. clever.   d. stupid.

Read the following selection. Then choose the best answer for each question.
Mark your answers on the answer sheet.

The Great Pyramid of Egypt

1. The Great Pyramid of Egypt has long been one of the wonders of the world. Built more than 5,000 years ago, it is the largest and most impressive of the many pyramids that dot the Egyptian desert. There are many aspects that make the Great Pyramid of Egypt so impressive.

2. The Great Pyramid covers 13 acres of land. It stands almost 500 feet high, as tall as a 42-story skyscraper. The pyramid is made of more than 2 million stones, each weighing about 2.5 tons.

3. The pyramid is not only very large but also precisely made. Its corners are almost perfect right angles. The four sides face exactly north, south, east, and west. The stones are so perfectly shaped that they fit snugly together without mortar, which is a mixture of cement, water, and sand used to hold stones together. Not even a knife blade can be inserted between the stones.

4. How were the ancient Egyptians able to move and raise such huge stones? How did they acquire their knowledge of geometry and architecture?

5. Most experts believe that the Egyptians knew enough about geometry and astronomy to build and position the pyramid, even though they lived so long ago. History books explain that thousands of laborers worked more than 20 years to construct the pyramids. They pulled the stones across the desert with ropes or on wooden rollers. They used ramps to pull the stones to the top of the pyramid. Even today, building a pyramid would be a difficult task.

29. What is the main idea of paragraph 1?
    a. The Great Pyramid was built more than 5,000 years ago.
    b. The Great Pyramid is the largest in the Egyptian desert.
    c. The Great Pyramid has long been one of the wonders of the world.
    d. The Great Pyramid covers 13 acres of land.

30. When was the Great Pyramid of Egypt built?
    a. more than 500 years ago
    b. more than 2,000 years ago
    c. more than 5,000 years ago
    d. more than 200 years ago

31. Why would building a pyramid be a difficult task even today?
    a. It would be difficult because labor is more expensive today.
    b. The right stones are difficult to find today.
    c. The project would take too long to complete.
    d. The Egyptians had a greater understanding of geometry and architecture.

32. In paragraph 3, the word *mortar* means
    a. explosive material.
    b. different kinds of stones.
    c. something that fits snugly.
    d. a mixture of cement, water, and sand.

Read the following selection. Then choose the best answer for each question.
Mark your answers on the answer sheet.

If Great-Grandpa Did It, So Can He

To the Editor:

1. Well, here we are again! Coming as I do from a long line of people whose skills have become obsolete or whose occupation became outdated because of modern technology, I am not surprised that I must now acquire new skills.

2. My great-grandpa was a blacksmith until Henry Ford invented the automobile. A weaker person might have been overcome with despair, but not Great-Grandpa. He just studied those newfangled machines, changed the sign on his shop, and became an auto mechanic. He said he was tired of shoeing horses anyway.

3. What about me? Well, I used to be the chief of the bobbin-making crews at Bodwell Industries. Unfortunately, bobbins aren't big sellers these days. So Bodwell decided to go high-tech. Microchips made by robots are the Bodwell mainstay now.

4. Am I unemployed and depressed? No, someone realized that even a robot can break down. So Bodwell enrolled me in classes to learn how to repair those intricate little fellows.

5. Change—even a massive economic change—need not be fearsome if we plan for it. I'm told that my children could have as many as three separate careers. If they grow up knowing that change is inevitable, they won't fear it. And if they know that they can retrain, they won't have the fears that some of my neighbors have every time they hear rumors of their plant closing down or of automation being introduced in factories.

6. As Great-Grandpa said, there's good and bad coming from a change in technology. "You can't feed one of those newfangled automobiles a lump of sugar when you've changed a tire. On the other hand, it won't try to rear back and kick you, either."

Sincerely yours,
T. Alvah Becker

33. What is the main idea of the letter?
    a. Workers need to adapt to changes in the workplace.
    b. T. Alvah Becker's great-grandfather was a blacksmith.
    c. T. Alvah Becker's children might have three separate careers.
    d. Bodwell Industries stopped making bobbins and started making microchips.

34. Why did Becker's great-grandfather become an auto mechanic?
    a. Cars were invented and there was little need for horseshoes.
    b. Cars were easier to work on than horses were.
    c. He was tired of shoeing horses.
    d. He preferred cars to bobbins.

35. How are Becker's ideas and his great-grandfather's ideas similar?
    a. Both believe that people should stick with the job they do best.
    b. Both believe that people can adapt to change.
    c. Both believe that jobs are hard to find.
    d. Both believe that people should have only one job in their careers.

36. In paragraph 1, the word *obsolete* means
    a. valuable.
    b. important.
    c. ancient.
    d. outdated.

Read the following selection. Then choose the best answer for each question.
Mark your answers on the answer sheet.

Ecosystems

1. Kangaroos jump from place to place, eating grass and shrubs. Foxes and dingoes lurk in the shadows, waiting for a joey, or baby kangaroo, to stray from its mother. Insects feed on plants and some feed on other insects. Mouselike animals pounce on any insects they can catch, while unusual-looking cats stalk the mice.

2. Although this scene takes place in Australia, the description could apply to the relationships between organisms, or individual animals or plants, in any area. You need only to change the names of the organisms. The description is that of an ecosystem, which is a group of organisms and their physical surroundings.

3. A basic fact of life is that all organisms must have energy, or food, to survive. Plants make their own food. They use the energy of sunlight to convert carbon dioxide and water into glucose and oxygen. The glucose is used as food immediately or stored for later use. Because plants can make their own food, they are called producers.

4. Unlike plants, animals must find their own food. Organisms that consume, or eat, other organisms are referred to as consumers. They are the second type of organism in an ecosystem.

5. The third type of organism in an ecosystem is decomposers. Decomposers are organisms that break down organic material, which is dead plants and animals, and return it to the soil, where producers reuse it. This process is known as decay. Examples of such decomposers are one-celled organisms called bacteria, and fungi, such as mushrooms.

6. These three types of organisms—producers, consumers, and decomposers—make up an ecosystem. They need each other to survive and flourish.

37. What is the main idea of paragraph 3?
    a. Plants make their own food.
    b. Plants are called producers.
    c. A basic fact of life is that all organisms must have energy to survive.
    d. Glucose is used as food immediately or stored for later use.

38. What type of organism are plants?
    a. consumers
    b. producers
    c. decomposers
    d. ecosystems

39. Why do you think removing one organism from an ecosystem could be harmful?
    a. The remaining organisms might destroy each other.
    b. Removing one organism might destroy the ecosystem's balance.
    c. The remaining organisms might not be able to find a place to live.
    d. Removing one organism would not be harmful at all.

40. In paragraph 2, the word *organisms* means
    a. organs, such as the heart.
    b. individual animals or plants.
    c. animals only.
    d. plants only.

Read the following selection. Then choose the best answer for each question.
Mark your answers on the answer sheet.

Silent World

1. Elliot evaded his partner's glances; he was disgusted. What a terrific weekend this was going to be, he thought, with more than a trace of sarcasm. He'd thought that it would be exhilarating to clear last winter's debris from the hiking trails with the local high school conservation clubs. How was he to predict that he would be working with a student from the Madison School for the Deaf?

2. Elliot made numerous attempts to talk to Caroline, but it was hopeless. He couldn't understand a word she said, although he pretended that he did. He simply smiled, nodded pleasantly, and continued to work.

3. Elliot began collecting trash he found in the brush, while Caroline tramped along behind him, eager to help her partner. When she caught up with him, Caroline couldn't believe her eyes— Elliot was standing on the edge of a huge patch of poison oak.

4. Caroline tried to tell Elliot about the poison oak, but he couldn't understand her. Caroline began to pantomime. She pantomimed somebody whose body is itching all over. As Elliot stared at her, fascinated with her performance, Caroline pointed at the brush again. This time Elliot turned and looked in the direction she was pointing. Suddenly, Elliot realized what Caroline was pantomiming. Elliot stepped away carefully, all the while feeling fortunate because he was allergic to poison oak.

5. Elliot decided to talk with her teacher to find some way to thank Caroline. His mission accomplished, he walked up to Caroline. He put his fingertips to his lips, palm flat and then moved his hand away from his face. He felt foolish, wondering if he was making sense, but then he saw a smile break over Caroline's face. He had made the gesture that meant "thank you" in sign language.

41. What is the main idea of the selection?
   a. Elliot and Caroline find a way to communicate.
   b. Elliot is very allergic to poison oak.
   c. At first, Elliot was disgusted with his partner.
   d. Elliot learned how to say "thank you" to his partner.

42. Initially, why was Elliot disappointed by the partner he received?
   a. Elliot thought he would be partners with one of his friends.
   b. His partner was deaf, and they couldn't communicate well.
   c. His partner didn't know what she was supposed to do.
   d. Elliot thought he would be working alone.

43. What do you think Elliot learned during his weekend cleaning the trails?
   a. He learned that he was allergic to poison oak.
   b. He learned how to use sign language to warn people about poison oak.
   c. He learned that he should not be so quick to judge other people.
   d. He learned that picking up debris from the hiking trails was difficult.

44. In paragraph 1, the word *exhilarating* means
   a. hopeless.
   b. disgusting.
   c. boring.
   d. exciting.

Read the following selection. Then choose the best answer for each question.
Mark your answers on the answer sheet.

The Daily Life of the Anasazi

1. Although the Anasazi settled in the Southwest more than 2,000 years ago, we know a lot about the daily lives of these people.

2. The Anasazi planted and tended corn, squash, and beans. They gathered wild plants—roots, berries, nuts, seeds, and fruits—and hunted deer, rabbits, and other animals. Animal skins and woven robes and blankets provided warm coverings. The Anasazi twisted fibers from the yucca plant into cords to make baskets, sandals, ropes, and snares for catching small animals.

3. Women had important roles in Anasazi society. Women were responsible for preparing and cooking food. They made cornmeal by grinding dried corn with a hand-held stone against a flat stone slab. The coarse cornmeal was mixed with water and baked in flat cakes on a stone griddle or formed into small balls and boiled in soups or stews. The Anasazi women cooked beans and squash alone or with meat, and they flavored foods with salt and wild plants, such as onion and mustard.

4. Women also cared for the young children. They snugly tucked their babies into cradleboards that they wore on their backs or propped up nearby as they worked. Girls learned how to prepare food, weave baskets, and make clothing, while boys practiced hunting with smaller versions of the men's bows and arrows.

5. Men were responsible for clearing land and building houses and other structures. With stone axes, they cut logs to make wooden supports for floors and roofs and to chip large sandstone chunks into rectangular blocks for building.

6. In 1276, a 23-year drought began. When the crops failed, people became malnourished. Groups of Anasazi began to move south and east and merged with other native peoples. They lost many of their old customs and adopted new ones. The present-day Pueblo people of the Southwest are descendants of the Anasazi.

45. What is the main idea of paragraph 3?
    a. There were many uses for cornmeal in Anasazi society.
    b. The Anasazi cooked beans and squash.
    c. Women made cornmeal by grinding dry corn.
    d. Women had important roles in Anasazi society.

46. How did men's and women's roles differ in Anasazi society?
    a. Men built houses, and women cared for the children and prepared the food.
    b. Women built houses, and men cared for the children and prepared the food.
    c. Men harvested the crops, and women prepared the food.
    d. Men cleared land, and women built houses.

47. How might a long drought have affected the Anasazi's lives?
    a. It might have made growing crops difficult.
    b. It might have made drying clothes more difficult.
    c. It might have caused difficulties preparing food.
    d. It might have made building houses difficult.

48. In paragraph 6, the word *malnourished* means
    a. frustrated.
    b. tired.
    c. poorly fed.
    d. unhappy.

Read the following selection. Then choose the best answer for each question.
Mark your answers on the answer sheet.

Captain's Hill

1. Pete woke up earlier than usual, put on his in-line skates, and headed for the park. It had taken a long time, but the city had finally cleared a place for in-line skaters. Now Pete could practice turning and skating backward, and more importantly, dance to the music from his headphones.

2. When he arrived at the park, Pete saw some kids from his school. Unfortunately, he didn't like them, and they didn't like him. As Pete deftly skated around the circle, the kids harassed him, calling him names and laughing.

3. One of the kids said, "You think you're an expert skater or something. I bet you're too afraid to skate down Captain's Hill."

4. Pete knew that Captain's Hill was one of the steepest hills around. Even worse, at the bottom of the hill was a busy intersection. Pete knew he could handle the hill, but he knew avoiding the cars at the intersection would be impossible. Drivers wouldn't see him coming and he wouldn't be able to stop quickly enough.

Nevertheless, Pete didn't want to appear afraid in front of these kids, so he told them he'd skate down Captain's Hill that afternoon.

5. Pete regretted agreeing to this ridiculous challenge, but he knew he'd be a laughingstock at school if he didn't do it. Suddenly, he had an idea. There was a sign on the right at the bottom of the hill that blocked the sightlines from the top of the hill. If Pete timed it right, he could duck behind the sign without being seen. It would appear to everyone at the top of the hill as if he had crossed the intersection.

6. When Pete arrived at Captain's Hill, a crowd of 50 classmates eagerly awaited his skate down the hill. Pete stood at the top of the hill, pushed off, and started his descent. As he reached the sign, he veered sharply and ducked behind it. When he reappeared, the kids at the top of the hill began to cheer. They never suspected that it was Pete's brains, and not his bravery, that had saved the day—and Pete's life.

49. What is the main idea of the selection?
   a. Pete was able to save himself using his brains and not bravery.
   b. Pete should have tried to go down Captain's Hill without his trick.
   c. Captain's Hill was not really dangerous.
   d. Pete was an excellent in-line skater.

50. Why did Pete try to trick his classmates?
   a. He wasn't a good skater.
   b. He knew he'd be killed if he skated into the intersection.
   c. He wanted to keep up his image as the best in-line skater.
   d. He wanted to impress his girlfriend.

51. How do you think Pete's classmates would describe his skate down the hill?
   a. He fell at the bottom of the hill.
   b. He skated right through the intersection.
   c. He was not a very talented skater.
   d. He was not a very fast skater.

52. In paragraph 2, the word *deftly* means
   a. fortunately.   c. skillfully.
   b. awkwardly.   d. unfortunately.

Read the following selection. Then choose the best answer for each question.
Mark your answers on the answer sheet.

Africa's Climate Zones

1. Because of its size and placement, Africa has a wide variety of climates. Africa is the second largest continent on Earth. Straddling the equator, Africa stretches 4,970 miles from its northernmost point, Cape Blanc in Tunisia, to its southernmost tip, Cape Agulhas in South Africa. At its widest point (measured from Cape Verde, Senegal, in the west to Ras Hafun, Somalia, in the east), Africa is about 4,700 miles wide. Africa is about three times the size of Europe and covers one-fifth of the total land surface of Earth.

2. From north to south, the continent is cut almost equally in half by the equator, so that most of Africa lies within the tropical regions. Because of the "bulge" formed by West Africa, the greater part of Africa's territory lies north of the equator. The continent's position astride the equator heavily influences its climates.

3. Temperatures in Africa are high for most of the year in northern and southern tropical zones. In high altitudes in parts of the interior, however, temperatures are much cooler because of the height of the mountains. This is especially true in the mountains of eastern Africa and parts of central and southern Africa.

4. The climate in Africa is further modified, or changed, by the impact of ocean currents—for example, the cooling Benguela Current, which flows north from the Cape of Good Hope toward the Congo, and the warming Mozambique Current, which passes through the channel between the island of Madagascar and the southeast coast of Africa. In addition, the climate is affected by the absence of mountain chains, which serve as climactic barriers.

5. All in all, Africa has six primary climate zones: tropical rain forest climate, tropical wet-and-dry climate, steppe climate, desert climate, Mediterranean climate, and vertical climate.

53. What is the main idea of paragraph 1?
    a. Africa has a wide variety of climates.
    b. Africa is 4,700 miles wide.
    c. Africa is three times the size of Europe.
    d. Cape Verde is located in Senegal.

54. Where does the greater part of Africa's territory lie?
    a. north of the equator
    b. south of the equator
    c. east of the equator
    d. west of the equator

55. Why might mountain chains act like climactic barriers?
    a. Mountain chains have an impact on the movement of weather fronts.
    b. Mountain chains are covered in snow.
    c. Mountain chains cause tornadoes.
    d. Mountain chains do not act as climactic barriers.

56. In paragraph 4, the word *modified* means
    a. changed.
    b. remained the same.
    c. improved.
    d. worsened.

Read the following selection. Then choose the best answer for each question.
Mark your answers on the answer sheet.

The Gift

1. "Hi, Grandmother."

2. "Hello, Martina, how was school?"

3. "The same as usual," Martina replied.

4. Grandmother knew not to press her grandchild any further. She knew Martina would talk to her when she was ready.

5. Martina sat quietly at the kitchen table. She loved watching her grandmother's fingers scooping up the colored beads on her needle.

6. Martina didn't know much about the Navajo culture. She lived in the city. She had never lived on a reservation. Her parents wanted her to fit in with the other children.

7. "Why are you still making my dress for a powwow I'm not going to?" Martina asked.

8. "I'm just making it to keep my mind and hands busy. I may not even give it to you. Maybe I'll just sell it."

9. "So you don't want me to go to the powwow?"

10. "You have to make your own decisions, dear. Do what is right for you," Grandmother said softly, as she continued to bead Martina's dress.

11. Lost in thought, Martina continued to watch her grandmother's knotted fingers work the beads gracefully.

12. After some time had passed, Martina broke the silence.

13. "Grandmother, tell me the story of the dress."

14. Grandmother sat quietly after finishing her story. She knew the power of silence. Words didn't always need to be spoken. Grandmother knew that Martina was deep in thought and allowed her the time to think things through on her own.

15. "I've got homework to do. Good night, Grandmother."

16. "Good night."

17. When Martina woke up the next day, she could hear the rustling of her parents making breakfast and getting ready for work. Martina waited for her parents to leave so she could have time alone with her grandmother before going to school. Martina had had trouble sleeping. She had too many thoughts and feelings running through her head.

18. "Hey, Grandmother," Martina cheerfully said to her grandmother after returning home from school.

19. Grandmother briefly looked up to give her granddaughter a warm smile.

20. "Grandmother," Martina said slowly.

21. "Humm," Grandmother replied, without looking up from or stopping her beadwork.

22. "Grandmother, I want to take part in the powwow. I want to know more about where I come from. I know that I need lots of practice in a short amount of time. Will you help me?"

23. Grandmother nodded again, but kept her head down on her beadwork to hide her smile.

24. For days, Martina practiced her dance for the competition. Grandmother helped Martina on her style. All the while, she was busily working on finishing Martina's dress.

25. Grandmother had not spoken much since Martina's decision to dance. Finally, Grandmother said, "You have one more part of the dance to learn—the meaning and use of the sacred eagle feather. The most important lesson to learn is that the eagle feather must never fall from your hand or touch the ground. If it does, you lose."

26. "Grandmother, I think I'm ready, and I'm going to win that dance competition. I want you to be proud of me. I want to know for myself what it means to be proud of who I am."

27. Once again, Grandmother said nothing. She touched her granddaughter lovingly on the arm and went back to work on the final stage of Martina's dress.

28. The day of the competition finally arrived. It would be the best powwow ever, Martina thought. She knew that she would win. She wanted to win to please her grandmother.

29. That morning, Grandmother helped pack all of the pieces of Martina's outfit into a

small suitcase. Her grandmother and parents prepared lunch and snacks. They loaded their lawn chairs, cooler, and Martina's suitcase into their car and drove to the dance grounds.

30. Martina nervously sat during the competition for the younger children. Feeling the sunbeams gave Martina a sense of pride and confidence. Finally, the announcer called for Martina's age and dance category. Grandmother helped Martina make the final adjustments to her outfit. Martina confidently walked to the center of the dance arena. Her outfit was perfect.

31. Twelve young women gathered in a circle, clutching their eagle feathers. The music started, and Martina lost herself to the music. She danced in perfect rhythm to the drum. The singers' voices uplifted Martina's heart, and she felt light, quick, and agile on her feet.

32. Martina sized up her performance against those of the other dancers. She believed she was the best and would easily win.

33. Martina moved and pounded her feet against the soft earth. She felt the warmth of the earth through the soles of her brightly beaded moccasins. But with the next beat, Martina stepped on a rock and lost her balance. Trying to steady herself, she lost hold of her feather. The feather drifted in the air before finally settling on the ground. Martina knew she had lost the competition, but she kept dancing. In that instant, Martina realized that the purpose of dancing was not to win. The purpose was to enjoy the dancing itself. She thought about all of those who had danced before her.

34. Martina glanced at her grandmother on the last beat of the drum. She saw her grandmother's wide grin and sparkling eyes. Martina was proud and smiling herself. She walked out of the arena toward her grandmother's outstretched arms.

1. The main, or most important, character in the story is
    a. Grandmother.
    b. Martina.
    c. the mother.
    d. the father.

2. Choose the words that best describe the main character.
    a. sad and lonely
    b. confused and curious
    c. shy and unhappy
    d. friendly and helpful

3. You can infer from the story that Martina
    a. doesn't know about her culture but is curious about it.
    b. doesn't want to live in the city with her grandmother.
    c. wants to learn how to do beadwork like her grandmother.
    d. has no interest in learning to dance.

4. The story takes place
    a. in the distant past.
    b. in the recent past.
    c. in the present.
    d. in the future.

5. The setting of most of the story is a house
    a. in a small town.
    b. on a reservation.
    c. at the powwow grounds.
    d. in a city.

6. The most exciting part of the story occurs
    a. when Martina asks her grandmother to tell her a story.
    b. when Martina practices dancing with her grandmother.
    c. when Martina waits nervously for her time to dance.
    d. when Martina drops her eagle feather.

7. At the end of the story,
    a. Martina learns how to be proud of herself and her culture.
    b. Martina is angry about losing the dance competition.
    c. Grandmother is ashamed of her granddaughter for losing.
    d. Martina stops dancing when she drops the eagle feather.

8. The main problem is
   a. within Martina's mind.
   b. with Martina's grandmother.
   c. with Martina's parents.
   d. with an outside force.

9. Martina wants to
   a. move in with her grandmother.
   b. move to a reservation.
   c. please her grandmother.
   d. learn nothing about her culture.

10. You can infer from the grandmother's reaction at the end of the story that she
    a. is showing Martina how proud she is of her.
    b. is ashamed of her granddaughter's performance.
    c. is happy that Martina lost the competition.
    d. understands how Martina must feel.

11. Choose the statement that best states the theme of the story.
    a. Competition makes people stronger.
    b. Where there's a will, there's a way.
    c. Success can be achieved in many ways.
    d. Don't count your chickens before they are hatched.

12. The word *agile* in paragraph 31 means
    a. steady.
    b. controlled.
    c. weak.
    d. graceful.

Read the following selection. Then choose the best answer for each question.
Mark your answers on the answer sheet.

Ancient Egypt

1. When people think of ancient Egypt, they often think first of the pyramids. The pyramids at Giza are considered one of the Seven Wonders of the World. They are the only wonders of the ancient world to have survived. Three different pharaohs, or rulers, built the pyramids.

2. Large groups of people built the pyramids by hand. A Greek historian wrote that it took 100,000 men 20 years to build the Great Pyramid, the largest of the three pyramids at Giza. This pyramid stands 481 feet (147 meters) tall.

3. The ancient Egyptians built the pyramids for their pharaohs. They believed that when a king died, he traveled to the underworld. In the underworld, his deeds on Earth were judged. If he had ruled and lived with a good heart, he would live on in the underworld. The pharaoh would be buried deep in his pyramid with all of his possessions. This way, the king would have what he needed even in the underworld.

4. The Great Sphinx is another famous site. The Sphinx has a lion's body and a human head. It guards the pyramids. The Sphinx is 66 feet (20 meters) tall. The Sphinx stands for the ancient Egyptian sun god.

5. The ancient Egyptians believed in many gods and goddesses. These gods and goddesses often had a human body with an animal's head. One of the most well-known gods is Ra, the sun god. He is the most important god of the ancient Egyptians. The goddess Nut swallowed Ra every night. Ra was then reborn every morning. He created himself. He also created humankind with his tears.

6. The most well-known pharaoh of ancient Egypt was King Tutankhamen (known as King Tut). King Tut was a boy king. He rose to power when he was only nine years old. He ruled until his death at the age of eighteen. How the boy king died is unknown. Some believe he was murdered.

7. The people who study ancient Egypt are called Egyptologists. Egyptologists have studied the ancient Egyptians for centuries. Egyptologists found King Tut's tomb in an area called the Valley of the Kings. The valley holds 62 tombs that we know about. Mystery surrounds not only King Tut's death, but also his tomb.

8. When Egyptologists found King Tut's tomb, they saw a warning above the doorway. The sign said that death would come to any who entered the tomb. No one paid attention to the mummy's curse. At least not until one of the people who entered the tomb died five months after discovering it.

9. Egyptologists and scientists learned a great deal from the boy king's tomb and remains. They learned much about how the ancient Egyptians buried their dead. They learned that pharaohs were mummified. Their bodies were carefully prepared after death so that they would look in death as they had looked in life. To create a mummy, the organs were removed. Then the body was dried, wrapped in linen strips, and laid in a coffin of gold.

Ancient Egypt

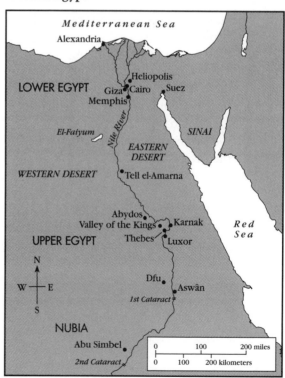

13. Which sentence in paragraph 9 states the main idea?
    a. the first sentence
    b. the second sentence
    c. the third sentence
    d. the last sentence

14. Think about the main idea of paragraph 5. Then choose the detail below that would support the main idea.
    a. Ra was often combined with the god Atum to form Ra-Atum.
    b. Egyptologists learned about the ancient Egyptians through their writings.
    c. Modern movies have taken ideas from the stories of and discoveries about ancient Egypt.
    d. The god Osiris is also well known.

15. Which of the following is *not* part of making a mummy?
    a. The organs are removed.
    b. The people place a curse on the body.
    c. The body is wrapped in strips of linen.
    d. The body is dried.

16. The ancient Egyptians built pyramids for their rulers because
    a. they wanted to hide them.
    b. they wanted them to travel safely to the underworld.
    c. they believed they would return to life on Earth.
    d. they wanted people to know where they were buried.

17. Mystery surrounds King Tutankhamen's tomb because
    a. he was a boy king.
    b. the boy king did not get his own pyramid.
    c. Egyptologists thought they would never find his tomb.
    d. a warning above the doorway said death would come to any that entered it.

18. You might infer from the selection that the ancient Egyptians
    a. knew little about how to survive.
    b. had strong beliefs about life and death.
    c. cared little about one another.
    d. could not build long-lasting buildings.

19. Which of these statements is an opinion?
    a. King Tutankhamen ruled from the age of nine until his death.
    b. The ancient Egyptians believed in many gods and goddesses.
    c. The Great Pyramid at Giza stands 481 feet tall.
    d. The Egyptians lived in mysterious ways.

20. Which of these statements is a fact?
    a. King Tutankhamen was the most friendly of all the Egyptian rulers.
    b. Mummies are scary to see.
    c. The Sphinx has a lion's body and a human head.
    d. The pyramids at Giza are the most beautiful of the Seven Wonders of the World.

21. Based on what you have read in the selection, why was King Tut's tomb important to Egyptologists?
    a. Egyptologists learned a lot about how ancient Egyptians buried their dead.
    b. King Tut was a boy king.
    c. King Tut's tomb was cursed.
    d. Some believe King Tut was murdered.

22. The word *pharaoh* in paragraph 1 means
    a. Egyptian.
    b. Greek historian.
    c. ruler.
    d. survivor.

Use the map on page 33 to answer questions 23 and 24.

23. The Valley of the Kings is located in
    a. lower Egypt.
    b. upper Egypt.
    c. Nubia.
    d. near the Red Sea.

24. Which city is Giza near?
    a. Karnak
    b. Thebes
    c. Alexandria
    d. Cairo

Read the following selection. Then choose the best answer for each question.
Mark your answers on the answer sheet.

Venus—"The Morning Star"

1. Venus is called "the Morning Star." Other than the Moon, Venus is the brightest object in the sky at dawn. If you look in the sky early in the morning, you will probably see a very bright star. That star is actually the planet Venus. Venus was named after the Roman goddess of love and beauty. The Romans probably named the planet Venus because it was the brightest of the planets known to these ancient peoples. It is the only planet in our solar system that was named after a Roman goddess.

2. Throughout history, Venus has also fascinated many other cultures, such as the Maya. The Maya were an ancient culture who lived in what is now Mexico. The Maya believed that Venus was the planet of warfare. They made offerings to Venus, perhaps to give them strength in battle or to secure a victory. The Aztec were another ancient culture in Mexico. Venus was a symbol for one of the Aztec gods. They believed this god ruled the night.

3. Venus was once called Earth's sister planet because both planets were thought to be similar. Venus and Earth are alike in three ways. The first way is their distance from the Sun. Venus is the second planet from the Sun. Earth is the third planet from the Sun. Venus and Earth are also similar in their size and weight. The other seven planets in our solar system either are much smaller and lighter, or they are much bigger and heavier. But the similarities end here.

4. The United States and Russia have studied Venus more than any other planet. These studies show that Venus and Earth are really quite different from one another. For example, Earth rotates, or moves, on its axis from west to east. Venus rotates from east to west. This means that if you lived on Venus, you would see the Sun rising in the west instead of the east, as we do on Earth. It takes Earth 365 days to travel around the Sun. Venus takes 225 days to make its way around the Sun. Earth's day is 24 hours. A day on Venus lasts about 116 Earth days!

5. The surface of Earth is land and water. Earth's surface is 74 percent water. The surface of Venus is mostly land. The land is mostly flat and shows signs of former volcanic action. There are no signs of Venus having water.

6. Venus probably could not support human life for several reasons. First of all, Earth and Venus have very different temperatures. Earth's mean, or average, temperature is 59 degrees Fahrenheit. The mean temperature on Venus is 867 degrees Fahrenheit. That's hot! Venus is so hot because the thick clouds that cover Venus trap the heat.

7. Second, Earth's air is made up of a lot of oxygen. Venus' atmosphere contains a lot of carbon dioxide. Humans and other animals cannot breathe carbon dioxide. It is toxic to our systems, and we would die.

8. Finally, Venus' atmosphere is more than 90 times heavier than Earth's. Even if we could somehow survive the heat and carbon dioxide on Venus, we would be crushed by the weight of its air.

Planetary Facts

	Diameter (miles)	Mean temp.(°F)	Air Pressure (lbs/in.^{2})	No. of Moons	Ring System
Mercury	3,032	333°F	0	0	no
Venus	7,521	867°F	91	0	no
Earth	7,926	59°F	1	1	no
Mars	4,222	−85°F	0.01	2	no
Jupiter	88,846	−166°F	unknown	17	yes

25. What is the main idea of the selection?
    a. how similar Earth and Venus are
    b. how Venus got its name
    c. how different Earth and Venus are
    d. why Venus is called Earth's sister planet

26. What is the main idea of paragraph 2?
    a. The Aztec worshiped Venus.
    b. Venus was the Mayan god of warfare.
    c. Only the Maya knew about Venus.
    d. Venus has fascinated other cultures.

27. Which of the following is probably *not* a cause of Venus' hot temperatures?
    a. heat from the Sun
    b. thick clouds that surround the planet
    c. volcanic activity
    d. no seasons

28. Which is *not* a reason supporting why Earth and Venus were once called sister planets?
    a. The planets are similar in size.
    b. Both planets are relatively close to the Sun.
    c. The planets were created about the same time.
    d. Both planets are similar in their weight.

29. Why is Venus called "the Morning Star"?
    a. It was the only planet that the Romans knew about.
    b. It is the brightest object in the sky at dawn.
    c. Venus is the goddess of love and beauty.
    d. It is the only planet in our solar system that can be seen with the naked eye.

30. *Venus is the second planet from the sun.* This statement is an example of
    a. a fact.
    b. an opinion.
    c. both a fact and an opinion.
    d. neither a fact nor an opinion.

31. What is the meaning of *mean* in paragraph 6?
    a. constant
    b. degrees
    c. average
    d. rude

Use the chart on page 36 to answer questions 32 through 34.

32. Which of the four planets listed below has a ring system?
    a. Jupiter
    b. Mars
    c. Earth
    d. Venus

33. Which of the four planets listed below does not have any moons?
    a. Jupiter
    b. Mars
    c. Earth
    d. Venus

34. Which of the four planets listed below is the smallest?
    a. Jupiter
    b. Mars
    c. Earth
    d. Mercury

Questions 35 and 36 are word problems. Use the space on this page for your calculations.

35. Earth's average temperature is 59°F. The average temperature on Venus is 867°F. What is the difference in the mean temperatures?
    a. 573°F
    b. 808°F
    c. 926°F
    d. 1,243°F

36. It takes Earth 365 days to go around the Sun. It takes Venus 225 days. How many more days does it take the Earth to travel around the Sun?
    a. 110 days
    b. 120 days
    c. 130 days
    d. 140 days

A. Study the following dictionary entry. Then answer questions 37 through 39.

> **home** (hōm) *n.* **1.** one's place of residence [Let's go *home*.] **2.** the social unit formed by a family living together [My *home* is where my family is.] **3.** a familiar or usual setting [It's good to be back *home* in North Dakota.] **4.** a place of origin [The salmon return to their *home* to spawn.] **5.** one's own country [We are having troubles at *home* and abroad.] *v.* to go toward a source [The missiles *homed* in on their target.]
> **—homed, —hom´ing**

37. How many noun meanings are given?
    a. three
    b. four
    c. five
    d. six

38. How many verb meanings are given?
    a. none
    b. one
    c. two
    d. three

39. Which of the following is a verb form?
    a. at home
    b. go home
    c. homing
    d. a home

B. Study the following part of an index. Then answer questions 40 and 41.

> **NATIVE AMERICANS**
> **Architecture**
>   Earth lodges, 227–228 *with diagram*
>   Hogans, 228–231 *with picture*
>   Longhouses, 232–233 *with picture*
>   Pueblos, 271–274 *with pictures*
>   Tipis, 294–297 *with diagram and pictures*
> **Artists**
>   Bad Heart Bull, Amos, 119, 122, 123 *color pictures*
>   Grigg, Carol, 143–147 *color picture A23*
>   Howe, Oscar, 337–342 *color pictures C12–C17*
>
>   Peña, Amado, 421–426 *color pictures E1–E7*
> **Contributions**
>   Foods, 28–40 *with chart*
>   Medicines, 20–33 *with chart*
>   Science, 52–61
>   Words, 1–22 *with chart*
> **Leaders and Chiefs**
>   Chief Joseph, 92, 100–110
>   Crazy Horse, 119–125
>   Geronimo, 126–132 *with picture*
>   Powhatan, 70–75 *with picture*
>   Sitting Bull, 109, 110, 112–119 *with map*

40. Where would you look to find information about longhouses?
    a. Leaders and Chiefs
    b. Contributions
    c. Artists
    d. Architecture

41. Where would you look to find artwork by Oscar Howe?
    a. E1–E7
    b. C12–C17
    c. 119, 122, 123
    d. A23

C. Think about words and word parts to answer questions 42 through 50.

42. Choose the prefix that will make the word *like* mean "not like."
    a. re-
    b. anti-
    c. un-
    d. pre-

43. Choose the suffix that will make the word *easy* mean "with ease."
    a. -able
    b. -ily
    c. -er
    d. -ness

44. Choose the correct way to divide the word *collection* into syllables.
    a. col lec tion
    b. co llec tion
    c. coll ec tion
    d. collec tion

45. Choose the word that has the same vowel sound you hear in *chief*.
    a. fried
    b. relief
    c. lied
    d. spied

46. Which of the following words has a soft *g* sound?
    a. garden
    b. garnish
    c. giant
    d. gaze

47. Choose the word with the *r*-controlled sound.
    a. dart
    b. rope
    c. helper
    d. drum

48. Choose the correct possessive form of the noun *beach*.
    a. beaches
    b. beachs
    c. beach's
    d. beachs'

49. Choose the correct possessive form of the noun *girls*.
    a. girl's
    b. girls
    c. girls'
    d. girl

50. Choose the word with the same vowel sound as *now*.
    a. know
    b. blow
    c. blue
    d. proud

Read the following selection. Then choose the best answer for each question.
Mark your answers on the answer sheet.

The Bucket Line

1. "Get up, Mandy!" Jane cried from downstairs. "The town's on fire!" Rubbing her eyes, Mandy stared out the window. In the darkness, a strange orange glow shone over Main Street. Down in the kitchen, Mandy's sister Jane was pumping water onto blankets. "Papa needs wet blankets right away to save the newspaper!"

2. Outside, a cold north wind whistled off the prairie, biting into the girls' faces. Rounding the corner, they hurried down Main Street, the only big street in town. The fire had started in the hardware store, but now the blacksmith shop was burning, too. The hotel would be next. After that, it would be Papa's newspaper office. "Thanks, girls," Papa said, grabbing the blankets. "If I can just keep sparks off the roof . . ."

3. The other townspeople had started a bucket line to save the hotel. Pail after pail of water passed from hand to hand. Mandy and Jane tried to join the line, but big Mr. Campbell shook his head. "Go home, girls," he shouted. "You'll only be in the way here." Furious, Mandy turned to see if she could help Papa. But he was already up on the roof. She shivered as she watched him spread out the half-frozen blankets. What good were wet blankets against such a fire?

4. As the girls watched the fire, the wind shifted. Smoke and burning ash began to drift south, toward their house. Loud explosions inside the hardware store sent blazing bits of timber high into the air. "Our roof has wooden shingles," Mandy thought aloud. "If anything lands on it . . ." Fearing the worst, the girls raced home. There they struggled to raise Papa's wooden ladder against the house, but it was hopeless.

5. Inside the house, Jane began packing things in a basket, just in case. After packing the family's silverware, she grabbed Papa's suits. Next she loaded the big clock from the mantelpiece. Mandy snatched a box and headed to her room. What should she pack first—her clothes, her dolls, or her books? That

was easy. Emptying both her bookshelves, she quickly filled the box.

6. Meanwhile, Jane had gone back outside to check the roof. Her screams of "Fire!" brought Mandy racing to the yard. A sheet of burning roofing paper from town had whirled down onto their roof. "Help!" the girls cried, as the flame spread over the roof. But their voices were lost in the wind. It was up to them to save the house.

7. That's when Mandy thought of the tree! A tall maple tree grew right beside the house. Last summer, Mandy had gotten into trouble climbing out her window onto it. "You could be killed!" Papa had warned her. Now she'd have to risk it. While Jane carried a bucket to the kitchen, Mandy ran to the stable to look for a rope. Finally, she found one, lying under the hay between the carriage and the pony's stall. Seconds later, she was crawling out her bedroom window, the rope tied around her waist. She inched up the trunk to a limb that spread out over the roof. Holding her breath, she stepped down onto the shingles.

8. On the ground, Jane had a full bucket. Mandy untied the rope, dropped one end, and Jane tied it onto the bucket. Anxious, Mandy pulled too hard on the rope, and the bucket swung wildly, spilling its load. "Hurry! Jane! More water!" Mandy screamed. Jane refilled the bucket. This time the rope slipped through Mandy's icy fingers, and the bucket crashed to the ground. Again, Jane made her way back to the kitchen pump to get another bucket of water. Mandy waited helplessly as the flames leaped higher on the roof.

9. The next bucket reached the roof, and Mandy tossed the water onto the flames. It didn't seem to do a thing. Four, five, six— Mandy lost count of how many buckets it took to douse the flames. With aching arms, she continued pouring water on the fire-darkened patch of roof until sunrise. By then, the wind had died down, and the house was safe.

10. Dressed in warm, dry clothes, the girls were eating toast and eggs when Papa returned. The back of his plaid jacket was charred black. The front was coated with ice. "Saved the newspaper," he announced proudly, "and the hotel! How come you girls didn't help out on the bucket line?"

11. Mandy and Jane smiled at each other. "We girls would only have been in the way," Jane said. "Besides, we were busy here."

1. The main character in the story is
   a. Mandy.
   b. Mr. Campbell.
   c. Papa.
   d. Jane.

2. Choose the words that best describe the main character.
   a. shy and unhappy
   b. lively and daring
   c. friendly and kind
   d. mean and angry

3. Judging from what Jane and Mandy packed, you might guess that
   a. Jane does not own any important belongings.
   b. neither girl cares about belongings.
   c. Mandy loves to read.
   d. the girls didn't care what they packed.

4. By the end of the story, the main character has learned that
   a. it's better to be concerned about others than yourself.
   b. it's foolish to get upset over little problems.
   c. imaginative solutions to problems can be found.
   d. fighting fires isn't very difficult.

5. The main problem in the beginning of the story is that
   a. Jane and Mandy's house is on fire.
   b. Mandy can't decide whether to save her dolls or her books.
   c. It's cold outside and all the blankets are wet.
   d. Papa's newspaper office might burn down.

6. The most important event in the middle of the story occurs when the girls
   a. bring wet blankets to their father.
   b. are not allowed to join the bucket line.
   c. discover the fire on the roof of their house.
   d. see that the town is burning.

7. The most exciting part of the story occurs when
   a. Mandy finds a way to put out the fire.
   b. the girls have to decide what to pack in their house.
   c. Papa returns and says he saved the newspaper.
   d. the townspeople form the bucket line.

8. At the end of the story,
   a. the fire on Main Street is still burning.
   b. Papa doesn't know his daughters put out a fire.
   c. the girls have packed up everything in their house.
   d. Mandy's house is destroyed.

9. This story takes place
   a. in the present time.
   b. in the past.
   c. in the near future.
   d. in the distant future.

10. The setting of the story is
   a. a small country town.
   b. a city.
   c. a log cabin in the wilderness.
   d. a suburban neighborhood.

11. The events in this story occur
   a. in summer.
   b. in autumn.
   c. in winter.
   d. in spring.

12. The part of the setting that was most important in the story was
   a. the temperature.
   b. the wind.
   c. the night.
   d. the town.

13. Papa needed blankets because
    a. the night was cold.
    b. he wanted keep his daughters busy.
    c. he wanted to protect the roof with wet blankets.
    d. all the towels were already used.

14. Mandy is furious at Mr. Campbell because he won't
    a. help her father save the newspaper.
    b. let her help on the bucket line.
    c. let her go into the hotel.
    d. help her save her house.

15. The girls raced home from the fire in town because
    a. Papa needed more blankets.
    b. Mr. Campbell told them to leave.
    c. it was very cold outside.
    d. they were worried about their house.

16. Mandy climbed the maple tree in order to
    a. get into her bedroom.
    b. see whether the fire on Main Street was still burning.
    c. get onto the roof.
    d. get a better view of the town.

17. The title of this story best describes
    a. how the townspeople saved the hotel.
    b. how Papa saved his newspaper office.
    c. how Mandy saved her house.
    d. how Jane put out a fire.

18. By the end of the story, the girls learn that
    a. adults usually know what's best.
    b. they are clever enough to solve big problems.
    c. fires and other disasters are just part of life.
    d. the townspeople didn't need their help.

19. Choose the statement that best expresses a theme of this story.
    a. Where there's a will, there's a way.
    b. Don't count your chickens before they hatch.
    c. Too many cooks spoil the broth.
    d. Don't cry over spilled milk.

20. You can infer that what Mandy best likes to do for enjoyment is
    a. collect stamps.
    b. play with dolls.
    c. climb trees.
    d. read books.

21. You can infer that the girls didn't use Papa's ladder because
    a. he had it at the newspaper office.
    b. it was too heavy to lift.
    c. it wasn't long enough to reach the roof.
    d. it was broken.

22. You can infer from Papa's appearance at the end of the story that he
    a. was very close to the flames.
    b. was badly hurt in the fire.
    c. didn't have to work on the bucket line.
    d. didn't put out the fire.

23. The word *trunk* in paragraph 7 means
    a. a strong, heavy box.
    b. the main part of a tree.
    c. a body, not including the head, arms, and legs.
    d. part of an elephant.

24. The word *stable* in paragraph 7 means
    a. a fenced-in yard.
    b. a building in which horses are kept.
    c. a toolshed.
    d. a sturdy object.

25. The word *douse* in paragraph 9 means
    a. to struggle with something.
    b. to soak something with water.
    c. to recognize a problem.
    d. to ignite something.

Read the following selection. Then choose the best answer for each question.
Mark your answers on the answer sheet.

The Age of the Vikings

1. The name *Vikings* refers to the people living in Norway, Sweden, and Denmark from about A.D. 800 to about A.D. 1100. During the Viking Age, other Europeans called these people Danes, Northmen, or Norsemen. The term *Viking* was not used until later. It probably came from the Scandinavian word *vic*, meaning "bay." To most Europeans, Vikings were robbers from the north. They roamed the bays and seas, raiding towns along the way.

Causes of the Viking Age

2. What brought about the Viking Age? By the end of the eighth century, many Scandinavians were growing restless in their homelands. They had already begun trading with merchants in England and France. They had seen the precious metals, silk, gems, and spices that these merchants had. Now the Vikings craved more of these goods for themselves. However, they did not have the means to buy them.

3. A fast-growing population and a paucity of good farmland in Scandinavia also brought about the Viking Age. The Vikings knew that the land in other countries of Europe was more fertile than theirs. Also, those lands were poorly defended. That's because their inhabitants were often fighting among themselves. To the Vikings, the time was right to invade and settle those lands.

Vikings as Shipbuilders

4. As master shipbuilders, the Vikings set out in vessels that were far better than those of other countries. Viking ships were light and easy to steer. The hulls were *clinkerbuilt*; that is, the planks overlapped one another for extra strength. The ships were called long boats because of their long, narrow design. Each boat had between 15 and 30 pairs of oars and a large woolen sail. On the bow was the carved head of a snake or dragon. The dragon was intended to ward off evil and frighten away the enemy.

5. Some Viking ships, preserved in clay, have been dug up in Norway. Scientists have learned much from these ships. The *Gokstad*, for example, was uncovered in 1880. Built around A.D. 900, the ship was 76 feet long, 6 feet wide, and 6 feet deep. In 1893, a Norwegian named Magnus Andersen built a replica of the *Gokstad*. He sailed from Norway to Canada in it in less than a month. The ship was fast and easy to steer. Another ship, the *Oseberg*, was dug up in 1903. Smaller and more richly carved, the *Oseberg* may have been the ship of a Viking queen.

Viking Navigation

6. In addition to building well, the Vikings navigated well. This is amazing, for they did not have compasses. Instead, they watched for landmarks, such as mountains, islands, and rocks. They also carried ravens aboard their ships. When a raven was let loose, it would fly to the nearest land. The Vikings would then follow the bird.

7. By the late 900s, the Norsemen had learned how to determine latitude. So, they no longer needed to rely on landmarks. To find their position on the sea, the Vikings used the North Star and a *husanatra*. This instrument was a wooden stick about a yard long. It had notches carved in it at equal spaces. At night, a navigator held the stick in front of him as he gazed at the North Star. He noted which notch lined up with the star. If a different notch lined up with the star the next night, he knew the ship was off course. Then he changed direction to get back on course.

Viking Invasions

8. The Viking invasions began in A.D. 793. In that year, Norwegian Vikings raided a monastery off the coast of England to steal its treasures. A wave of raids against England,

Ireland, and Scotland followed. By the mid-800s, the Norwegians were raiding towns as far away as France, Italy, and Spain. By the late 800s, the Vikings even dared to cross the rough North Atlantic Ocean and to migrate to Iceland.

9. In the year 982, a Norwegian Viking named Eric the Red left his home in Iceland and sailed west. He landed in a country he named Greenland. Later, in a voyage from Iceland to Greenland, a Viking named Bjarni Herjulfsson was blown off course in a storm. Eventually, he spotted the mainland of North America. He did not stop to explore it. By the year 1000, cropland in Greenland was in short supply. So Lief Ericson, the son of Eric the Red, sailed westward to find the land that Herjulfsson had spotted. He landed at a place he called Vinland, on the northern tip of Newfoundland. Despite these voyages, the Vikings made no permanent colonies in North America.

10. The Swedish Vikings went east, as far as the Black and Caspian Seas. They set up many trade centers in what is now western Russia. By the late 800s, they founded the first Russian state of Kiev.

11. The Danish Vikings traveled south to Germany, France, Spain, Italy, and the Mediterranean coast. In 1016, they conquered England. In France, they controlled the region called Normandy. This name means "land of the Northmen."

12. By 1100, the Viking Age had come to a close. The Vikings had set up trade centers and colonized some of the lands they had invaded. They had also realized that trading offered a more stable and prosperous life than raiding and looting did. In time, they learned the ways of the people living in the countries they had settled. Today, Vikings are credited with having found many trade routes still in use today. The Vikings and their way of life will not soon be forgotten.

Viking Exploration, A.D. 700–1000

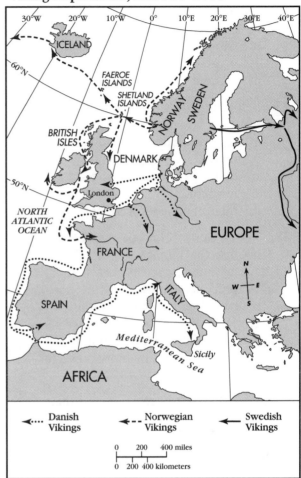

26. The Vikings invaded England in A.D. 793 because they
    a. needed more farmland.
    b. wanted to find trade routes.
    c. wanted to raid a monastery.
    d. wanted to settle there.

27. Before the 900s, the Vikings tended to sail close to land because
    a. they navigated by landmarks.
    b. their ships were not sturdy.
    c. they were in search of good farmland.
    d. their compasses were not accurate.

28. Viking raids in Europe eventually ended because the Vikings
    a. lost interest in silk, gems, and precious metals.
    b. preferred trading to raiding.
    c. were unable to fight against powerful European armies.
    d. were defeated by more powerful people.

29. Vikings carried ravens aboard their ships because the birds
    a. were thought to ward off evil.
    b. were a symbol of good luck.
    c. were used to carry messages back to Scandinavia.
    d. led the ships to land.

30. In what way were the Vikings of 800 different from other Europeans?
    a. They had larger populations.
    b. They built better ships.
    c. They were kind to their neighbors.
    d. all of the above

31. Both the Norwegian and Danish Vikings
    a. explored North America.
    b. avoided Iceland.
    c. went south to the Mediterranean coast.
    d. made raids on England.

32. Contrasted with the *Gokstad*, the *Oseberg* was
    a. in much better condition.
    b. larger.
    c. more richly carved.
    d. more difficult to find.

33. Which of the following statements is a fact?
    a. The Vikings were amazing navigators.
    b. By the late 900s, the Norsemen had learned to determine latitude.
    c. Using ravens was a clever navigation device.
    d. The Vikings took advantage of their opportunities.

34. Which of the following statements is an opinion?
    a. The Viking invasions of Europe began in 793.
    b. The *Gokstad* was 76 feet long.
    c. The Vikings were wrong to raid and loot neighboring countries.
    d. The Vikings used the North Star to navigate by.

35. *The Swedish Vikings went east, as far as the Caspian Sea.* This statement is
    a. a fact.
    b. an opinion.
    c. both a fact and an opinion.
    d. neither a fact nor an opinion.

36. *The Vikings should have made a permanent colony in North America.* This statement is
    a. a fact.
    b. an opinion.
    c. both a fact and an opinion.
    d. neither a fact nor an opinion.

37. Based on paragraphs 1 through 3, you can infer that most Europeans
    a. copied the Vikings.
    b. feared the Vikings.
    c. learned from the Vikings.
    d. told stories about the Vikings.

38. You can infer that the Vikings originally settled Greenland to
    a. find lumber for their ships.
    b. find and use new cropland.
    c. find gold and precious goods.
    d. find people to conquer.

39. You might infer from paragraph 12 that many Vikings
    a. tried to return to Scandinavia.
    b. died in battle.
    c. were not successful as traders.
    d. grew tired of looting and raiding.

40. Which sentence expresses the main idea of paragraph 3?
    a. To the Vikings, the time was right for invading these lands.
    b. The Vikings knew that the land in other countries of Europe was more fertile than their own was.
    c. A fast-growing population and a paucity of farmland in Scandinavia also brought about the Viking Age.
    d. Also, those lands were poorly defended.

41. Which sentence expresses the main idea of paragraph 5?
    a. Viking ships were fast and easy to steer.
    b. Scientists have learned much from Viking ships dug up in Norway.
    c. The *Gokstad* was discovered by archaeologists in 1880.
    d. The *Oseberg* was a burial ship.

42. Which sentence in paragraph 7 states the main idea?
    a. the first sentence
    b. the second sentence
    c. the fourth sentence
    d. the last sentence

43. Think about the main idea of paragraph 8. Then choose the detail below that would support the main idea.
    a. These invasions brought the Vikings great wealth.
    b. Viking invasions of England helped unify that country.

c. The Vikings recalled their deeds in long stories called sagas.
    d. The Vikings sacked Kiev.

44. Think about the main idea of paragraph 12. Then choose the detail below that would support the main idea.
    a. Vikings gave up raiding after being defeated.
    b. For a Viking, raiding was a way to attain wealth and honor.
    c. No records exist of Viking settlements in North America.
    d. Vikings set up trade centers in the lands they conquered.

45. The word *replica* in paragraph 5 means
    a. a copy.   c. a sailor.
    b. a motorboat.   d. a statue.

46. The word *craved* in paragraph 2 means
    a. created.   c. desired.
    b. owned.   d. stole.

47. The word *paucity* in paragraph 3 means
    a. shortage.   c. oversupply.
    b. awareness.   d. fertility.

Use the map on page 45 to answer questions 48 through 50.

48. Which Viking group reached Sicily in the Mediterranean Sea?
    a. the Norwegians c. the Swedish
    b. the Danish   d. none of the above

49. About how far did the Vikings have to sail from Norway to their settlement on Iceland?
    a. about 500 miles
    b. about 1,000 miles
    c. about 1,500 miles
    d. more than 2,000 miles

50. In sailing from Norway to the British Isles, a Viking ship might stop at
    a. the Faeroe Islands.
    b. the Shetland Islands.
    c. Iceland.
    d. Denmark.

Read the following selection. Then choose the best answer for each question. Mark your answers on the answer sheet.

Why Do Earthquakes Happen?

1. The Earth is made up of four main layers. The topmost layer, where we live, is a thin layer called the crust. Underneath the crust is the mantle. Next comes the outer core. Finally, the inner core makes up the center of the Earth. The closer to the center of the Earth, the hotter the temperature. The mantle, for example, is about 1,600°F and is formed mainly of molten, or melted, rock. The temperatures of the inner and outer cores are much hotter than the mantle.

2. The crust of the Earth floats on the molten rock of the mantle the way a boat floats on water. The crust, however, is not one solid piece. It is broken up into about 15 pieces called plates. Each plate moves freely as it floats on the mantle. On the gigantic plates rest the Earth's continents and oceans.

3. In some places, plates have crashed together to form mountains. Sometimes, one plate rides up over another plate. This causes deep ocean trenches to form. Other plates rub and slide past each other, causing earthquakes. Shocking things happen where giant plates meet.

4. A fault zone is an area where two plates rub against each other. In some places, a fault is a crack in the ground or a small valley. It might be a lake, if the fault fills in with water. In other places, a fault might lie buried under a development, a shopping center, or a highway.

5. North America sits almost entirely on one plate—the North American plate. A small region of southern California and Mexico, however, rests on another plate, the Pacific plate. Those two plates come together in a fault zone that includes the San Andreas fault. The city of San Francisco is partly built on top of the San Andreas fault.

6. Like all the plates in the Earth's crust, the North American and Pacific plates move slowly. But they do not move in the same direction. The Pacific plate moves northward along the North American plate. As they rub against each other, the plates create friction. This friction makes the plates stick together. But they don't stick together for long.

7. Remember that plates float on molten rock in the mantle. Deep inside the Earth,

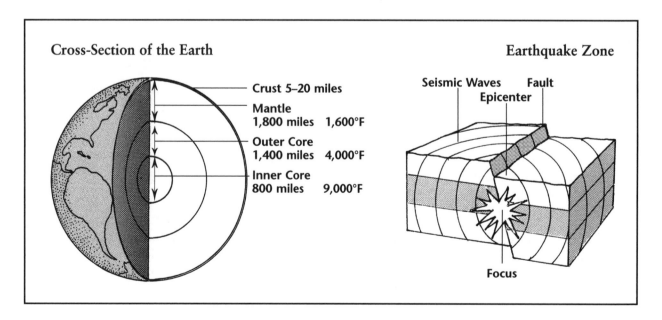

Cross-Section of the Earth

Crust 5–20 miles
Mantle 1,800 miles 1,600°F
Outer Core 1,400 miles 4,000°F
Inner Core 800 miles 9,000°F

Earthquake Zone

Seismic Waves   Fault
Epicenter
Focus

pressure builds up underneath the point where the two plates rub together. In time, that pressure separates the plates with a sudden jerk. Shock waves move out from the point where the plates move. Those shock waves are the earthquake. After the earthquake, smaller movements, called aftershocks, can occur.

8. Earthquakes cause destruction in different ways. Often, buildings simply aren't able to stand up to such violent shaking, so they crumble. Another problem is liquefaction. In some places, the ground isn't tightly packed. Ground that is loose gravel or sand can mix with underground water during an earthquake. The ground becomes a liquid mass, and buildings actually sink into it. More destructive than liquefaction is a tsunami. This is a huge wave, sometimes 100 feet high (30 meters), that forms when the ocean bottom rises and falls from the shock of an earthquake.

51. Ocean trenches are caused when
    a. one plate rides up over another.
    b. two plates crash into each other.
    c. two plates rub and slide against each other.
    d. the Earth's crust cracks.

52. The reason two plates don't stick together very long is because
    a. they are always rubbing against each other.
    b. pressure deep in the Earth forces them to move.
    c. the heat inside the core is too great.
    d. earthquakes break them apart.

53. Liquefaction can damage buildings because
    a. the Earth beneath them shakes violently.
    b. the ocean bottom near them rises and falls.
    c. sand and gravel mixed together make the ground unstable.
    d. the ground beneath them mixes with water causing them to sink.

54. Which is *not* one of the four main layers of the Earth?
    a. the outer core
    b. the mantle
    c. the plates
    d. the inner core

55. A tiny portion of California lies on the
    a. North American plate.
    b. San Andreas plate.
    c. Atlantic plate.
    d. Pacific plate.

56. Which type of disaster is *not* related to earthquakes?
    a. liquefaction
    b. tsunamis
    c. hurricanes
    d. all of the above

57. The word *molten* in paragraph 1 means
    a. melted.
    b. heavy.
    c. moving.
    d. floating.

Use the diagrams on page 48 to answer questions 58 through 61.

58. The thickest layer of the Earth is the
    a. mantle.
    b. outer core.
    c. inner core.
    d. crust.

59. What is the temperature of the outer core?
    a. 800°F
    b. 1,600°F
    c. 4,000°F
    d. 9,000°F

60. Which of the following is *not* part of the earthquake zone?
    a. epicenter
    b. fault
    c. mantle
    d. focus

61. Which of the following is *not* located on the Earth's surface?
    a. crust
    b. fault
    c. seismic waves
    d. focus

62. The main idea of paragraph 1 is stated in the
    a. first sentence.
    b. second sentence.
    c. third sentence.
    d. last sentence.

63. The main idea of paragraph 3 is stated in the
    a. first sentence.
    b. second sentence.
    c. third sentence.
    d. last sentence.

64. The main idea of paragraph 8 is stated in the
    a. first sentence.
    b. second sentence.
    c. third sentence.
    d. last sentence.

65. Which detail supports the main idea of paragraph 8?
    a. Most earthquakes pass without being noticed.
    b. Sometimes liquefaction causes buildings to sink into the ground.
    c. Scientists are looking for ways to predict earthquakes accurately.
    d. Plates in the Earth's crust move slowly.

66. The main idea of paragraph 2 is that the Earth's crust is broken up into plates that move freely. Which detail supports this idea?
    a. The Earth's crust is 5–20 miles thick.
    b. The continents on the Earth's crust are actually moving slowly in different directions.
    c. No life exists beneath the Earth's crust.
    d. The Earth is made up of four main layers.

67. Choose the correct definition of the word *crack* as it is used in the second sentence of paragraph 4.
    a. a sharp noise
    b. a narrow opening
    c. a sudden blow
    d. a highway

68. Choose the correct definition of the word *development* as it is used in the last sentence of paragraph 4.
    a. the act of becoming larger, fuller, or better
    b. a piece of land with newly built homes
    c. an event or happening
    d. the act of appearing

69. The word *liquefaction* in paragraph 8 comes partly from the word
    a. liquid.
    b. fraction.
    c. leak.
    d. fluid.

70. The English words that mean about the same as the word *tsunami* in paragraph 8 are
    a. earthquake shock.
    b. giant ocean wave.
    c. ocean bottom.
    d. aftershock.

Questions 71 through 75 are word problems. Use the space below each one for your calculations.

71. The Earth's outer core is 1,400 miles thick. The inner core is 800 miles thick. How thick is the core as a whole?
    a. 600 miles
    b. 1,480 miles
    c. 2,200 miles
    d. 14,800 miles

72. A scientist in Japan recorded 24 minor earthquakes one month. A scientist in Chile recorded twice as many. How many earthquakes did the scientist in Chile record?
    a. 12
    b. 24
    c. 36
    d. 48

73. 850 people became homeless during an earthquake. 230 were able to move in with relatives. How many people still needed housing?
    a. 1,080
    b. 730
    c. 620
    d. 520

74. A tsunami in Japan in 1896 was 115 feet high. Another in 1912 was 94 feet high. How much higher was the 1896 tsunami?
    a. 7 feet
    b. 15 feet
    c. 21 feet
    d. 26 feet

75. Between 1900 and 1920, Japan had three tsunamis. The first tsunami was 97 feet, the second tsunami was 110 feet, and the third tsunami was 91 feet. What is the total number of feet of the three tsunamis combined?
    a. 289 feet
    b. 298 feet
    c. 389 feet
    d. 398 feet

A. Study the following dictionary entry. Then answer questions 76 through 80.

face (fās) *n.* **1.** the front part of the head, including the eyes, nose, and mouth **2.** a look that shows meaning or feeling [The clown made a sad *face.*] **3.** surface or side; especially the main, front, or top side [the *face* of the Earth.] **4.** dignity or reputation [to lose *face*] *v.* **1.** to turn toward or have the face turned toward [Please *face* the door.] **2.** to meet or oppose with boldness [*face* the enemy] **3.** to put material on the surface of [The school is *faced* with marble.]
—faced, fac′ ing —face to face, **1.** with each facing the other **2.** very close —in the face of, **1.** in the presence of. **2.** in spite of.
—on the face of it, as far as can be seen.

76. How many noun meanings are given?
    a. two
    b. three
    c. four
    d. five

77. Which of the following is a noun meaning?
    a. very close
    b. to meet with boldness
    c. in the presence of
    d. the main, front, or top side

78. How many verb meanings are given?
    a. two
    b. three
    c. four
    d. five

79. Which of the following is a verb form?
    a. facing
    b. fast
    c. face to face
    d. in the face of

80. Which noun definition would apply to the following sentence? *James lost face when his teacher caught him cheating.*
    a. definition 1
    b. definition 2
    c. definition 3
    d. definition 4

B. Study the following encyclopedia index. Then answer questions 81 through 85.

MIDDLE AGES
    Art and Architecture **M:**442–447
        Castle **C:**212–214 *with diagram*
        Cathedral **C:**232–233 *with picture*
        Gothic Art **G:**267 *pictures* on **G:**269
        Stained Glass **S:**848
    Defense
        Armies (Medieval) **A:**641
        Armor **A:**685 *with pictures*
        Sword **S:**831
    Government
        City-State **C:**450
        Feudalism **F:**250
        Free City **F:**387–388 *with map*
        Magna Carta **M:**49
        Middle Ages **M:**438–440
    Health and Welfare
        Bubonic Plague **B:**531
        Medicine **M:**306

81. Where would you look to find information about armies in the Middle Ages?
    a. A:641
    b. A:685
    c. S:831
    d. M:438–440

82. Where would you look to find pictures of Gothic art in the Middle Ages?
    a. C:232–233
    b. G:267
    c. G:269
    d. M:442–447

83. The information about castles in the Middle Ages includes a
    a. chart.
    b. picture.
    c. map.
    d. diagram.

84. Where would you look to find a map showing free cities in the Middle Ages?
    a. F:250
    b. F:387–388
    c. M:49
    d. C:450

85. Where would you look to find information about the plague in the Middle Ages?
    a. B:531
    b. P:531
    c. M:306
    d. M:438–440

C. **Think about word parts to answer questions 86 through 100.**

86. Choose the base word in *unbelievable*.
    a. live
    b. leave
    c. believe
    d. able

87. Choose the base word in *unimaginable*.
    a. imagine
    b. able
    c. imaginable
    d. image

88. Choose the base word in *remover*.
    a. remove
    b. over
    c. mover
    d. move

89. Choose the base word in *uninterested*.
    a. arrest
    b. interest
    c. rest
    d. rested

90. Choose the suffix that will make the word *fight* mean "one who fights."
    a. -able   c. -er
    b. -ly   d. -ing

91. Choose the suffix that will make the word *happy* mean "in a happy way" when the *y* is dropped and *i* is added.
    a. -ly   c. -er
    b. -ness   d. -est

92. Choose the suffix that will make the word *like* mean "possible to like."
    a. -able   c. -un
    b. -ly   d. -ness

93. Choose the prefix that will make the word *respect* mean "without respect."
    a. un-   c. re-
    b. dis-   d. im-

94. Choose the prefix that will make the word *ice* mean "remove ice."
    a. under-   c. pre-
    b. de-   d. un-

95. Choose the prefix that will make the word *paid* mean "paid again."
    a. un-   c. under-
    b. pre-   d. re-

96. Choose the prefix that will make the word *heat* mean "heat before."
    a. un-   c. re-
    b. pre-   d. de-

97. Choose the prefix that will make the word *named* mean "not named."
    a. re-   c. pre-
    b. un-   d. dis-

98. Choose the correct way to divide the word *unsaddle* into syllables.
    a. un sad dle   c. un sa ddle
    b. un sadd le   d. un s addle

99. Choose the correct way to divide the word *pamper* into syllables.
    a. pa mper   c. p am per
    b. pamp er   d. pam per

100. Choose the correct way to divide the word *together* into syllables.
    a. to get her   c. to geth er
    b. tog eth er   d. to ge th er

Read the following selection. Then choose the best answer for each question.
Mark your answers on the answer sheet.

A Tale of Terror

1. I was once traveling in Calabria, a region in southwest Italy. It is a land of wicked people. I believe they hate everyone, particularly French people like me. The reason would take too long to explain. It is enough to say that they hate us. French people get on very badly when they fall into the hands of Calabrians.

2. I had a young man for a companion. In those mountains, the roads are steep. Our horses had great difficulty. My companion went first. A path that seemed to be a shortcut led us astray. It was my own fault. An old man like me shouldn't have trusted a 20-year-old!

3. While daylight lasted, we tried to find our way through the woods. But the harder we tried, the more lost we became. It was pitch dark when we came to a very evil-looking house. We entered fearfully. What else could we do?

4. We found a coal miner and his family at the table. They asked us to join them. My young companion did not wait to be asked twice. Soon we were eating and drinking. He was, at least, but I looked around the house, which seemed more like an arsenal than a home. There were pistols, swords, and knives of all kinds. Everything about the place displeased me. And I saw very well that I displeased our host.

5. My young friend, however, acted as though he were one of the family. He laughed and talked with them. I should have foreseen his stupidity! He told them where we came from. He told them where we were going. He told them that we were French. Just imagine! We were among our worst enemies. We were alone, lost, and far from help. To make matters worse, he even pretended to be a rich man. For helping us, he promised to give the family money when we left.

6. Then he spoke of his bag. He begged them to help him care for it. He wanted it put at the head of his bed. He said he didn't want a pillow, just his bag. What a foolish youth! Our hosts must have thought we carried the king's diamonds.

7. After supper, our hosts left us. They slept in quarters beneath the main floor. A loft 7 or 8 feet high was to be our resting place. It was a nest reached by a ladder. One got into it by creeping under beams loaded with dried hams and other provisions. My companion climbed up alone. Nearly asleep, he laid himself down with his head on the bag.

8. Deciding to remain awake, I made a good fire in a small stove and sat down beside it. There, not daring to sleep, I passed the night.

9. When the night was nearly over, I heard the voices of our host and his wife talking and arguing below. I put my ear to the floor and clearly heard these words spoken by the husband. "Well, let's see, must they both be killed?" To this, his wife replied, "Yes."

10. I heard no more. How shall I go on? I stood scarcely breathing. My body was cold as stone. You could hardly have known if I were alive or dead. We were against a large family, and they had so many weapons!

11. My companion was still dead with sleep. To call him, or make a noise, I dared not. To escape alone was impossible. The window was not high, but outside were two large dogs howling like wolves.

12. At the end of a long quarter-hour, I heard someone on the ladder. I looked through the crack in the door and saw the miner. In his hand, he carried a long knife. He came up, his wife after him. I was behind the door when he opened it and entered, barefoot. From the outside, the woman said in a low voice, "Softly, go softly." Getting up as high as the bed—the poor young man lying with his throat bare—he took his knife and—cut a slice from a ham that hung from the ceiling. Then he left, closing the door, and I was left with my thoughts.

13. Soon the sun rose. The family came to awaken us, as we had asked. They brought us something to eat. It was a very good breakfast, I assure you. Two capons formed part of it. We must eat one, our hostess said, and take the other with us on our journey. When I saw the chickens, I understood the meaning of those terrible words: "Must they both be killed?" And I think I don't have to say now what they meant.

1. The main character in the story is
   a. an old man.
   b. a young man.
   c. a coal miner.
   d. an old woman.

2. Choose the word that best describes the main character.
   a. independent
   b. suspicious
   c. generous
   d. innocent

3. Judging from the way the two travelers act, you might guess that
   a. the young man is more trusting than the old man.
   b. the young man is more fearful than the old man.
   c. the old man is more trusting than the young man.
   d. evil-looking creatures lurk in the dark.

4. By the end of the story, the main character has learned that
   a. few people can be trusted.
   b. it's easy to jump to conclusions.
   c. first impressions are usually correct.
   d. it's not safe to travel at night.

5. The main character's conflict is really with
   a. his own feelings.
   b. another character.
   c. the forces of nature.
   d. supernatural forces.

6. Which sentence best describes this conflict?
   a. The miner wants to kill the main character.
   b. The main character is lost at night in the woods.
   c. Neither of the men are very trusting.
   d. The main character struggles against groundless fears.

7. How is this conflict finally resolved?
   a. The travelers find the house.
   b. The young man is friendly to his hosts.
   c. The hosts are generous to the men.
   d. The travelers leave before daybreak.

8. The old man has a conflict with the young man because
   a. he feels the young man is too trusting.
   b. he feels the young man gives the hosts too much money.
   c. he thinks the young man is trying to kill him.
   d. he thinks the young man wants to take his bag of money.

9. The first important event in the story occurs when
   a. the young man says he is French.
   b. the travelers are attacked.
   c. the travelers get lost.
   d. the travelers stumble across an evil-looking house.

10. The most exciting part of the story occurs when
    a. the travelers find the miner's house.
    b. the old man watches his host approach with a knife.
    c. the young man promises to give his hosts money.
    d. the hosts discover the travelers are French.

11. The story ends with the travelers
    a. being killed at the house.
    b. having breakfast at the house.
    c. preparing to leave the house.
    d. sneaking out of the house.

12. Where does the main action of this story take place?
    a. in Italy
    b. in France
    c. in the American South
    d. in Germany

13. The action in the story probably takes place
    a. over 100 years ago.
    b. in the present time.
    c. in the near future.
    d. in the distant future.

14. In the opening scene, the travelers are
    a. next to a large coal mine.
    b. in a small Calabrian village.
    c. in a house in the woods.
    d. on a mountain trail.

15. The scene in paragraph 12 occurs in
    a. a barn.
    b. a loft of the miner's house.
    c. the kitchen of the house.
    d. sleeping quarters beneath the main floor.

16. What is the author's message in this story?
    a. You can't be too careful.
    b. Our fears are often groundless.
    c. Life goes on no matter what.
    d. All good things must come to an end.

17. By the end of the story, the Frenchman has learned that he should
    a. trust strangers less.
    b. always travel alone.
    c. have a more open mind.
    d. always travel in pairs.

18. The story's title refers to the terror
    a. of the murders in the house.
    b. that the younger traveler commits.
    c. of being lost in a dark forest.
    d. that the older traveler imagines.

19. Which of the following titles would also be appropriate for this story?
    a. "A Frenchman's Travels"
    b. "A Tale of Two Murders"
    c. "Imagining the Worst"
    d. "Life in Calabria"

20. Who is the narrator of the story?
    a. the coal miner
    b. the young traveler
    c. the older traveler
    d. the old woman

21. Why is first-person point of view a good way of telling this story?
    a. The narrator understands the situation he is in.
    b. The narrator's thoughts and fears are important to the story.
    c. The narrator can explain how the hosts feel.
    d. The narrator knows what others are thinking.

22. Which of these events did the narrator *not* see or hear?
    a. the killing of the capons
    b. the host climbing the ladder
    c. his companion offering money to the host
    d. the hosts talking to each other

23. The word *arsenal* in paragraph 4 means
    a. a place to eat a meal.
    b. a place to store weapons.
    c. a place that is dirty or messy.
    d. a place far away from others.

24. The word *capon* in paragraph 13 means
    a. bacon.
    b. chicken.
    c. fruit.
    d. goat.

25. The word *nest* in paragraph 7 means
    a. a place built by birds to lay their eggs.
    b. a snug resting place.
    c. a set of things that fit within each other.
    d. a basement.

Read the following selection. Then choose the best answer for each question.
Mark your answers on the answer sheet.

The French Explore North America

1. Jacques Cartier, a French sailor, was an early explorer of North America. Between 1533 and 1535, Cartier made two trips to the area we know today as Canada. Cartier was searching for a water route to Asia. Although he failed to find one, Cartier was the first French sailor to discover the St. Lawrence River.

2. Besides failing to discover a sea route to Asia, Cartier also failed to find gold to pay for further voyages. After Cartier's travels, France lost interest in North America for nearly 50 years. The only French on the continent were fishermen. They lived on the eastern coast and traded with Native Americans.

3. The desire for furs reawakened France's interest in the New World. The French king encouraged traders and colonists to settle there. In 1603, one company set up a small trading post in Nova Scotia. Samuel de Champlain was that company's mapmaker.

4. For several years, Champlain mapped the coastlines of what are now Maine and New Hampshire. In 1608, Champlain sailed up the St. Lawrence River, searching for a water route to Asia. He built a trading fort called Quebec on the river.

5. Champlain learned that the land around Quebec was held by a group of Native Americans called the Huron. He encouraged the Huron to sell him beaver skins. To prove his friendship, Champlain joined the Huron in 1609 in a war against their enemies, the Iroquois. Champlain traveled with a Huron war party through what is now Vermont and New York State. There he helped the Huron defeat the Iroquois. As a result, the powerful Iroquois nation became enemies of the French settlers.

6. Champlain worked hard to attract French merchants and settlers to Quebec. Settlers in New France faced many problems, though. The oak, maple, and birch forests were difficult to cut and clear for planting. Many colonists felt cut off from the rest of the world.

Quebec's climate was bitterly cold. Winter ice prevented ships from making contact with France for six months each year. By 1663, only 2,500 people from France had settled in New France.

7. After 1663, the French made a greater effort to settle New France. The king put New France under his direct control. To end the danger from the Iroquois, the king sent troops to invade their lands. French missionaries began to build missions along the Great Lakes.

8. One missionary in New France was Father Jacques Marquette. The Huron told him about a great river to the west. This river was said to lead all the way to the Pacific Ocean and Asia. Could this be the passage explorers had been seeking?

9. In 1673, Father Marquette decided to find out if the story was true. From Lake Michigan, he set out with a fur trader named Louis Joliet. The explorers portaged, or carried, their canoes to the Wisconsin River. Then they paddled down that river and onto the Mississippi. For three weeks, they sailed southward. At last, Marquette realized that the river did not turn west. Instead, it flowed south to the Gulf of Mexico. Marquette and Joliet feared they would be captured by Spanish troops in that area, so they returned to Quebec.

10. Marquette and Joliet had not found a passage to Asia. But they did chart the course of the Mississippi River. Now New France could build forts and trading posts along the river. That would expand the profitable fur trade.

11. In 1682, Robert LaSalle led an exploring party down the Mississippi River. Along the way, the French made friends with Native Americans. They found good sites for forts and trading posts. LaSalle reached the mouth of the Mississippi River. He claimed the entire midsection of North America for France. He named this land Louisiana for the French king, Louis XIV.

12. In Europe, wearing furs was very fashionable. Therefore, French fur traders made

more of the skins, fur traders explored much of North America. Those traders did not want farmers to clear forests and drive off wild animals. For that reason, farmers often felt unwelcome in New France. As a result, France did not settle much of the land it claimed in North America. This became a problem in later years, when the French were greatly outnumbered by English settlers in North America.

Early French Explorers of North America, 1600s

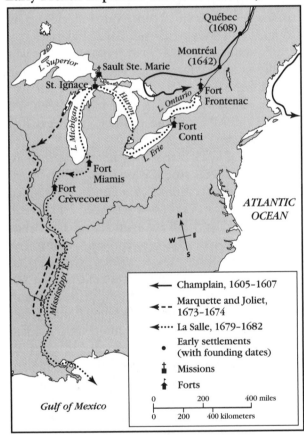

26. What is the main idea of paragraph 2?
    a. Cartier failed to discover a sea route to Asia.
    b. The French traded with Native Americans.
    c. The only French on the continent were fishermen.
    d. After Cartier's travels, France lost interest in North America for nearly 50 years.

27. What is the main idea of paragraph 6?
    a. Champlain worked hard to attract French settlers to Quebec.
    b. Settlers in New France faced many problems, though.
    c. By 1663, only 2,500 people from France had settled in New France.
    d. Quebec's cold climate prevented ship passage for many months.

28. Which sentence in paragraph 7 states the main idea?
    a. the first sentence
    b. the second sentence
    c. the third sentence
    d. the last sentence

29. What is the unstated main idea of paragraph 9?
    a. Marquette and Joliet were the first French to explore the Mississippi River.
    b. Marquette and Joliet were almost captured.
    c. The Mississippi River was a water route to Asia.
    d. The Mississippi River was the water passage explorers had been seeking.

30. What is the unstated main idea of paragraph 12?
    a. Furs made New France rich.
    b. The fur trade helped and hurt New France.
    c. Settling New France was a serious problem.
    d. The French were fashionable people.

31. Find the main idea of paragraph 5. Then choose the detail that supports the main idea.
    a. Champlain was one of the early French explorers of North America.
    b. Champlain sailed to Mexico in 1599.
    c. Later in his life, Champlain explored Lake Ontario.
    d. Champlain learned the Huron language and customs.

32. Champlain fought against the Iroquois in 1609 because
    a. they wouldn't sell him furs.
    b. he was a friend of the Huron.
    c. they wouldn't let the French clear the forests.
    d. they had gold.

33. Cartier's discoveries didn't interest the French because
    a. he found no gold.
    b. the New World was too far away.
    c. he found no furs.
    d. the land was too harsh.

34. Marquette and Joliet did not complete their journey down the Mississippi because
    a. the Native Americans had no furs to trade.
    b. they feared capture by the Spanish troops.
    c. they realized the river did not flow east.
    d. the cold prevented further travel.

35. The fur trade slowed down the settlement of New France because
    a. fur traders did not want farmers to clear forests.
    b. the demand for furs in Europe was high.
    c. the fur trade was not very profitable.
    d. animals were scarce in the cold climate.

36. Like Marquette and Joliet, LaSalle
    a. was a French missionary.
    b. seized land from the Spanish.
    c. explored the Mississippi River.
    d. built forts.

37. Unlike the Huron, the Iroquois
    a. trapped animals for their furs.
    b. were enemies of the French.
    c. went to the French missions.
    d. knew where to find gold.

38. Both Cartier and Champlain
    a. made friends with the Huron.
    b. set up fur trading posts.
    c. searched for a route to Asia.
    d. set up missions.

39. What is the meaning of the word *portaged* in paragraph 9?
    a. explored
    b. paddled
    c. searched
    d. carried

40. What is the meaning of the word *pelts* in paragraph 12?
    a. profits
    b. trade goods
    c. money
    d. animal skins

41. Which statement is a fact?
    a. The French and the Huron had a good relationship.
    b. Fighting the Iroquois was Champlain's worst mistake.
    c. By 1663, 2,500 French had settled in New France.
    d. The Huron were good traders.

42. Which statement is an opinion?
    a. Cartier searched for a passage to Asia.
    b. Life in Quebec was very difficult.
    c. LaSalle reached the Gulf of Mexico in 1682.
    d. Between 1533 and 1535, Cartier made two trips to what is now known as Canada.

43. *The French were the first Europeans to explore the Great Lakes.* This statement is
    a. a fact.
    b. an opinion.
    c. both a fact and an opinion.
    d. neither a fact nor an opinion.

44. *The French were foolish to focus so much on fur trading.* This statement is
    a. a fact.
    b. an opinion.
    c. both a fact and an opinion.
    d. neither a fact nor an opinion.

45. The lakes and rivers of New France
    a. made it difficult for settlers.
    b. blocked trade in many areas.
    c. provided ready transportation.
    d. could not be traveled because of the cold climate.

Use the map on page 58 to answer questions 46 through 50.

46. The mission of St. Ignace is located where Lake Michigan meets
    a. Lake Superior.
    b. Lake Huron.
    c. Lake Erie.
    d. Lake Ontario.

47. According to the map, LaSalle began his journey at
    a. Fort Frontenac.
    b. Fort Conti.
    c. Sault Ste. Marie.
    d. the Gulf of Mexico.

48. Before turning back, Marquette and Joliet traveled south about
    a. 600 miles.
    b. 1,000 miles.
    c. 1,800 miles.
    d. 2,000 miles.

49. What was the founding date of Montréal?
    a. 1605
    b. 1608
    c. 1630
    d. 1642

50. In what direction did LaSalle travel to go from Fort Miamis to Fort Crèvecoeur?
    a. southeast
    b. southwest
    c. northeast
    d. northwest

Read the following selection. Then choose the best answer for each question. Mark your answers on the answer sheet.

The Water Cycle

1. A typical water molecule doesn't stay in the same place for long. It might start out in the air. The next day, it could be drawn up into a pine tree. The next week, it might be in a pond or in the cells of your body. The following month, it might be back in the air. The movement of water around the Earth is called the **water cycle**. Here's how it works.

2. Water left outside in a bowl eventually disappears. It changes from water to water vapor through the process of evaporation. On a larger scale, as the Sun heats the Earth, water evaporates into water vapor from the surfaces of lakes, rivers, oceans, and from the soil.

3. People, animals, and plants also give off water vapor. Try breathing on a mirror. Notice the cloud that forms on the glass. Each time you breathe out, or exhale, water from your cells is released as water vapor. Plants also add water vapor to the air. During the process of transpiration, water stored in plant cells is released as water vapor, passing from the leaves into the air.

4. Evaporation and transpiration add moisture to the air. Winds carry this moisture over the Earth. Temperature decreases with altitude, so the higher water vapor goes, the colder the temperature of the air. As water vapor rises, or is blown higher into the atmosphere, it cools and changes to drops of water. Clouds are formed, just as exhaled water vapor forms a "cloud" when it hits the cool

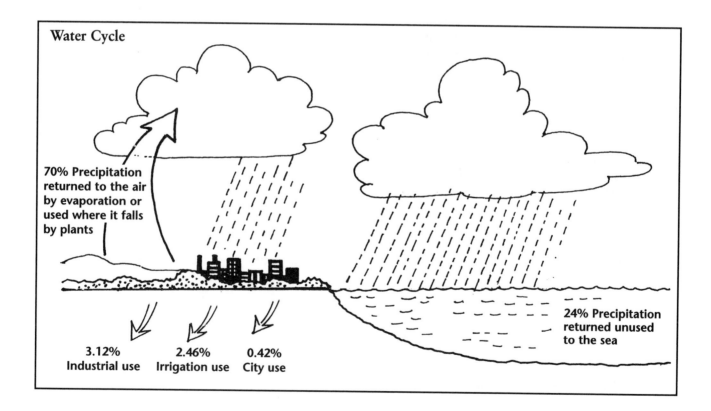

Water Cycle

70% Precipitation returned to the air by evaporation or used where it falls by plants

24% Precipitation returned unused to the sea

3.12% Industrial use

2.46% Irrigation use

0.42% City use

surface of a mirror. In time, the drops of water fall back to Earth as precipitation—rain, snow, sleet, or hail.

5. Some precipitation that strikes the ground runs off the land and flows into rivers, lakes, and oceans. The rest soaks into the soil.

6. Precipitation that runs off or falls directly into the oceans and other bodies of water is immediately ready to start the cycle over again. However, water that soaks into the soil may have a longer journey. Some soil water will evaporate from the ground and return to the atmosphere. Some will be taken in by plants that will release it back into the atmosphere. Most of the soil water will become part of the groundwater supply. Like surface runoff, groundwater also flows back into lakes, rivers, and oceans—only much more slowly. Thus, the water cycle continues.

7. In the United States, about 48 percent of the people in cities and towns get their water directly or indirectly from the ground. About 52 percent get their water from lakes and rivers. In rural areas, about 95 percent of the population depends on groundwater pumped from wells.

8. Water is a renewable resource. Over time, all the water on Earth is recycled, so there is always the same amount of water on Earth. The water that people use is a small part of the total amount of water on the planet. Although the unused water will not disappear, much of it is too salty or otherwise unusable.

51. Water vapor forms clouds as it rises because
    a. less evaporation occurs at high altitudes.
    b. air temperature decreases at high altitudes.
    c. it remains part of the water cycle.
    d. it releases moisture into the air.

52. What is one effect of the Sun's heating the Earth?
    a. Plants release more water vapor into the air.
    b. Humans and animals exhale.
    c. Water evaporates into the air.
    d. The water cycle stops.

53. Precipitation that doesn't soak into the soil is immediately able to begin the water cycle because
    a. it is released as water vapor by plants.
    b. it evaporates from rivers, lakes, and oceans.
    c. it is a renewable resource.
    d. the Sun dries it up.

54. According to the selection, one form of precipitation is
    a. runoff.
    b. hail.
    c. clouds.
    d. oceans.

55. A large forest releases water to the atmosphere through
    a. precipitation.
    b. condensation.
    c. transpiration.
    d. evaporation.

56. Compared to cities, rural areas have
    a. greater rainfall.
    b. more groundwater wells to supply water.
    c. more lakes and rivers.
    d. fewer sources for water.

57. Like surface runoff, water that soaks into the ground
    a. will flow back into lakes, rivers, and oceans.
    b. changes to liquid water.
    c. is released into the atmosphere through transpiration.
    d. will evaporate into the air.

58. Unlike people in rural areas, more than half of city residents get their water from
    a. lakes and rivers.
    b. groundwater.
    c. transpiration.
    d. condensation.

59. The main idea of paragraph 1 is stated in
    a. the first sentence.
    b. the second sentence.
    c. the third sentence.
    d. the sixth sentence.

60. The main idea of paragraph 3 is stated in
   a. the first sentence.
   b. the second sentence.
   c. the fourth sentence.
   d. the last sentence.

61. The main idea of paragraph 8 is stated in
   a. the first sentence.
   b. the second sentence.
   c. the third sentence.
   d. the last sentence.

62. Choose the correct definition of the word *strikes* as it is used in paragraph 5.
   a. has a strong effect on
   b. hits
   c. finds or comes upon
   d. soaks into

63. The word *exhale* in paragraph 3 means
   a. release.
   b. add.
   c. breathe out.
   d. form.

Use the diagram on page 61 to answer questions 64 through 66.

64. How much precipitation is returned unused to the sea?
   a. about 24%
   b. about 50%
   c. about 5%
   d. about 70%

65. What percentage of the precipitation is used for irrigation?
   a. 3.12%
   b. 2.46%
   c. 0.42%
   d. 0.24%

66. What percentage of the precipitation evaporates or is used by plants where it falls?
   a. 70%
   b. 59%
   c. 42%
   d. 24%

67. *Water stored in plant cells is released as water vapor.* That sentence describes
   a. evaporation.
   b. condensation.
   c. transpiration.
   d. precipitation.

68. *Water left outside in a bowl eventually disappears.* That sentence describes
   a. evaporation.
   b. condensation.
   c. transpiration.
   d. precipitation.

69. *Try breathing on a mirror. Notice the cloud that forms on the glass.* Those sentences describe
   a. evaporation.
   b. condensation.
   c. transpiration.
   d. precipitation.

70. Moisture is carried over the Earth by
   a. clouds.
   b. temperature.
   c. winds.
   d. the Earth's rotation.

71. Much of the water on Earth that is unusable is
   a. too deep in the ground.
   b. in the air.
   c. too salty.
   d. evaporated into the air.

Questions 72 through 75 are word problems. Use the space below each one for your calculations.

72. A swimming pool holds 8,900 gallons of water. One week, 296 gallons evaporate. How much water is left in the pool?
   a. 9,196 gallons
   b. 8,764 gallons
   c. 8,700 gallons
   d. 8,604 gallons

73. A small pond has 11,400 gallons of water. During a storm, 750 gallons of runoff water enter the pond. How much water is in the pond after the storm?
    a. 10,650 gallons
    b. 12,150 gallons
    c. 14,250 gallons
    d. 17,150 gallons

75. During a storm, 800,000 gallons of water fall in a certain area. One-fifth of the water infiltrates into the soil. How many gallons are runoff?
    a. 640,000 gallons
    b. 400,000 gallons
    c. 160,000 gallons
    d. 100,000 gallons

74. A forest releases 17,200 gallons of water a day by transpiration. If half the forest is cut down, how much water will it release?
    a. 34,400 gallons
    b. 25,500 gallons
    c. 8,600 gallons
    d. 5,733 gallons

A. Use the following dictionary entry to answer questions 76 through 80.

---

kick (kik) **v. 1.** to strike out with the foot or feet, as in striking something or in dancing, swimming, etc. **2.** to move by kicking with the foot **3.** to spring back suddenly, as a gun does when fired **4.** to complain or grumble: *used only in everyday talk* **5.** to get rid of: *slang in this meaning* [to *kick* a habit] **n. 1.** a blow with the foot **2.** a way of kicking **3.** a springing back; recoil **4.** a thrill or excited feeling: *used only in everyday talk* **kicked, kick´ ing —kick in,** to pay, as one's share: *a slang phrase* **—kick off, 1.** to put a football into play **2.** to start, as a campaign **3.** to die: *slang in this meaning* **—kick out,** to get rid of or put out: *used only in everyday talk*

---

76. How many verb meanings of the entry word are given?
    a. two
    b. three
    c. four
    d. five

77. How many idioms, or phrases, using *kick* are given?
    a. two
    b. three
    c. four
    d. five

78. Which of the following is a noun meaning of the entry word?
    a. to complain or grumble
    b. a thrill or excited feeling
    c. to spring back suddenly
    d. to pay, as one's share

79. Which idiom is *always* slang?
    a. kick off
    b. kicking
    c. kick out
    d. kick in

80. Which is the respelling of the entry word?
    a. kick ing
    b. kik
    c. to strike out with the foot or feet
    d. verb

B. Think about word parts to answer questions 81 through 100.

81. Which prefix would you add to change the meaning of *governed* to "badly governed"?
    a. *pre-*
    b. *mis-*
    c. *dis-*
    d. *un-*

82. Which prefix would you add to change the meaning of *loyal* to the opposite of loyal?
    a. *trans-*
    b. *dis-*
    c. *pre-*
    d. *in-*

83. Which prefix would you add to change the meaning of *heat* to "heat too much"?
    a. *over-*
    b. *mis-*
    c. *pre-*
    d. *un-*

84. Which prefix would you add to change the meaning of *paid* to "paid ahead"?
    a. *re-*
    b. *dis-*
    c. *pre-*
    d. *un-*

85. Which suffix would you add to change the meaning of *worth* to "without worth"?
    a. *-en*
    b. *-ly*
    c. *-y*
    d. *-less*

86. Which suffix would you add to change the meaning of *wonder* to "full of wonder"?
    a. *-ful*
    b. *-ment*
    c. *-ly*
    d. *-less*

87. Which suffix would you add to change the meaning of *dark* to "make dark"?
    a. *-en*
    b. *-ly*
    c. *-ful*
    d. *-ness*

88. Choose the correct way to divide the word *sticky* into syllables.
    a. sti cky
    b. stic ky
    c. stick y
    d. st icky

89. Choose the correct way to divide the word *begin* into syllables.
    a. be gin
    b. beg in
    c. be g in
    d. b eg in

90. Choose the correct way to divide the word *bellow* into syllables.
    a. bell ow
    b. bel low
    c. be llow
    d. b el low

91. Choose the correct way to divide the word *tunnel* into syllables.
    a. tu nnel
    b. tun nel
    c. tunn el
    d. t un nel

92. What is the base word in *unacceptable*?
    a. accept
    b. acceptable
    c. table
    d. able

93. What is the base word in *disarrangement*?
    a. disarrange
    b. arrange
    c. range
    d. men

94. What is the base word in *transplantable*?
    a. plant
    b. transplant
    c. plantable
    d. table

95. What is the base word in *endlessly*?
    a. less
    b. end
    c. endless
    d. endlessly

96. What is the base word in *evaporation*?
    a. ration
    b. pore
    c. vapor
    d. evaporate

97. What is the base word in *unusable*?
    a. sable
    b. use
    c. unusual
    d. able

98. What is the base word in *condensation*?
    a. sensation
    b. dens
    c. condense
    d. sat

99. What is the base word in *renewable*?
    a. new
    b. renew
    c. able
    d. renewable

100. What is the base word in *missionary*?
    a. is
    b. miss
    c. on
    d. mission

Read the following selection. Then choose the best answer for each question.
Mark your answers on the answer sheet.

Arachne Weaves a Web

1. In our tiny village in Ancient Greece, we were all poor shepherds or farmers. No one was famous except Arachne. Not that she was rich or powerful or even beautiful. In fact, she was rather small and pale from weaving indoors all day at her loom. She lived alone with her father, Demetrius, who dyed wool.

2. All day long, Arachne spun her father's raw wool into fine thread. Then she wove it into cloth, extraordinary cloth. Her weaving and stitching were so marvelous that people came from all over Greece to buy it. In that way, she became famous. The other village girls and I would stand in her doorway sometimes and watch her. We all assumed that Athena, goddess of households, must have taught Arachne the secrets of her marvelous craft. Where else could such talent come from?

3. "Did Athena herself come to your cottage and teach you to weave?" I once asked Arachne. She looked up from her loom and gazed at me in scorn. What had I said wrong?

4. "With my own fingers, I learned to weave," Arachne muttered angrily. "For years, I practiced hard from morning until night. No one taught me, and I owe nothing to Athena! Indeed," the weaver continued, "if the goddess were to come here today and compete with me, she could weave no better than I."

5. I shuddered at Arachne's brazen words. I was 12, and even at that age, I knew that nothing good could come of daring the gods in this fashion. Perhaps that is why the amazing events I am about to recount did not surprise me as much as they did the other villagers.

6. It was a summer morning, and I was helping Demetrius wash wool. Arachne was in the yard, too, selling cloth to a trader. Marveling at the cloth, he vowed that her talents must have come from Athena. Arachne's reaction was quick and proud. "Neither Athena nor any other god or goddess has anything to teach me," she told the trader, pushing the cloth toward him angrily.

7. No sooner were the words said than a dark cloud hid the bright sun over Greece. The Earth itself seemed to tremble briefly. Suddenly, an old woman, bent and poor, appeared in the yard. Demetrius and I watched wide-eyed. Who could she be? Surely she was not from our village. "Arachne," the old woman called, "how dare you claim to be the equal of a god! Take my advice, and ask Athena's pardon. Be content with who you are: the best weaver that humans will ever know."

8. "Mind your own business, woman," replied Arachne, "and I'll mind mine. If Athena has a problem with me, let her come down here from Mount Olympus. I challenge her to a weaving contest. Then we will see who is the better weaver!"

9. At those words, the old woman grew tall and fair and her robes turned dazzling white. The sun blazed once again in the sky. Demetrius and I threw ourselves to the ground. We knew we were standing before Athena herself! Arachne blushed. She had never imagined the old woman might be the goddess in disguise! Still, Arachne was too proud to apologize or to ask forgiveness. Instead she led the goddess into the cottage where two looms stood.

10. Demetrius and I crept to the doorway on our hands and knees. Inside, the weavers began sorting bundles of wool in as many colors as the rainbow. Threading the wool on their looms, Arachne and Athena went to work. Neither woman spoke a word, but the whirring and creaking of the looms filled the tiny cottage.

11. As my eyes got used to the light, I slowly made out the scene Athena was weaving. In the center was an olive tree, Athena's favorite, in magnificent greens and yellows. Each corner of the weaving, however, showed humans who had tried to vie with the gods. In bright detail, Athena wove the terrible fate that had befallen each of them. Even I could see that this was Athena's last warning to Arachne.

12. My eyes turned toward Arachne. Her face was red, and beads of sweat formed on her upper lip. I could see how determined she was. Racing to keep up with the goddess, she

dropped her yarn several times. She was having trouble with the thread, too.

13. At one point, Arachne glanced up to see Athena's work. The scenes the goddess wove seemed to make Arachne furious. Perhaps that is why she chose her fateful design.

14. I couldn't see much of Arachne's design as she was working. But when she finished and stood up, I gasped in shock. Arachne had chosen a pattern of scenes that showed the gods at their worst! There was Zeus tricking a poor maiden. There was Hermes, stealing cattle. Any god or goddess who had ever done anything unworthy was captured on Arachne's tapestry.

15. Athena's eyes blazed with anger when she saw Arachne's design. There would be no final judging of the finished work. Tearing the cloth from Arachne's loom, Athena destroyed it. Poor Arachne stood there a moment, struggling with anger, fear, and pride. "I cannot live with this insult," she cried at last.

16. "You have angered the gods," replied Athena. "Live on and spin, and all your children, too! Help everyone remember that it is not wise to compete with the gods." With that, I hid my eyes and ran from the doorway. Later, Demetrius told me how poor Arachne's body shriveled up, how her legs and arms grew tiny and misshapen. Finally, she became a spider. This is the way that spiders first came into our village and the world.

1. Arachne's main conflict is with
   a. Zeus.   c. Athena.
   b. Demetrius.   d. herself.

2. Which sentence best describes this conflict?
   a. Arachne is too good at her craft.
   b. Arachne is unkind to the villagers.
   c. Arachne's pride angers a goddess.
   d. Arachne doesn't realize how talented she is.

3. Arachne increases her conflict by
   a. becoming a better weaver.
   b. competing with a goddess.
   c. becoming a spider.
   d. taking weaving lessons from Athena.

4. By the end of the story, Arachne has learned that
   a. fame has many disadvantages.
   b. pride can cause one's downfall.
   c. a good worker finishes the job.
   d. everyone has a special talent.

5. The first event in the story that hints of conflict occurs when
   a. traders buy Arachne's cloth.
   b. Arachne denies that she owes her skill to Athena.
   c. Athena weaves quickly and well.
   d. Arachne's fame spreads.

6. Arachne becomes more deeply involved in her conflict when
   a. people come to the village to watch her work.
   b. Athena appears in the village.
   c. she drops the thread.
   d. Athena challenges her.

7. How is this conflict finally resolved?
   a. Arachne's work is judged better than Athena's.
   b. Athena's work is judged better than Arachne's.
   c. Athena tears down Arachne's work.
   d. Athena's and Arachne's works are judged as equal.

8. The story ends when
   a. the old woman reveals she is Athena.
   b. Arachne apologizes to Athena.
   c. Arachne turns into a spider.
   d. Zeus tricks a maiden.

9. When does the story take place?
   a. in ancient times
   b. about 100 years ago
   c. in the present day
   d. in the future

10. Where does the main action of the story take place?
    a. in Athens
    b. in Rome
    c. on Mount Olympus
    d. in Arachne's cottage

11. What feature of or change in the setting announces an important event?
    a. The village is small and ordinary.
    b. A dark cloud hides the sun.
    c. An olive tree suddenly appears.
    d. An old woman appears.

12. What is the main message of this story?
    a. The Greek gods had little use for humans.
    b. Not everyone can be famous.
    c. Humans should not put themselves above the gods.
    d. Human talent can equal that of the gods.

13. This story may also have tried to explain
    a. how weaving originated.
    b. how spiders originated.
    c. how children should behave around adults.
    d. how Arachne became famous.

14. Athena's weaving was a warning because
    a. she completed it so quickly.
    b. it showed what happened to humans who vied with gods.
    c. it showed a spider on an olive tree.
    d. she used it to record history.

15. Arachne's weaving was insulting because
    a. it was not done skillfully.
    b. it was ripped in half.
    c. it was completed too quickly.
    d. it showed misdeeds of gods.

16. Which of these alternate titles is most appropriate for the story?
    a. "The Household Goddess"
    b. "The Spider That Would Not Spin"
    c. "Arachne Angers Athena"
    d. "Along Came a Spider"

17. What is the unstated main idea of paragraph 5?
    a. Arachne was proud of her work.
    b. The gods would punish Arachne's boastful pride.
    c. The gods were involved in the everyday lives of the Greeks.
    d. The gods were not concerned with what humans were doing.

18. What is the unstated main idea of paragraph 12?
    a. Arachne was not a very good weaver.
    b. Competing with Athena made Arachne nervous.
    c. The competition was unfair.
    d. Arachne would easily beat Athena.

19. What is the unstated main idea of paragraph 14?
    a. Arachne deliberately offended Athena.
    b. The Greek gods liked to hurt people.
    c. Athena was much too sensitive.
    d. Arachne's weaving was not her best work.

20. Who is the narrator of the story?
    a. Arachne   c. a young village girl
    b. Athena   d. Demetrius

21. Why is first person a good point of view for telling this story?
    a. The narrator heard about these events from others.
    b. The narrator reports only the facts, and not her feelings.
    c. The narrator knows what everyone is feeling and thinking.
    d. The narrator sees the events, which lets readers feel that they are present.

22. A disadvantage of this story's point of view is that the narrator cannot
    a. make judgments about events.
    b. describe her feelings.
    c. know what other characters are thinking.
    d. accurately tell the events.

23. What is the meaning of *design* in paragraph 14?
    a. a scheme or evil plan
    b. a sketch from which to work
    c. the arrangement of details in a work
    d. a story

24. The word *brazen* in paragraph 5 means
    a. angry.   c. truthful.
    b. weak.   d. bold.

25. The word *vie* in paragraph 11 means
    a. compete.   c. work.
    b. communicate. d. help.

Read the following selection. Then choose the best answer for each question. Mark your answers on the answer sheet.

Ancient Empires in West Africa

1. Three great empires developed in West Africa long ago: Ghana, Mali, and Songhai. These empires were called the "kingdoms of gold and salt" because they were built around the trade in gold and salt. Gold, of course, has long been valued all over the world. Salt was also very valuable in ancient times. People needed salt to preserve food. Africans paid high prices for salt that was mined in the Sahara Desert.

The Empire of Ghana

2. The empire of Ghana was established around A.D. 600. It lay along an important trade route across the Sahara Desert. So Ghana became a major trade center, and the king of Ghana taxed goods bought and sold in his country. As trade grew, Ghana became rich.

3. Gold was an all-important word in Ghana. In fact, the name *Ghana* came to mean gold to Africans. In A.D. 1000, Ghana's powerful ruler was called "king of gold." His servants had swords decorated with gold. His guard dogs had collars of gold.

4. Over the years, Ghana's kings used their gold to pay for large armies. At times, the kings had 200,000 warriors to fight battles. The warriors of Ghana also had iron swords and spears, which were better than the wooden weapons their neighbors used. So Ghana was able to control a large territory in West Africa.

5. In the eighth century, Islamic traders settled in Ghana. The newcomers built mosques and introduced Arabic learning. Most of Ghana's rulers and farmers kept their old religion. In the eleventh century, however, Islamic forces from North Africa conquered Ghana.

The Empire of Mali

6. The empire of Mali arose in West Africa about A.D. 1250. The city of Timbuktu was at its center. Like Ghana, Mali controlled trade routes across the Sahara. Mali also dominated the all-important gold mines in West Africa.

7. Mansa Musa, emperor of Mali, used his great wealth to improve Timbuktu. He invited famous Islamic scholars to live in the city. Mansa Musa built fine buildings and universities in Timbuktu so it would become a center of learning. Students from all over Africa studied there.

8. Mansa Musa was an Islamic, a believer in Islam. In 1324, he set out on a pilgrimage to the holy city of Mecca in Arabia. On this journey, he took 6,000 people with him for safety. He also brought lots of money. Each of his 80 camels was loaded with hundreds of pounds of gold. In Egypt, Mansa Musa spent his gold at an incredible rate. He spent so much that the price of gold fell and stayed low for many years.

9. Mansa Musa died in 1332. After that, the empire of Mali began to fall apart. Raiders from other lands attacked its cities. Some cities in Mali broke away to set up their own kingdoms. In the 1400s, one former city of Mali began to build the empire of Songhai.

The Empire of Songhai

10. Like Ghana and Mali, Songhai grew rich from trade. Its main trade goods were gold and ivory. Songhai expanded trade to Europe and Asia. Some of Songhai's gold was sent to Egypt. From there, it went on to other areas. In return, Songhai got cloth, copper, beads, and other goods.

11. In 1493, Askia Mohammed began to rule Songhai. His armies expanded the empire. Askia Mohammed also brought more scholars to Timbuktu, and once again, the city became an important center of learning. Leo Africanus, from Spain, visited Timbuktu around 1500. He described the city in a report to the Pope in Rome. Africanus wrote that ". . . here [Timbuktu] are brought . . . written books

which are sold for more money than any other merchandise."

12. In 1591, soldiers from Morocco in North Africa crossed the desert in search of gold. These soldiers carried guns, but the Songhai warriors still had only bows and arrows. The defenders didn't have a chance against the better-armed Moroccans, so the last great empire of West Africa came to an end.

Africa's Early Kingdoms

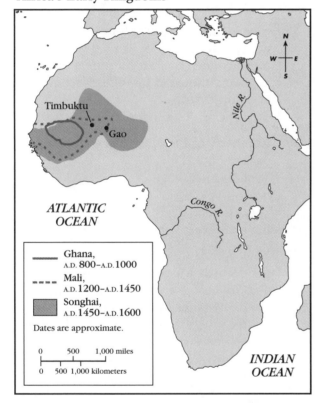

26. The main idea of paragraph 3 is stated in the
   a. first sentence.
   b. second sentence.
   c. third sentence.
   d. last sentence.

27. The main idea of paragraph 4 is stated in the
   a. first sentence.
   b. second sentence.
   c. fourth sentence.
   d. last sentence.

28. The main idea of paragraph 7 is stated in the
   a. first sentence.
   b. second sentence.
   c. fourth sentence.
   d. last sentence.

29. What is the unstated main idea of paragraph 11?
   a. Leo Africanus came from Spain.
   b. Askia Mohammed fought with Spain.
   c. Askia Mohammed wanted Timbuktu to become a center of learning.
   d. The Pope expanded the Songhai empire.

30. What is the unstated main idea of paragraph 12?
   a. The warriors of Songhai never had guns.
   b. Morocco conquered Songhai in 1591.
   c. Morocco was a kingdom in North Africa.
   d. Songhai warriors found gold.

31. Find the main idea of paragraph 8. Then choose the detail that best supports the main idea.
    a. Mansa Musa took control of the important trading city of Gao.
    b. After Mansa Musa's death, his son Mansa Maghan I became the ruler of Mali.
    c. Six thousand people accompanied Mansa Musa on his way to Mecca.
    d. The city of Timbuktu was the center of the empire of Mali.

32. Ghana became a very wealthy empire because
    a. it taxed the goods that moved along its trade route.
    b. the name *Ghana* meant "gold."
    c. it was established as early as A.D. 600.
    d. Ghana's kings were great rulers.

33. Ghana's warriors were able to conquer their neighbors because
    a. Ghana's warriors had iron weapons.
    b. the king of Ghana had so much gold.
    c. Ghana lay along an important trade route.
    d. they had a powerful ruler.

34. The empire of Mali fell apart because
    a. Mansa Musa went on a pilgrimage.
    b. cities in the kingdom began to break away to form their own kingdoms.
    c. there was conflict between Ghana and Mali.
    d. Mansa Musa spent all of his gold.

35. The soldiers of Songhai were defeated by the army from Morocco because
    a. the Moroccans had a larger army.
    b. the soldiers of Songhai surrendered without fighting.
    c. the Moroccans had guns.
    d. the Songhai had too much land to defend.

36. Like Mansa Musa, Askia Mohammed
    a. was called the "king of gold."
    b. spent his gold foolishly.
    c. expanded his trade network to Europe and Asia.
    d. brought scholars to Timbuktu.

37. All three of the empires
    a. included the city of Timbuktu.
    b. controlled important trade routes.
    c. had local leaders who broke away and formed their own kingdoms.
    d. were defeated by more powerful enemies.

38. Like Songhai, the kingdom of Ghana
    a. rebuilt the city of Timbuktu.
    b. expanded trade to Europe and Asia.
    c. was conquered by soldiers from North Africa.
    d. kept its old religion.

39. Another word for *pilgrimage* in paragraph 8 is
    a. holy city.
    b. journey.
    c. believer.
    d. wonderer.

40. You can infer that the price of gold fell after Mansa Musa's visit to Egypt because
    a. no one else could afford the prices that Mansa Musa paid.
    b. there was so much more gold in the city.
    c. there was little left to buy in the city.
    d. no more gold could be found.

41. The cities in Mali began to break away after Mansa Musa's death. You can infer this occurred because
    a. there was no one strong enough to stop them.
    b. they admired Askia Mohammed so much.
    c. they were tired of the gold and salt trade.
    d. they wanted to leave West Africa.

42. You can infer that the soldiers of Songhai didn't have guns to fight the Moroccans because
   a. it was against their religion to carry them.
   b. they had nothing to trade for them.
   c. there was no gold in Songhai to pay for them.
   d. the new invention had not reached them.

43. From the selection, you can infer that the city of Timbuktu
   a. kept getting bigger and better between 1300 and 1600.
   b. was important to the empire of Ghana.
   c. is still a center of learning in Africa today.
   d. was a holy city.

44. Choose the correct definition of the word *preserve* as it is used in paragraph 1.
   a. protect from harm
   b. keep from spoiling
   c. maintain or keep in a certain condition
   d. make taste better

45. The word *dominated* in paragraph 6 means
   a. controlled.
   b. closed down.
   c. accepted.
   d. fought.

Use the map on page 71 to answer questions 46 through 50.

46. The kingdom that reached farthest east was
   a. Ghana.
   b. Mali.
   c. Gao.
   d. Songhai.

47. Which kingdom was largest in area?
   a. Ghana
   b. Mali
   c. Songhai
   d. Timbuktu

48. The city of Timbuktu was not part of
   a. Ghana.
   b. Mali.
   c. Africa.
   d. Songhai.

49. The kingdom of Mali from east to west covered a distance of about
   a. 400 miles.
   b. 600 miles.
   c. 800 miles.
   d. 1,200 miles.

50. The kingdom of Songhai lasted about
   a. 150 years.
   b. 200 years.
   c. 250 years.
   d. 300 years.

Read the following selection. Then choose the best answer for each question.
Mark your answers on the answer sheet.

Jet Streams and Weather Fronts

1. Near the end of World War II, a group of U.S. planes took off from a base in the Pacific Ocean. The planes could fly higher than any other planes had before. At an altitude of about 9,000 meters, the planes found themselves surrounded by a fast-moving river of air. The planes tried to fly upstream against this river, but the speed of the air matched the speed of the planes. Thus, the planes were standing still in midair.

2. The river of air was a very powerful wind. Up until that time, no one knew the river of wind existed. Today, we call the river of wind a jet stream. Other jet streams have been discovered, too. Found at altitudes between 6,000 and 12,000 meters (19,680 and 39,360 feet), those air currents flow around Earth from west to east. Winds in the jet streams may reach speeds of up to 500 kilometers (805 miles) per hour.

Jet Streams Affect Air Masses

3. Jet streams affect weather patterns around the world. Scientists are not sure how the high-speed, high-altitude winds control air along Earth's surface, but they seem to steer Earth's air masses.

4. When you hear a weather forecast, the term *air mass* is often used. An air mass is a large body of air in which the temperature and water content are the same at a certain altitude. In other words, in any air mass, all points at the same altitude will have the same temperature and contain the same amount of moisture.

5. Your weather depends on the type of air mass covering your region. Air masses are influenced by the climate of the region over which they form. For example, an air mass that collects near the North or South Pole over land will be cold and dry. One that collects near the North or South Pole over water will be cold and wet. Air masses that gather near the equator will be warm. If they form over inland terrain, they will be warm and dry. If they start over water, they will be warm and wet.

Fronts Are Boundaries

6. The boundaries between air masses are called *fronts*. A mass of cold air moving into a mass of warm air forms a cold front. The opposite movement—warm air into cold air—forms a warm front. Each different front produces a certain pattern of weather. Most weather changes take place along the fronts where two air masses meet.

7. Weather maps show fronts in three ways. A map will represent a cold front as a heavy black line with small triangles. The triangles indicate the direction in which the front is moving. A warm front is shown by a dark line, too, but small half-circles point its direction. A stationary front is a front that hasn't moved for 48 hours. That kind of front is shown by a black line with both triangles and half-circles on either side of it.

8. Cold fronts travel twice as fast as warm fronts. When a cold front approaches, the heavy cold air sinks below the warm air and forces it to rise rapidly. High, towering clouds form in the rising air. The rain or snow from the clouds is quite heavy, but it does not last long. Soon after the cold front passes, the sky most often clears, and a mass of cool, dry air follows.

9. Warm fronts produce more gradual weather changes than cold fronts do. As a warm front approaches, the warm air slowly rises up over the colder air. Clouds form as the warm air cools. The first clouds to arrive are high, thin, cirrus clouds. As the front gets closer, the clouds get lower and thicker. Then a light, steady rain or snow starts. Often it will fall for several hours or days as the warm front passes. When the warm front has passed, a rise in temperature and clearing skies usually follow.

High and Low Pressure

10. Warm air can hold more water vapor than cold air can. Warm air is also lighter than cold air. When warm, moist air is surrounded by cooler, drier air, a region of low pressure

forms. There are usually several low pressure areas across the United States on any day. Between the low pressure areas, the cooler, drier air presses down. Those areas become regions of high pressure.

11. Highs and lows are centers of weather systems. They are steered by the jet stream and moved by winds from the west. As these pressure areas move across the United States, the weather changes.

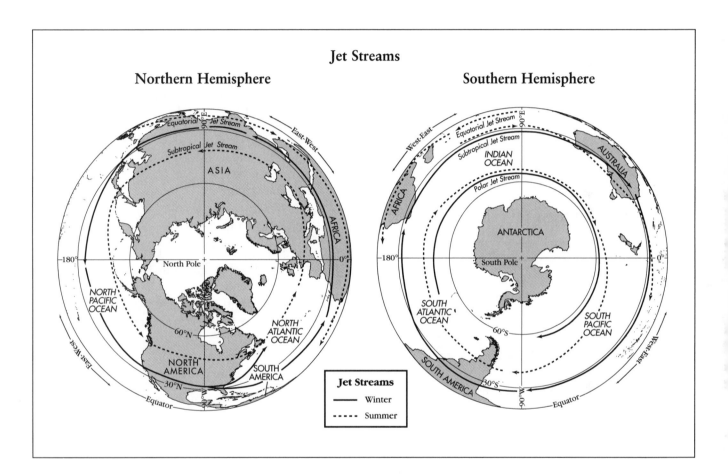

51. The main idea of paragraph 5 is stated in
   a. the first sentence.
   b. the second sentence.
   c. the fourth sentence.
   d. the last sentence.

52. Choose the main idea of paragraph 6.
   a. Each different front produces a certain pattern of weather.
   b. A mass of cold air moving into a mass of warm air forms a cold front.
   c. When warm air replaces cold air, a warm front forms.
   d. The boundaries between air masses are called *fronts*.

53. Think about the main idea of paragraph 2. Then choose the detail below that would best support the main idea.
   a. There are four main types of air masses.
   b. Jet streams are found at varying altitudes.
   c. High-altitude planes have led to many scientific advances.
   d. An air mass is a large body of air.

54. Think about the main idea of paragraph 9. Then choose the detail below that would best support the main idea.
    a. Cold fronts may bring heavy winds.
    b. As a warm front approaches, the warm air slowly rises up over the colder air.
    c. If the air is dry, a front may form no precipitation.
    d. Cold air is heavier than warm air.

55. World War II planes found the jet stream because
    a. they had equipment to track weather patterns.
    b. they were at the equator, where warm fronts originate.
    c. they were able to fly high enough.
    d. they knew what to look for.

56. Clouds form when a warm front approaches because
    a. the warm air cools.
    b. the cold air warms.
    c. the warm air rises rapidly.
    d. the cold air sinks.

57. The jet stream influences weather because
    a. it moves at a high speed.
    b. it lowers the temperature of Earth's surface.
    c. it moves the clouds high above Earth.
    d. it steers air masses that become fronts.

58. Warm air
    a. is heavier than cold air.
    b. can hold more water vapor than cold air.
    c. is faster than cold air.
    d. originates over the poles.

59. Compared to a cold front, a warm front tends to cause
    a. longer periods of rain or snow.
    b. shorter periods of rain or snow.
    c. periods of rain or snow of about the same length.
    d. no change in weather patterns.

60. Air masses that form over northern Canada would tend to be
    a. warm and dry.
    b. warm and wet.
    c. cold and wet.
    d. cold and dry.

61. On a weather map, the direction of a cold front is shown by
    a. triangles.
    b. half-circles.
    c. triangles and half-circles.
    d. black lines.

62. Several days of slow, steady rain would probably result from a
    a. warm front.
    b. cold front.
    c. stationary front.
    d. jet stream.

63. Airplanes traveling east can cross the United States in less time than those going west because
    a. they avoid stationary fronts.
    b. they are helped by jet streams.
    c. areas of high pressure form in the east.
    d. the west has hotter and drier air.

64. If an air mass is warm and dry, you can infer that
    a. it formed over water.
    b. it formed inland.
    c. it formed over the North Pole.
    d. it formed over the South Pole.

65. Based on their relative speeds, you can infer that
    a. cold fronts often catch up to warm fronts.
    b. warm fronts often catch up to cold fronts.
    c. warm fronts and cold fronts never meet.
    d. warm and cold fronts travel at the same speed.

66. The word *represent* in paragraph 7 means
    a. speak and act for.
    b. show or depict.
    c. be an example of.
    d. contain.

67. What is the meaning of the word *terrain* in paragraph 5?
    a. a mass of air
    b. a region of land
    c. a large lake
    d. a dry area

Use the diagram on page 75 to answer questions 68 through 71.

68. Which jet stream travels from east to west in the Northern Hemisphere?
    a. Polar Jet Stream
    b. Subtropical Jet Stream
    c. Equatorial Jet Stream
    d. all of the above

69. The Polar Jet Stream travels from
    a. east to west.
    b. north to south.
    c. west to east.
    d. south to north.

70. Which jet stream is found near Antarctica?
    a. Subtropical Jet Stream
    b. Equatorial Jet Stream
    c. Polar Jet Stream
    d. none of the above

71. The Equatorial Jet Stream travels
    a. over the North Pole.
    b. over the South Pole.
    c. over the North Atlantic Ocean.
    d. near the equator.

Questions 72 through 75 are word problems. Use a separate sheet of paper for your calculations.

72. A warm front traveling 35 mph causes low clouds and rain in Buffalo, New York, at 11 P.M. At what time will similar weather conditions occur in Albany, New York, 250 miles to the east?
    a. about 4 A.M.
    b. about 6 A.M.
    c. about 8 A.M.
    d. about 10 A.M.

73. The jet stream allows an airliner to make a flight from San Francisco, California, to New York City 7% faster than the return trip westward. The eastbound trip takes 248 minutes. About how long is the westbound trip?
    a. 257 minutes
    b. 265 minutes
    c. 287 minutes
    d. 295 minutes

74. A warm front is 34 times as long as it is high. If the front is 640 miles long, what is its altitude?
    a. about 15 miles
    b. about 19 miles
    c. about 20,000 miles
    d. about 674 minutes

75. The arrival of a cold front causes the temperature in a city to drop 4 degrees to 54°F. What percentage change in temperature does this represent?
    a. about 15%
    b. about 12%
    c. about 9%
    d. about 7%

A. Use the following dictionary entry to answer questions 76 through 80.

---

piece (pēs) *n.* **1.** a part broken from a whole thing [a *piece* of a broken bottle] **2.** a part or section of a whole, thought of as complete by itself [a *piece* of meat] **3.** any one of a set or group of things [a chess *piece*] **4.** a work of writing, music, or art **5.** a firearm, as a rifle **6.** a coin [a fifty-cent *piece*] **7.** a single item or example [a *piece* of information] *v.* **1.** to add a piece or pieces to in order to repair or make larger **2.** to join the pieces of, as in mending [*piece* together a broken vase] **3.** to eat a snack between meals: *used only in everyday talk* **pieced, piec´ ing —go to pieces, 1.** to fall apart **2.** to lose control of oneself, as in crying **—of a piece** or **of one piece,** of the same sort, alike **—speak one's piece,** to say what one really thinks about something

---

76. How many verb meanings of the entry word are given?
    a. seven　　c. three
    b. five　　　d. two

77. Which idiom, or phrase, using *piece* means "alike"?
    a. go to pieces
    b. of one piece
    c. speak one's piece
    d. piecing

78. Which noun definition of *piece* is used in the following sentence? *We bought a piece of land near Montvale.*
    a. definition 1　　c. definition 3
    b. definition 2　　d. definition 4

79. Which verb definition of *piece* is used in the following sentence? *I had to piece in another panel to make the skirt fit.*
    a. definition 1
    b. definition 2
    c. definition 3
    d. none of the above

80. Which is the phonetic respelling of the entry word?
    a. pēs
    b. piec´ ing
    c. —go to pieces
    d. of one's piece

B. Use the following part of an index to answer questions 81 through 85.

Warmblooded animals, 188–189
Water, 8, 9
　in air, 227–228
　freezing, 126
　running, and erosion, 109, 182, 211
　vapor, 78, 80, 113
Waves, 116–117, 146–147
Weather
　cold and warm fronts, 239–241
　forecasts, 247
　maps, 240
　temperature and humidity, 227–228
　thunderstorms and tornadoes, 144
Wegener, Alfred, 55, 56
Whale, 188, 223

---

81. On what page(s) would you find information on weather maps?
    a. 227–228
    b. 240
    c. 247
    d. 239–241

82. How many subtopics are listed under the topic *weather*?
    a. six　　c. four
    b. five　　d. three

83. On how many separate pages of the book would you find information on running water and erosion?
    a. one　　c. three
    b. two　　d. four

84. If this book had information about waterfalls, where would it be listed?
    a. after *weather*
    b. before *water*
    c. after *warmblooded animals*
    d. before *waves*

85. How many pages does the book have on water vapor?
    a. two　　c. four
    b. three　　d. five

C. **Think about word parts to answer questions 86 through 100.**

86. Which prefix would you add to change the meaning of *human* to "below human"?
    a. *non-*   c. *sub-*
    b. *semi-*   d. *in-*

87. Which prefix would you add to change the meaning of *skilled* to "partly skilled"?
    a. *non-*   c. *sub-*
    b. *in-*   d. *semi-*

88. Which prefix would you add to change the meaning of *frost* to "take away the frost"?
    a. *non-*   c. *re-*
    b. *de-*   d. *pre-*

89. Which suffix would you add to change the meaning of *fail* to "the act of failing"?
    a. *-ous*   c. *-ment*
    b. *-ness*   d. *-ure*

90. Which suffix would you add to change the meaning of *courage* to "having courage"?
    a. *-ly*   c. *-ity*
    b. *-ous*   d. *-ment*

91. Which suffix would you add to change the meaning of *direct* to "one who directs"?
    a. *-ly*   c. *-ship*
    b. *-or*   d. *-ness*

92. Choose the correct way to divide the word *lumber* into syllables.
    a. lum ber
    b. lumb er
    c. lu mber
    d. l um ber

93. Choose the correct way to divide the word *humble* into syllables.
    a. humb le
    b. hum ble
    c. hu mble
    d. h um ble

94. Choose the correct way to divide the word *gather* into syllables.
    a. ga ther
    b. gat her
    c. gath er
    d. ga th er

95. Choose the correct way to divide the word *middle* into syllables.
    a. mid dle
    b. mi ddle
    c. midd le
    d. mi dd le

96. Which of the following shows the accent mark placed correctly?
    a. de´ cent ly
    b. de cent´ ly
    c. de cent ly´
    d. decent´ ly

97. Which of the following shows the accent mark placed correctly?
    a. for´ get ting
    b. for get´ ting
    c. for get ting´
    d. forget´ ting

98. Which of the following shows the accent mark placed correctly?
    a. por´ cu pine
    b. por cu´ pine
    c. por cu pine´
    d. porcu´ pine

99. Which word shows the schwa sound correctly circled?
    a. d⊙ cline
    b. l⊙ne some
    c. dis t⊙nt
    d. f⊙th er

100. Which word shows the schwa sound correctly circled?
    a. l⊙c o motive
    b. loc ⊙ mo tive
    c. loc o m⊙ tive
    d. loc o motiv⊙

Read the following selection. Then choose the best answer for each question.
Mark your answers on the answer sheet.

Imperfect Game

1. I darted to my left, fielded the hard grounder, and fired the ball to the first baseman. "Out!" barked the umpire. That was the fifteenth batter in a row that our Falcon pitcher, Marv Gilson, had gotten out. Marv had a perfect game going. After five innings, none of the Jaguars had gotten on base.

2. I was the Falcon shortstop. I'd driven in both our runs with a second-inning homer over the left-field fence. Still, the hero of the game was clearly Marv, and he would have been the first to say so. "I'm the best pitcher in the Southside Conference," he once told the team. "Get me a run or two, and we'll win every game." He wasn't kidding. He had won every game he pitched this spring, and a win today would make us conference champs.

3. Yes, Marv was our ace, but he had an ego the size of Texas. When I had hit my second-inning home run, for example, he never said a word to me. He didn't even look at me. Other teammates gave me high-fives and cheered, but Marv just sat there on the bench with a self-satisfied grin. Clearly, this game was *his* game, not the team's. The crowd was in his corner, too. Sure, they cheered for my homer. But they cheered even louder every time Marv threw a strike.

4. The sky was growing darker. Rain had been threatening all day. For a moment, I actually found myself hoping we'd get rained out. If the umpires called off the game before the seventh inning, Marv's perfect game would be a washout. I guess that tells you how much I disliked Marv Gilson.

5. In the sixth inning, Marv easily struck out the first two Jaguars. Then Roscoe Jones, the Jaguar catcher, slashed the ball between the third baseman and me. I was playing deep. Without thinking, I dove to my left, made a perfect trap, and got the ball off to first base. The throw was low, but our first baseman, Jeff Garcia, scooped it up like a pro. Jones, a fast runner, was out by an inch. "Way to go, Larry! Way to go, Jeff!" came the cries from the fans.

But Marv didn't even look our way. A drop of rain fell on my face, which was hot with anger. "Let it rain!" I thought.

6. In the bottom of the sixth inning, my anger for Marv turned to hate. We had two outs and two men on base and I was up. The Jaguar pitcher caught me looking at a fastball for the first strike. I lined the second pitch deep to left, out of the stadium and into the suburbs beyond. Too bad it was foul. The next pitch must have been 6 inches outside. Too bad the umpire didn't see it that way. "Strike three!" he called. I knew better than to argue, but I stared at him in disbelief. Everyone knew he had made a bad call.

7. Everyone knew but Marv Gilson, that is. Coming out of the dugout, he laughed at me. "Where's our slugger, Larry Rodriguez, when we need him?" he asked derisively. "You could have sealed the championship for us. Instead, you choked and struck out. Oh, well," he sneered, "I guess it's all up to me."

8. I couldn't believe his nerve! Didn't he see my long drive out of the park and the ump's bad call? Suddenly everything I ever knew about good sportsmanship was gone. "You've got a lot of nerve," I heard myself screaming. I grabbed Marv's arm, and for a second, I thought about hitting him.

9. Coach Chen and the other players started out of the dugout. The last thing they wanted was an altercation at the championship game. With the coach approaching, Marv gave me a hard look and pulled away. "Let go, jerk," he sneered. "I need this arm to pitch my perfect game." I followed him onto the infield, shaking my head, disgusted with Marv and with myself for acting so childishly.

10. He certainly was pitching a perfect game, though. For two more innings, there were no hits, walks, or errors. Even the sky seemed to cooperate, clearing up so there would be no chance of a rainout. Here we were about to win the title, and I was furious!

80

11. At last, it was the top of the ninth inning. This was the Jaguars' last chance. Marv got the first batter out on three straight strikes. The crowd went wild. The second batter hit a long fly to left field. Fortunately, Dusty Wilson, our left fielder, can really run. He chased the ball and caught it inches from the fence for out number two. I glanced over at the mound. Marv's perfect game had come within inches of disappearing, but he was as cool as ever.

12. This was it. Marv threw two fast strikes past Jack Chang, the Jaguar batter. Inwardly, I groaned. Was Marv really going to get a perfect game so easily? Marv wound up and threw again. Chang poked in vain at the ball. He got a piece of it, sending a weak fly toward left-center field. The outfielders were playing too deep, and the second and third basemen didn't have a chance either. It was up to me, and it wouldn't be an easy play.

13. How can I describe what was going through my mind as I went back to make the catch? Instinctively, I wanted to catch the ball. That's what ballplayers do. But there was also this strong voice inside me saying, "Miss the ball! Miss the ball, and Marv misses his perfect game!" I'm not proud of that, and maybe the thought of deliberately missing the catch threw me off stride. Or it could have been the grass, still slick from the rain. In any event, I stumbled as I ran backward, tumbled, and rolled head over heels. After that, it's all a blur. I certainly didn't have my eye on the ball, but I guess my glove was still outstretched.

14. Maybe it was a miracle. For suddenly I heard the crowd cheering wildly. I looked down, and there was the ball in the pocket of my glove. It must have just landed there; I didn't even see or hear it. The next thing I knew, old Marv was running up to me, clapping me on the back. "Good play, Larry!"

15. I felt a little sheepish about his compliment. The play could just as easily have gone the other way. For some reason, though, I wasn't feeling so angry now. Maybe Marv wasn't such a bad guy after all. Even if he was, the Falcons were now headed for the state finals. It wouldn't pay for me to have a grudge against our ace pitcher.

1. This story takes place in
   a. the past.
   b. the present.
   c. the near future.
   d. the distant future.

2. One aspect of the setting that might affect the story's plot is
   a. the cold.
   b. the bright, hot sun.
   c. the unfriendly crowds in the surrounding neighborhood.
   d. the possibility of rain.

3. The mood of the story is mainly
   a. humorous.
   b. tense.
   c. mysterious.
   d. joyous.

4. Who is the main character of the story?
   a. Jeff Garcia
   b. Jack Chang
   c. Coach Chen
   d. Larry Rodriguez

5. Choose the word that best describes the main character.
   a. jealous
   b. destructive
   c. unselfish
   d. friendly

6. The main character's main goal throughout the story is to
   a. make sure his team wins the championship no matter what.
   b. gain the recognition he thinks he deserves.
   c. spoil the ending of the game.
   d. prove he is the best player of the league.

7. For the most part, the main character's conflict is with
   a. his own abilities.
   b. another character.
   c. an outside force.
   d. a supernatural force.

8. Which sentence best describes the source of the conflict?
   a. Larry Rodriguez is not as good a player as he thinks he is.
   b. Marv Gilson is full of himself.
   c. The Falcons place too much importance on winning.
   d. The Jaguars have a stronger team.

9. By the end of the game, the conflict
   a. has long been resolved.
   b. has no hope of being resolved.
   c. has just begun to be resolved.
   d. is in the middle of being resolved.

10. What event in the beginning of the story introduces the conflict?
    a. Marv does not cheer Larry's home run.
    b. Larry hopes it will rain.
    c. Larry almost fights with Marv.
    d. Marv strikes out the batter.

11. Larry and Marv almost fight when
    a. Larry asks the umpires to call off the game because of the weather.
    b. Larry almost misses a fly ball.
    c. Marv insults Larry for striking out.
    d. Larry hits a home run.

12. The story reaches its climax when
    a. Larry and Jeff Garcia make a great play in the infield.
    b. Larry stumbles on slick grass and catches a ball.
    c. the coach and players come out of the dugout to stop the fight.
    d. Coach Chen pulls Larry out of the game.

13. At the end of the story, we wonder whether
    a. Marv pitched a perfect game.
    b. Larry really tried to catch the ball or not.
    c. the Jaguars really tried to beat the Falcons for the championship.
    d. Larry and Marv are best friends.

14. To what does the story title refer?
    a. Larry's and Marv's attitudes made the game imperfect.
    b. Marv was the perfect pitcher he often claimed to be.
    c. Larry actually didn't catch the fly ball at the end of the game.
    d. The Falcons didn't make it to the state finals.

15. What do you think is the author's message?
    a. People take athletics too seriously.
    b. Competition always brings out the worst in people.
    c. Every team has to have one or two stars who make all the difference.
    d. Athletes shouldn't let their egos influence their play.

16. Which of the following might also be a good title for this story?
    a. "Homer Fever"
    b. "Fair Ball or Foul?"
    c. "The Shortstop's Dilemma"
    d. "The Unfair Umpire"

17. What is the unstated main idea of paragraph 5?
    a. The Falcon fans are very loyal.
    b. Larry isn't trying hard to win.
    c. Larry wants to be the best player.
    d. Marv doesn't appreciate his teammates' efforts.

18. What is the unstated main idea of paragraph 13?
    a. The ball would have been easy to catch if Larry focused on it.
    b. Larry has a conflict about whether to catch the ball or not.
    c. Larry definitely wants to spoil Marv's perfect game.
    d. Marv wants the best for his teammates.

19. What is the unstated main idea of paragraph 15?
   a. Larry decides that he really likes Marv after all.
   b. Larry realizes it is not worth it to be angry at Marv.
   c. Marv realizes that Larry might have missed the ball on purpose.
   d. Larry understands why he wants to win so badly.

20. In this story, the narrator is
   a. a participant in the events.
   b. a fan watching from the stands.
   c. an outsider who heard about events.
   d. an outsider who sees everything happening.

21. One disadvantage of the story's point of view is that the narrator cannot
   a. explain the actions of the characters.
   b. give details of what happened.
   c. explain his own feelings.
   d. tell what other characters are thinking or feeling.

22. Which event happened before the story begins?
   a. Larry's home run
   b. Marv's complaint about Larry striking out
   c. Larry hoping it might rain
   d. Marv's heroic pitching

23. What is the meaning of the word *derisively* in paragraph 7?
   a. in an offhand way
   b. in a sneering way
   c. in a joking way
   d. in a nice way

24. What is the meaning of the word *sheepish* in paragraph 15?
   a. angry
   b. embarrassed
   c. curious
   d. bold

25. What is the meaning of the word *altercation* in paragraph 9?
   a. annoyance
   b. agreement
   c. harmony
   d. fight

Read the following selection. Then choose the best answer for each question. Mark your answers on the answer sheet.

Korea—A History of Struggle

1. Korea, known to its people as the Land of Morning Calm, has a 3,000-year history. For much of that time, Korea recognized the Emperor of China as its overlord. Nevertheless, Koreans had an identity of their own. Unlike the people of China, who could be quite different in racial background, the Koreans were very much alike racially and in language and customs. The Korean spoken language was very different from Chinese. Their written language was based on an alphabet, not the thousands of picture symbols used by the Chinese.

2. Throughout their history, the Koreans have been inventive. They used movable type in printing long before that system developed in Europe. They also developed small, iron-covered warships more than 400 years ago. With these boats, they destroyed a large Japanese naval force that attacked their country in 1592. That was more than 250 years before the American iron ships the *Merrimac* and the *Monitor* met during the American Civil War.

3. Like the Chinese and the Japanese, the Koreans had little contact with Americans or Europeans until the 1800s. Before that time, Korea only knew about the West from what they learned from shipwrecked sailors. A few Christian missionaries tried to enter Korea secretly, but they were taken captive. Koreans considered foreigners to be uncivilized. Such barbarians were forbidden to enter Korea.

4. Between 1839 and 1842, the British waged war against the Chinese. When the British won, they forced the Chinese to give them trading rights along the coast. Other European countries demanded and got similar rights in China. Then, in 1854, the U.S. government used its navy to open Japan to world trade. All over Asia, the West was making its influence felt.

5. Korea was determined to resist Western influence. When a group of French missionaries entered Korea illegally, they were put to death. When the French sent a fleet to Korea in 1866 to fight back, the French ships were destroyed. In that same year, an American merchant vessel, the *General Sherman*, ignored the Korean ban on Western trade. The Koreans burned the American ship, and the crew was probably put to death.

6. In 1871, an American fleet sailed to Korea. Its purpose was to persuade the Koreans to sign a trade treaty with the United States. The Koreans refused to negotiate and demanded that the Americans leave. Eventually, the Koreans opened fire on the American ships. The Americans returned fire with much larger guns, destroying a Korean fort. Nevertheless, the Koreans still refused to trade with the Americans.

7. Meanwhile, Japan did open its ports to the West and quickly began to adopt Western ways. The Japanese industries and their military were reorganized and outfitted with modern equipment from Europe and the United States. As a growing industrial power, Japan wanted Korea's iron ore, coal, and forest products. Recognizing the superior force of Japan, the Koreans finally made a trade agreement with the Japanese in 1876 and later with the United States.

8. Japan gradually gained control over Korea. In 1894, Japan waged war on China, Korea's traditional overlord. By defeating China, Japan removed one of its rivals for control of the Korean peninsula. At this time, however, Russia also wanted to control Korea. The clashing interests of the Russians and the Japanese led to war in 1904.

9. Japanese soldiers moved through Korea and China to strike at Russia. After Russia was defeated, however, the Japanese troops stayed in Korea. Then, in 1910, Japan took over Korea, making it an official part of the Japanese empire.

10. The Japanese closed all Korean schools, hoping the Koreans would forget they were once an independent nation. Privately owned land was taken from Koreans and given to Japanese settlers. Newspapers and books were censored. The Japanese occupied all government positions in Korea.

11. Thousands of Koreans fled their country to escape the Japanese. These exiles formed patriotic organizations in other lands, waiting for a chance to restore freedom to their homeland. The defeat of Japan in World War II finally presented Korean patriots with an opportunity for independence. The United Nations made plans to hold elections that would create a new Republic of Korea. The new republic would have the same boundaries as the old kingdom of Korea.

12. A military agreement between the Americans and the Russians prevented the Korean patriots' dreams of a single, free homeland. The two larger countries agreed that the Soviet Union would accept the surrender of Japanese forces stationed north of the 38th parallel. South of the 38th parallel, the United States would accept the Japanese surrender. Americans saw this agreement as a temporary arrangement. But the Soviets regarded it as the division of Korea into two countries. There would be a Communist North Korea and a non-Communist South Korea. The United States could not persuade the Soviet Union to accept a unified Korea. Eventually, U.S. officials relegated the problem of a divided Korea to the United Nations.

Korea, 1950s

26. The main idea of paragraph 1 is stated in
 a. sentence 1.
 b. sentence 2.
 c. sentence 3.
 d. the last sentence.

27. What is the main idea of paragraph 2?
 a. Throughout their history, Koreans have been inventive.
 b. Koreans used movable type long before Europeans.
 c. Koreans developed small, iron-covered ships over 400 years ago.
 d. The *Merrimac* and the *Monitor* met during the Civil War.

28. The main idea of paragraph 4 is stated in
 a. sentence 1. **c.** sentence 3.
 b. sentence 2. **d.** sentence 5.

29. What is the unstated main idea of paragraph 6?
 a. The Koreans actively resisted trading with America.
 b. The United States and Korea engaged in a naval battle in 1871.
 c. Korean weapons were not as powerful as American weapons.
 d. Koreans tried to persuade the United States to sign a trade treaty.

30. What is the unstated main idea of paragraph 10?
    a. After the takeover, the Japanese did not allow Koreans to hold political office.
    b. The Koreans suffered under the harsh rule of the Japanese.
    c. Under the Japanese, the Koreans had no way to regain their freedom.
    d. The Koreans prospered under Japanese rule.

31. Think about the main idea of paragraph 12. Then choose the detail below that would support the main idea.
    a. Korea seemed caught between U.S. and Russian interests.
    b. Most of the Korean people lived in South Korea.
    c. Americans saw this agreement as a temporary arrangement.
    d. Korean exiles formed patriotic organizations in other countries.

32. The Japanese became interested in Korea in the 1870s because
    a. it provided a route to attack Russia.
    b. Korea resisted Western influence.
    c. China was threatening to attack Korea.
    d. Korea had important natural resources.

33. The Koreans attacked American ships that entered their ports in the 1870s because
    a. the United States was at war with China, Korea's overlord.
    b. they did not want Western influences in Korea.
    c. the United States wanted to take over Korea.
    d. the United States was blocking trade routes.

34. The United States handed the problem of Korea over to the United Nations after World War II because
    a. Japanese forces would not leave Korea.
    b. the Soviets refused to allow a unified Korea.
    c. Korean patriots could not agree on a plan for independence.
    d. Koreans had been removed from political office.

35. Unlike the Chinese, the Koreans
    a. were alike in racial background.
    b. had an alphabet based on picture symbols.
    c. did not want to trade with the West.
    d. gained political independence.

36. Like the Japanese, the Koreans
    a. signed trade treaties.
    b. recognized China as their overlord.
    c. encouraged Western missionaries.
    d. had little contact with the West until the 1800s.

37. Both China and Russia
    a. fought with Japan around 1904.
    b. were overlords of Korea in the nineteenth century.
    c. discouraged Korea from trading with the West.
    d. influenced Korean culture.

38. Which of the following statements is a fact?
    a. The Koreans have always been inventive.
    b. The Japanese ruled Korea harshly.
    c. Between 1839 and 1842, the British waged war against the Chinese.
    d. Korea rightly resisted Western influence.

39. *In 1910, Japan took over Korea and made it part of its empire.* This statement is
    a. a fact.
    b. an opinion.
    c. neither a fact nor an opinion.
    d. both a fact and an opinion.

40. *The Soviet position on a unified Korea was quite unfair.* This statement is
    a. a fact.
    b. an opinion.
    c. neither a fact nor an opinion.
    d. both a fact and an opinion.

41. From the use of Korea's early iron boats against their enemy, you can infer that
    a. Korea was a technologically advanced country.
    b. Korea had once hoped to invade China.
    c. Korea was involved in the American Civil War.
    d. Japan had long desired to control Korea.

42. From the description of Japan's takeover of Korea, you can infer that
    a. many Koreans supported the Japanese.
    b. Korean soldiers fought the Japanese along the peninsula.
    c. the Japanese tried to weaken the Koreans' sense of identity.
    d. thousands of Koreans fled their country.

43. The Soviet Union probably wanted Korea divided into two countries
    a. to make sure Korea would not invade Russia again.
    b. to establish another Communist country in Asia.
    c. to express its disagreement with the United Nations.
    d. to show the Koreans how powerful Russia is.

44. The outcome of World War II seemed favorable to Korea because
    a. Western powers were too busy to try to influence Korea.
    b. the new United Nations would work for a unified Korea.
    c. the Japanese empire was defeated.
    d. the Russians lost interest in Korea.

45. What is the meaning of *exiles* in paragraph 11?
    a. citizens
    b. refugees
    c. officials
    d. prisoners

46. What is the meaning of *relegated* in paragraph 12?
    a. defeated
    b. solved
    c. communicated
    d. assigned

Use the map on page 85 to answer questions 47 through 50.

47. South Korea is about
    a. 150 miles wide.
    b. 250 miles wide.
    c. 350 miles wide.
    d. 450 miles wide.

48. The capital of South Korea is
    a. on the Yellow Sea.
    b. east of the Sea of Japan.
    c. south of the Demilitarized zone.
    d. north of Panmunjom.

49. The capital of North Korea is
    a. southeast of Hamhung.
    b. northwest of Seoul.
    c. northeast of Panmunjom.
    d. south of the 38th parallel.

50. Which battle of the Korean War occurred south of the 38th parallel?
    a. Heartbreak Ridge
    b. Changjin Reservoir
    c. Panmunjom
    d. Seoul

Read the following selection. Then choose the best answer for each question. Mark your answers on the answer sheet.

Glaciers on the Move

1. Glaciers are huge rivers of ice that slowly flow over land. The movement of glaciers has interested scientists for many, many years. As early as 1705, they noted that boulders in glacier ice changed position from year to year. Scientists also noted that after a glacier melted, deep abrasions in the rocky floor were left behind. Stones caught at the bottom of the glaciers had caused the scratching.

2. Gravity is a very important factor in the movement of glaciers. The huge ice sheets usually flow downhill. However, gravity alone cannot explain glacier movement because solid ice does not flow in the same way as liquid water. There are three other main causes of glacier movement.

Other Causes of Glacier Movement

3. Movement within and between tiny grains of ice, called crystals, causes some glacier movement. Even though ice crystals are locked together tightly, some slipping occurs between millions of grains of ice. Think of the way a snowball changes shape as you pack it. This is called intercrystalline movement. Studies show that tiny slips also occur inside each crystal. This intracrystalline movement adds to the overall flow of glaciers.

4. Glacier movement is also caused by the melting and refreezing of ice crystals inside the glacier. Ice expands, or increases in size, when it gets warmer. The expanding ice pushes the glacier forward. When the ice gets colder again, the crystals slip away from mountain walls as they shrink, and this action also pushes the glacier forward.

5. Melting also causes glacier movement. The meltwater fills in cracks in any surfaces that frame the glacier. When the water freezes, it puts pressure on the glacier. Meltwater on the sides and bottoms of a glacier also "grease" the ice, making it easier for a glacier to slip over rocks.

Measuring Glacier Movement

6. The movement of a glacier over its rocky valley floor is called basal slip. This process is like a blanket of snow sliding off a steep roof. Changes in the ice crystals can cause an internal flow of ice, a movement within the glacier. That motion allows a glacier to flow over uneven surfaces or around curves in mountains. Internal flow also explains how glaciers pick up rocks as they move.

7. Basal slip and internal flow cannot be easily seen. Scientists who study glaciers have drilled deep holes in glaciers and then sunk long steel pipes into the holes. Over time, the pipes bent forward as the ice flowed. Those experiments showed that the surface of the glacier moves faster than, and is often carried along by, the ice beneath it. Scientists have also driven straight lines of stakes across the surface of glaciers. Over time, they found that the center stakes moved farther than the stakes on either end of the line, meaning that the middle of a glacier moves faster than the sides. In fact, the middle can move as much as four times faster. The sides are usually slowed as they drag along the valley walls.

Zones of Ice

8. There are two basic zones of ice in glaciers. The zones help explain the different speeds of glacier flow. The zone of fracture is the upper layer, between 100 and 200 feet thick. There the ice is brittle and breaks sharply. The lower part of a glacier is called the zone of flow. The ice in the zone of flow is more flexible and better able to flow. In fact, the zone of flow carries the zone of fracture along on its back.

9. The ice in the zone of flow does not move at an even rate. It may slow down to pass over rocky humps or other things in its way. Since the ice in this zone is elastic, it can change the way it moves. But the brittle ice in the zone of fracture cannot. It shatters and cracks easily. Such cracks are the deadly

crevasses—openings—that have trapped many explorers. Some crevasses can be between 100 and 200 feet deep.

Kinds of Crevasses

10. Crevasses are formed by the stretching and fracturing of ice, but not all crevasses are alike. Transverse crevasses are most common. They form across the glacier. Usually they develop when the surface over which a glacier is traveling is steeply sloped. Marginal crevasses appear near the sides of a glacier. They form when the ice in the center of the glacier breaks away from the ice dragging along the valley walls. When the ice is suddenly able to spread out, longitudinal crevasses form. They are usually found at the snout, or end, of a glacier where the ice begins to fall apart.

11. Another interesting feature of glaciers is the icefall. Icefalls develop when a glacier passes over a particularly steep drop-off and shatters. An icefall appears as a huge mass of jagged, frozen blocks. Like the water in a waterfall, the broken ice eventually rejoins the glacier and continues to flow.

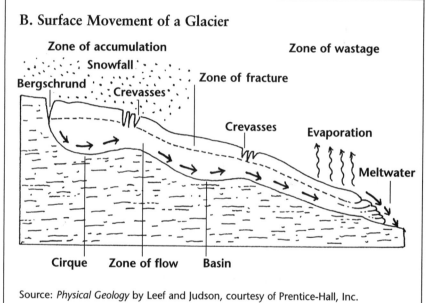

A. Cross-Section of a Glacier

Total surface movement

A → A1

Ice

Rock

Basal slip   Internal flow

Sources: Dr. Robert P. Sharp and University of Oregon Press

B. Surface Movement of a Glacier

Zone of accumulation   Zone of wastage

Snowfall

Bergschrund   Zone of fracture

Crevasses

Crevasses

Evaporation

Meltwater

Cirque   Zone of flow   Basin

Source: *Physical Geology* by Leef and Judson, courtesy of Prentice-Hall, Inc.

51. The main idea of paragraph 5 is stated in
   a. sentence 1.
   b. sentence 2.
   c. sentence 3.
   d. the last sentence.

52. What is the unstated main idea in paragraph 6?
   a. Glaciers tend to move very slowly.
   b. Basal slip and internal flow are types of glacier movement.
   c. Changes in ice crystals cause internal flow.
   d. Glaciers pick up rocks as they move.

53. What is the unstated main idea of paragraph 7?
    a. Scientists have found interesting ways to study the movement of glaciers.
    b. Studies show that the tops and centers of glaciers move the fastest.
    c. Glacial movement can be easily seen.
    d. Experiments on glaciers have failed.

54. One reason melting produces glacier movement is because
    a. the water fills in cracks in the surface of the glacier.
    b. the glacier gets smaller and can move more rapidly.
    c. the meltwater puts less pressure on the glacier.
    d. the water makes the glacier slide more easily.

55. The ice at the center of a glacier moves faster because
    a. there is a steep drop-off in the center of the valley floor.
    b. ice at the sides of a glacier hangs on to the valley wall.
    c. the ice can spread out at the snout of the glacier.
    d. it can melt quickly.

56. Crevasses occur in glaciers because
    a. the zone of fracture cannot easily change with the glacier's movement.
    b. intracrystalline movement occurs.
    c. expanding ice pushes the glacier forward.
    d. ice is brittle and breaks easily.

57. Glacier movement is caused by
    a. the zone of fracture.
    b. the melting and freezing of ice crystals.
    c. basal slip.
    d. abrasions on the rocky floor.

58. Unlike the zone of fracture, the zone of flow
    a. is marked by crevasses.
    b. contains brittle ice.
    c. has more flexible ice.
    d. moves at an even rate.

59. Transverse crevasses occur
    a. near the glacier's floor.
    b. across the glacier.
    c. when meltwater refreezes.
    d. near the sides of a glacier.

60. Unlike intracrystalline movement, intercrystalline movement occurs
    a. between crystals of ice.
    b. inside crystals of ice.
    c. during the melting and refreezing of ice.
    d. on the surface of the ice.

61. The type of crevasse most likely to be found across a glacier is
    a. transverse.
    b. longitudinal.
    c. marginal.
    d. icefall.

62. That the top zone of a glacier moves faster than the lower zone was shown by an experiment using
    a. deep holes and pipes.
    b. straight lines of stakes.
    c. six-sided ice crystals.
    d. careful observation.

63. Scientists probably cannot observe basal slip directly because
    a. glaciers move much too quickly.
    b. the ice is too thick to drill into.
    c. crevasses make the work too dangerous.
    d. the motion occurs deep within a glacier.

64. Crevasses are between 100 and 200 feet deep because
    a. at deeper levels, refreezing ice fills the cracks.
    b. rocks carried in the ice make deep cuts.
    c. the ice in the zone of flow does not move along at an even rate.
    d. that is the depth of the zone of fracture.

65. Based on abrasions left behind after glaciers melted, scientists inferred that
    a. glaciers were not moving.
    b. glaciers were moving.
    c. glaciers were unsafe.
    d. glaciers were safe.

66. What is the meaning of *abrasions* in paragraph 1?
    a. scratches   c. flows
    b. blocks   d. movements

67. What is the meaning of *intercrystalline* in paragraph 3?
    a. containing crystals
    b. within a crystal
    c. not including crystals
    d. between crystals

68. What is the meaning of *marginal* in paragraph 10?
    a. outside the mainstream of a group
    b. near the sides
    c. barely exceeding the minimum
    d. the main part

Use the diagrams on page 89 to answer questions 69 through 71.

69. Which of the following is not shown in diagram A?
    a. zone of fracture
    b. total surface movement
    c. basal slip
    d. internal flow

70. According to diagram B, a glacier forms in a region called the
    a. cirque.
    b. basin.
    c. zone of wastage.
    d. crevasses.

71. According to diagram B, at the end of the zone of wastage, you would expect to see
    a. snowfall accumulation.
    b. a stream.
    c. the bergschrund.
    d. another crevasse.

Questions 72 through 75 are word problems. Use a separate sheet of paper for your calculations.

72. A glacier in Canada moves 1.4 feet per day. About how far will a boulder in the glacier move over the course of a year?
    a. about 500 feet   c. about 600 feet
    b. about 550 feet   d. about 650 feet

73. A glacier in Norway is 35 miles long and 14 miles wide. A glacier in Alaska is 31 miles long and 13 miles wide. How much larger in area is the Norwegian glacier?
    a. 77 square miles   c. 97 square miles
    b. 87 square miles   d. 107 square miles

74. By one estimate, a glacier contains 400 million tons of snow and ice. In one year, 6% of the glacier melts or evaporates and 18 million tons of snow fall on the glacier. About how much snow and ice does the glacier contain at the end of the year?
    a. 368 million tons
    b. 386 million tons
    c. 394 million tons
    d. 407 million tons

75. Greenland has an area of 840,000 square miles. Approximately 78% of that is covered by a huge continental glacier, or ice sheet. How much of Greenland is not covered by ice?
    a. 184,800 square miles
    b. 176,600 square miles
    c. 172,400 square miles
    d. 164,900 square miles

A. Use the following dictionary entry to answer questions 76 through 80.

---

as so ci ate (ə so′ she āt, ə so′ se āt) **v.**
as so′ ci at ed, as so′ ci at ing 1. to connect in one's mind; think of together [We *associate* the smell of something with its taste.] **2.** to bring or come together as friends or partners [Don't *associate* with thieves.] **n.** (ə so′ she it, ə so′ se it) **1.** a person with whom one is joined in some way; friend, partner, or fellow worker **adj.** (ə so′ she it, ə so′ se it) **1.** joined with others in some way [an *associate* justice of the Supreme Court] **2.** having less than full rank; of a lower position [an *associate* professor]

---

76. How many adjective meanings of the entry word are given?
    a. one
    b. two
    c. three
    d. four

77. What part of speech is *associate* in the following sentence? *Let's call her associate from the office.*
    a. adverb
    b. verb
    c. adjective
    d. noun

78. *Associate* has a long *a* sound in its last syllable when used as
    a. a verb.
    b. a noun.
    c. an adjective.
    d. an adverb.

79. Which syllable of *associate* has two pronunciations?
    a. first syllable
    b. second syllable
    c. third syllable
    d. fourth syllable

80. The word *associated* is shown as
    a. a verb form.
    b. a noun form.
    c. an adjective form.
    d. an adverb form.

B. Use the following part of a science book index to answer questions 81 through 85.

Magnesium chloride, 118
Magnesium hydroxide, 71
Magnesium oxide, 54, 55
Magnet, 216
Magnetic
  domains, 216
  field, 220–221
  levitation, 236
  poles, 311
Matter, 1–2
  law of conservation of, 119
  measuring, 3–4
  phases, 11
  properties, 15, 29
Mechanical, 91
  advantage, 193
  energy, 162, 187
  magnesium, 46, 54, 63, 118

---

81. On what page would you find information about magnetic poles?
    a. 236   c. 311
    b. 193   d. 216

82. How many pages in the book tell about mechanical energy?
    a. two   c. four
    b. three   d. five

83. How many subtopics are listed under *matter*?
    a. two   c. four
    b. three   d. five

84. Which chemical is mentioned on page *55*?
    a. magnesium
    b. magnesium chloride
    c. magnesium hydroxide
    d. magnesium oxide

85. Which page(s) discuss the phases of matter?
    a. 3–4
    b. 11
    c. 15, 29
    d. 1–2

C. Think about word parts to answer questions 86 through 100.

86. Which word below would you use to complete the following sentence? *Be careful not to _____ the equipment.*
    a. disuse   c. nonuse
    b. misuse   d. preuse

87. Which word below would you use to complete the following sentence? *I'm paid _____; I get 24 checks a year.*
    a. midmonthly
    b. monthly
    c. bimonthly
    d. trimonthly

88. Which prefix would you add to change the meaning of *transparent* to "partly transparent"?
    a. *mid-*   c. *trans-*
    b. *semi-*   d. *non-*

89. Which suffix would you add to change the meaning of *avoid* to "act of avoiding"?
    a. *-ent*   c. *-ance*
    b. *-ment*   d. *-ness*

90. Which suffix would you add to change the meaning of *arrive* to "process of arriving"?
    a. *-al*   c. *-ance*
    b. *-able*   d. *-ment*

91. Which word below would you use to complete the following sentence? *The child _____ to apologize.*
    a. confused   c. perused
    b. defused   d. refused

92. Choose the correct way to divide the word *bitterly* into syllables.
    a. bitt er ly   c. bit te rly
    b. bit ter ly   d. bi tt erly

93. Choose the correct way to divide the word *follicle* into syllables.
    a. foll ic le
    b. fol lic le
    c. fol li cle
    d. fo lli cle

94. Choose the correct way to divide the word *transaction* in syllables.
    a. tran sact ion
    b. trans act ion
    c. trans ac tion
    d. tran sac tion

95. Choose the correct way to divide the word *renewable* into syllables.
    a. ren ew a ble
    b. re new able
    c. re new a ble
    d. ren ewa ble

96. Which of the following shows the accent mark placed correctly?
    a. reg´ u lar
    b. reg u´ lar
    c. reg u lar´
    d. regu´ lar

97. Which of the following shows the accent mark placed correctly?
    a. dra´ mat ic
    b. dra mat´ ic
    c. dra mat ic´
    d. drama´ tic

98. Which shows the schwa sound correctly circled?
    a. d⊙c o rate
    b. dec ⊙ rate
    c. dec o r⊙te
    d. dec o rat⊙

99. Which word is an antonym of *temporary*?
    a. passing
    b. reasonable
    c. permanent
    d. brief

100. Which word is a synonym of *fascinate*?
    a. bore
    b. repel
    c. regard
    d. charm

Read the following selection. Then choose the best answer for each question.
Mark your answers on the answer sheet.

Uncle Billy's Tricks

1. Most of the old-timers up in Monroe County don't remember my uncle, Billy Mudge, anymore, but from the stories I've heard, he had more tricks up his sleeve than hairs on his head. Best of all, there's a yarn for every trick.

2. My favorite tale about Billy was the time my great-grandfather hired him to dig a well on his farm up near Brewerton. Back then, folks excavated by hand, so Billy started shoveling one morning, and by lunchtime, he had a hole six feet deep. Exhausted, he clambered out of the pit and trudged over to Tug Pond for a little repast and relaxation.

3. Returning to the job after lunch, poor Billy saw that the loose, dry soil had caved into the well hole, almost filling it. Billy groaned in dismay, shaking his fist at the soil as if it had been out to get him personally. Then he took off his hat and vest, the way he always did when he was working. Instead of going back to work though, Billy laid the hat and vest next to the filled-in hole and climbed back up to Tug Pond for another nap.

4. By and by, Leroy and Atticus, two of great-grandpa's neighbors, meandered by to see how Old Billy was doing and maybe add some moral support. They took one look at the earth-filled hole, spotted Billy's hat and vest, and jumped to the only obvious conclusion. Rushing home for shovels, Leroy and Atticus returned posthaste, and began digging the soil out of the hole like there was no tomorrow. Needless to say, they were relieved, and a bit mystified, to find only more dirt and not Uncle Billy at the bottom of the hole.

5. Just about then, a relaxed and smug-looking Uncle Billy ambled down from the pond. "You had to dig out the well hole?" he asked, scratching his head, as the panting Leroy recounted the events of the previous half-hour. "Well, I suspect the walls of the well must have caved in while I was up at the pond having lunch. Boys, let me express my heartfelt gratitude for the concern you've shown for me."

6. Once news of Billy's well caper got out, folks were chuckling all over the county, but Leroy and Atticus didn't really mind. Monroe County wasn't the most exciting place to live in those days, and having a joker like Uncle Billy around to liven things up was a real asset. In fact, one of Leroy and Atticus's favorite pastimes was listening to the lies Billy made up. "Tell us a whopper," they'd beg, and Billy would spin some long, ludicrous yarn that would have both of them rolling with laughter.

7. One autumn day, Leroy and Atticus were out threshing wheat when Billy galloped by on his old dun mare. "Hey, Billy, slow down," yelled Atticus. "Come on over and tell us a whopper!"

8. "Can't today," cried Uncle Billy. "Grandma Hayes just hurt her foot with an ax while she was chopping kindling! I'm going for Doc Pierce right now." His horse was an arrow whizzing down the road to Pierce Corners.

9. Well, Leroy and Atticus started feeling bad for poor, old Grandma Hayes and decided to hustle up there to see if they could help her. Taking the shortcut through the briars and the swamp, the boys ran full tilt two miles up Sickle Hill to Grandma's farm. By the time they arrived, the veins in their faces were bulging like homemade sausages. Needless to say, they were flabbergasted to see Grandma, as spry as ever, out shearing her ewes in the barnyard. Grandma listened to the boys' story and assured them that her foot had never been better. "Why do you boys even listen to that Billy Mudge?" she cackled. "Don't you see he's just telling you another one of his whoppers?"

10. That year, Grandma Hayes's potato crop was almost worthless. The potatoes were no bigger than marbles, and the old lady figured she'd have to feed them to her pullets. Old Billy, whose shack was up near Grandma's, had a brainstorm, though, and persuaded her to let him haul the tiny spuds down to the county fair at Bigelow Falls. Even back in those days, lots of

city folks attended the fair for their annual taste of country living. Uncle Billy parked his wagon by the gate. "What are those little things, some new kind of vegetables?" the fairgoers inquired when they saw the tiny potatoes.

11. "These are Monroe County wild potatoes," Billy replied, doing his best to squelch a grin flickering at the corners of his mouth. "They're forest-grown, and taste ten times better than the ordinary field potatoes at your city markets. Best of all, these incredible vegetables are available for little more than you'd pay for ordinary potatoes!" Nobody could pass up a bargain like that. The crowd swelled around Uncle Billy's wagon, and in just a short while, he had sold every last potato.

12. Later that day at the fair, Billy encountered two young city fellows who wanted him to take them fishing up Long River. Billy agreed, against his better judgment, and indeed the trip was something of a disaster. For one thing, the mosquitoes were biting like crazy, but the fish weren't. Even worse, the city slickers, with their loud voices and clumsy movements, scared away just about any halfway hungry fish in the river. By sundown, Billy had caught only two measly trout. "This has to be divided three ways," thought Billy sourly, as he fried the fish over a campfire, "and it's not even enough for me."

13. Just then, nature decided to cooperate with Billy's growling stomach by having an owl hoot in the darkness. "A wolf," hissed Billy, "and from the sound of its howl, it's mighty hungry! Run for those trees, boys, climb up, and don't come down till I give you the all-clear." Those fellows didn't need much prompting; three seconds later, they were scrambling up into some birches, giving Billy time to wipe the smirk off his mouth. Billy made a big show of running off, too, then slyly circled back to the campfire for a bit. He let five minutes or so elapse and then sang out, "All clear, boys! Come on down! The wolf is gone! Too bad it got our dinner, though."

1. Based on details in the stories, you can assume that Billy Mudge
   a. lives in the present time.
   b. lived about 25 years ago.
   c. lived about 100 years ago.
   d. lived over 300 years ago.

2. Most of the action takes place
   a. in a typical small town.
   b. in a rural agricultural county.
   c. in a forest near Long River.
   d. in a mountain cabin.

3. Choose the words that best describe Billy.
   a. nervous and determined
   b. sly and quick-witted
   c. good-natured and relaxed
   d. cunning and malicious

4. The author reveals the kind of character that Billy is through
   a. Billy's thoughts and feelings.
   b. Billy's reactions to other characters' tricks.
   c. other characters' opinions of him.
   d. other characters' actions.

5. By the end of these four short stories about Billy Mudge, you can tell that he
   a. has grown tired of tricking people.
   b. has paid a price for his lies and pranks.
   c. has continued his trickery without changing.
   d. has vowed never to tell a whopper again.

6. In the story about digging the well, Billy's conflict is basically with
   a. Leroy.
   b. Atticus.
   c. the forces of nature.
   d. himself.

7. Billy resolves this conflict by
   a. refusing to dig in the soft, dry soil.
   b. apologizing for the mistake.
   c. telling whoppers to people in the county.
   d. getting Leroy and Atticus to dig out the well hole.

8. In the last story, Billy's main conflict is
   a. with the mosquitoes at Long River.
   b. with a wolf that comes into camp.
   c. with city folks over a shortage of food for dinner.
   d. with the fish that won't bite.

9. Which is the first event that causes the action to rise in the well-digging story?
   a. Billy digs a hole by hand.
   b. Billy leaves his hat and vest next to the filled-in well hole.
   c. Leroy and Atticus are surprised not to find Billy at the bottom of the hole.
   d. Leroy and Atticus dig to find Billy.

10. The climax of the story about Grandma Hayes occurs when
    a. Billy tells Leroy and Atticus that Grandma has hurt her foot.
    b. Leroy and Atticus discover that Grandma is unhurt.
    c. Grandma tells Leroy and Atticus not to listen to Billy Mudge's stories.
    d. Billy sells all his potatoes at the country fair.

11. The story about the fishing trip reaches its climax when
    a. Billy gets annoyed that there are so few fish to eat.
    b. the two men climb up a tree believing a wolf is nearby.
    c. the two men come down from the trees.
    d. Billy eats the fish.

12. Which of the following titles might be best for the story about Billy digging the well?
    a. "Tug Pond"
    b. "Billy the Digger"
    c. "Digging a Well Long Ago"
    d. "Free Labor"

13. What might be the author's message in the story about the wild potatoes?
    a. Variety is the spice of life.
    b. There's a fool born every minute.
    c. People who play tricks on others eventually get tricked themselves.
    d. Opportunity comes to those who look for it.

14. Which title might be best for the story about Billy's fishing trip?
    a. "Uncle Billy Fries Fish"
    b. "City Slickers"
    c. "Fishing on Long River"
    d. "The Owl That Was a Wolf"

15. What is the unstated main idea of paragraph 3?
    a. Billy wanted it to look as if he were buried in the hole.
    b. Billy really didn't care about the cave-in of the well hole.
    c. It was foolish to dig a well hole in such loose, dry soil.
    d. Billy was not good at digging holes.

16. What is the unstated main idea of paragraph 9?
    a. Leroy and Atticus were tricked once again.
    b. People in Monroe County found Billy's lies annoying.
    c. Leroy and Atticus enjoyed Billy's jokes and tricks.
    d. This time Billy was telling the truth.

17. What is the unstated main idea of paragraph 11?
    a. Billy really believed the wild potatoes were a good bargain.
    b. The fairgoers were amused by Billy's humorous language.
    c. Billy took advantage of people's desire to experience something new.
    d. The potatoes really tasted good.

18. We might say the author's attitude toward these events is
    a. confused.
    b. concerned.
    c. angry.
    d. sentimental.

19. When describing Billy's horse in the last sentence of paragraph 8, the author uses
    a. a simile.
    b. a metaphor.
    c. personification.
    d. exaggeration.

20. When describing Leroy and Atticus's faces in paragraph 9, the author uses
    a. a simile.
    b. a metaphor.
    c. personification.
    d. exaggeration.

21. What is the meaning of the word *caper* in paragraph 6?
    a. accident
    b. chicken
    c. escape
    d. prank

22. What is the meaning of the word *flabbergasted* in paragraph 9?
    a. angry
    b. surprised
    c. satisfied
    d. concerned

23. What is the meaning of the word *ludicrous* in paragraph 6?
    a. timely
    b. never-ending
    c. sarcastic
    d. absurd

24. Choose the correct definition of *relieved* as it is used in paragraph 4.
    a. gave or brought help to
    b. freed from pain or worry
    c. set free from work or duty
    d. increase or intensify

25. Choose the correct definition of *hustle* as it is used in paragraph 9.
    a. to force in a rough way
    b. to go or do quickly
    c. to get or sell in a bold or dishonest way
    d. to relax or take it easy

Read the following selection. Then choose the best answer for each question.
Mark your answers on the answer sheet.

The Mongols Rule China

1. In the steppes of the Mongolian plain, a leader called Temujin united the Mongol groups and other people of the area. In 1206, he received the title Genghis Khan, meaning Universal Ruler. Led by Genghis Khan, the Mongols burst from their homeland in Mongolia, raced into Central Asia, swept across Asia, and reached Central Europe. The Mongols' cruelty and ruthlessness were unparalleled. In a speech, Genghis Khan is reported to have said, "The greatest joy that a man can know is to conquer his enemies and drive them before him, to ride their horses and deprive them of their possessions, to make their beloved weep. . . ."

2. Genghis Khan's mounted warriors devastated North China, bringing ruin to cities and farming regions alike. The Mongols sacked Peking (Beijing) in 1215 and left it burning for more than a month. More than 90 Chinese cities and towns suffered similar devastation. The Khan's cruelty toward the Chinese did not end until he decided it would be more profitable to tax them than to kill them.

3. The Chinese returned the animosity felt by the Mongols. One Chinese scholar wrote, "The Mongols smell so heavily that one cannot approach them." The Mongol diet, which included mare's milk and cheese, was quite different from that of the Chinese. Mongol clothing was rough leather and fur, rather than the fine cloth favored by the Chinese.

4. By the time of his death in 1227, Genghis Khan controlled most of northern China, but the swampy lands to the south stopped his cavalry from further advance. His sons expanded Mongol control farther by conquering lands to the east and west. They divided the empire into four large khanates, in Persia, Central Asia, Russia, and East Asia. Thus, the Chinese people were for the first time linked to the world beyond their traditional borders.

5. In 1260, Genghis's grandson Kublai became the Great Khan. He moved his capital to Beijing and continued the Mongol conquests in China. In 1271, he took the title Emperor of China and established the Yuan (or "original") dynasty. By 1279, the Mongols had taken over the southern part of China as well. Kublai conquered by stealth as well as by military might. Chinese traitors, for example, were paid to turn over the navy in southern China to the Mongols. The Mongols then attempted to invade Japan, but failed when a typhoon destroyed the Mongol fleet.

6. Kublai Khan carried on large, warlike hunts to show that he kept Mongol traditions. Nevertheless, he also made improvements in China's waterways. Among his projects was a vast renovation of the Grand Canal. This waterway was important for the wealth and unity of the nation. Kublai Khan also directed the building of water control projects, such as dams and dikes, along the Yellow River. All in all, Kublai Khan was a vigorous and capable ruler.

7. As rulers of China, the Mongols treated other Mongols most favorably. Many Mongols received land and political appointments, and there were different laws for Mongols and Chinese. A second class of citizens included the non-Chinese, such as the Muslims who were hired by the Mongols. A third class was the northern Chinese. Because they dwelled close to the nomads, the Mongols regarded them with some favor and allowed them to keep low-level government jobs. At the bottom of the social scale were the southern Chinese, who made up the majority of the population. The Mongols distrusted them because they had resisted conquest and were hostile to Mongol rule.

8. During the Mongol rule, trade grew with Central Asia and the Middle East. Both of those areas were ruled by relatives of the Khan. Over time, the vast land controlled by the Mongols experienced a general harmony and decades of peace. It was said that "a maiden bearing a nugget of gold on her head could wander safely throughout the realm." Camel

caravans once more carried Chinese products such as tea, silk, and medicines to the Middle East and into Europe along the Silk Road.

9. Because the Mongols did not trust native Chinese people, they were willing to use the services of foreigners. People from Arabia, Central Asia, Persia, and Europe held government posts. One such person was Marco Polo, a native of Venice who served in the Mongol court for 17 years (1275–1292).

10. In his book, *Description of the World*, published in 1298, Marco Polo dictated an account of his experiences in China. Among other wonders, he described how the Chinese used paper money, which was accepted in all parts of the empire, and a postal system, in which mail carriers "travel a ten days' journey in a day and a night." Europeans doubted Marco Polo's report on China because of the unimaginable wealth he described. Even so, it became one of the most widely read books of its time. It also resulted in further European exploration of and interest in Asia.

11. The Mongols welcomed missionaries from foreign lands. During the Mongol reign, there was a Christian bishop of Beijing as well as leading Muslim religious leaders in the city. The court of Kublai valued traditional Chinese Confucianism for its requirements to obey

authority. However, the Mongols looked most favorably on Lamaism, a form of Buddhism that had developed in Tibet.

12. During the Yuan dynasty, the great painting that had graced the earlier Song dynasty continued. However, the forced departure of many scholars from government held back high culture. On the other hand, popular culture grew in this period. The development of the Chinese novel, written in the vernacular of the people rather than in scholarly language, was one high point. Drama became a popular entertainment, too, especially a combination of drama and music known today as the "Beijing opera."

13. After the death of Kublai, his descendants fought over the throne. The rivalries weakened the government while too much paper money led to inflation, weakening the economy. The hostility that the Chinese felt for the Mongols continued, causing further unrest. A Chinese resistance group, the Red Turbans, began to undermine Mongol control. Terrible floods devastated the Yellow River valley as the great river changed its course. In the popular mind, this suggested that the dynasty had lost the "mandate of heaven." Finally in 1368, a rebellion drove the Mongols out of Beijing.

Mongol Empire and China Under Kublai Khan, 1294

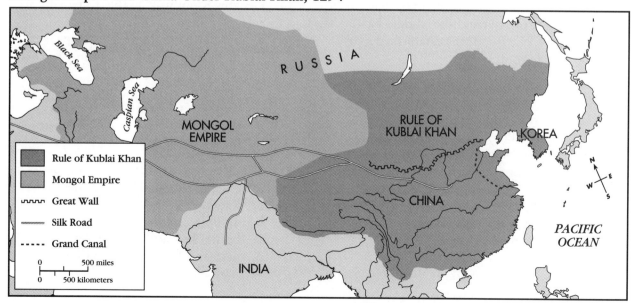

26. Choose the main idea of paragraph 2.
    a. Genghis Khan's mounted warriors devastated North China.
    b. The Mongols sacked Peking in 1215 and left it burning for a month.
    c. More than 90 Chinese cities and towns suffered devastation.
    d. Genghis Khan decided to tax the Chinese rather than kill them.

27. The main idea of paragraph 6 is stated in the
    a. first sentence.
    b. third sentence.
    c. fifth sentence.
    d. last sentence.

28. What is the unstated main idea of paragraph 7?
    a. The Mongols classified other Mongols into four groups.
    b. In general, the Mongols distrusted the southern Chinese.
    c. Not all subjects of the Mongols had the same opportunities.
    d. Kublai Khan was an effective leader.

29. What is the unstated main idea of paragraph 8?
    a. The Mongol rulers brought about an era of peace and prosperity.
    b. The Mongols did much to link China to the rest of the world.
    c. The Khan and his relatives ruled most of Asia and the Middle East.
    d. The Silk Road was established as a trade route.

30. What is the unstated main idea of paragraph 10?
    a. Most Europeans did not believe Marco Polo's account of China.
    b. Chinese society under Kublai Khan was more advanced than the West.
    c. Many Chinese read Marco Polo's book.
    d. China was a country of unimaginable wealth.

31. Choose the detail that best supports the main idea of paragraph 10.
    a. Polo's father and uncle accompanied him to China.
    b. Polo's book resulted in Europe's interest in the exploration of Asia.
    c. Kublai Khan liked Marco Polo and didn't want him to go back to Italy.
    d. Polo described how the Chinese used paper money.

32. Find the main idea of paragraph 1. Then choose the detail that best supports the main idea.
    a. Mongols originally were nomads who lived in felt tents.
    b. In 1206, he received the title Genghis Khan, the Universal Ruler.
    c. Genghis Khan's son, Ogotai, died while invading western Europe.
    d. No other Mongol leader matched Genghis Khan's greatness.

33. The Mongols were willing to hire foreigners because
    a. they lacked technology and a strong navy.
    b. they wanted to forge stronger ties with Europe and Central Asia.
    c. they tended not to trust the native Chinese people.
    d. they provided cheap labor.

34. Genghis Khan was unable to extend his rule over southern China because
    a. a typhoon destroyed his ships.
    b. the ground was too swampy for his warriors on horseback.
    c. he preferred to tax, not conquer, the southern Chinese.
    d. the Chinese army was able to stop his advances.

35. *The Mongols' cruelty and ruthlessness were unparalleled.* This statement is
    a. a fact.
    b. an opinion.
    c. both a fact and an opinion.
    d. neither a fact nor an opinion.

36. Which statement is an opinion?
    a. In 1260, Genghis's grandson Kublai became the Great Khan.
    b. Kublai's descendants fought over the throne.
    c. Kublai Khan was a vigorous and capable ruler.
    d. Genghis Khan ruled most of northern China by the time of his death.

37. From the details in paragraph 11, we can infer that the Mongols
    a. had little interest in religion.
    b. had little religious prejudice.
    c. tended to discourage Western religions.
    d. exploited the religions of others.

38. From the details in paragraph 12, we can infer that
    a. novels written in the vernacular were not very interesting.
    b. the Yuan dynasty was a time of high culture.
    c. Mongol painting was more highly developed than Chinese painting.
    d. rulers of China before the Mongols paid scholars to produce works of high culture.

39. We can infer from paragraph 13 that inflation is caused by
    a. an increase in the amount of goods to purchase.
    b. political rebellion.
    c. natural disasters, such as floods.
    d. an oversupply of money.

40. The "mandate of heaven," mentioned in paragraph 13, probably means
    a. "the will of the gods."
    b. "the support of the people."
    c. "the approval of the Great Khan."
    d. "with the gods' help."

41. Choose the definition of *appointments* as it is used in paragraph 7.
    a. arrangements to meet someone or be somewhere
    b. positions or jobs
    c. furniture or fittings in a place
    d. the act of appointing

42. What is the meaning of *vernacular* in paragraph 12?
    a. everyday language
    b. formal dress
    c. creative meeting
    d. religious scripture

43. What is the meaning of *animosity* in paragraph 3?
    a. hatred
    b. curiosity
    c. confusion
    d. kindness

44. How old is the primary source that includes a quotation by Marco Polo?
    a. about 500 years
    b. about 600 years
    c. about 700 years
    d. about 800 years

45. What type of primary source is used to give us the exact words of Genghis Khan?
    a. a book
    b. a letter
    c. a speech
    d. a diary

46. Based on the facts in the selection, which generalization is most valid?
    a. When a group of people invade a nation, they rarely govern it well.
    b. Conquered people can feel anger toward their conquerors for hundreds of years.
    c. Good transportation is all-important when ruling a large empire.
    d. Ruling with a cruel hand is better than ruling with a kind hand.

47. Based on the facts in the selection about Kublai Khan, which generalization is most valid?
    a. Mongolian rule in China greatly benefited the people of surrounding areas.
    b. A lack of respect for native culture often leads to a ruler's downfall.
    c. Rulers who focus on empire building rarely pay enough attention to detail to rule well.
    d. Foreign rulers can often revitalize a nation.

Use the map on page 99 to answer questions 48 through 50.

48. Compared to the area that was ruled by Kublai Khan, the area of the Mongol Empire was
    a. much larger.
    b. slightly larger.
    c. quite a bit smaller.
    d. exactly the same size.

49. Which region was *not* controlled by the Mongols or Kublai Khan?
    a. Korea
    b. Russia
    c. India
    d. all of the above

50. The Mongol Empire and the rule of Kublai Khan
    a. were linked by the Grand Canal.
    b. were crossed by the Silk Road.
    c. used the Great Wall as a border.
    d. bordered the Pacific Ocean.

Read the following selection. Then choose the best answer for each question. Mark your answers on the answer sheet.

Insect Metamorphosis

1. In the process of growth from egg to adult, most insects pass through a series of transformations, or changes, called metamorphosis. For most insects, there are four stages of development. The first, the egg stage, ends when the young insect, called the larva, emerges from the egg. During the second, or larval stage, the insect feeds constantly and molts, or sheds, its hard, outer exoskeleton several times. After that change is complete, it becomes an inactive pupa. The third stage, the pupal stage, is a period of inactivity in which the body of the insect undergoes striking changes. In the fourth and final stage, the insect is an adult.

2. If an insect goes through all four stages, the metamorphosis is said to be complete. About 87 percent of all insect species undergo complete metamorphosis. About 12 percent of insect species omit the pupal stage in their development. This is called incomplete metamorphosis. Less than 1 percent of insects undergo ametabolic metamorphosis. That is, they experience little change in their development; the young are much like the adults, only smaller. Such insects are small, wingless, and the most primitive on Earth.

3. Insect eggs may be round, oval, flat, or oddly shaped. Some have smooth surfaces, while others are covered with delicate patterns of ridges and grooves. Black, green, blue, brown, spotted, or white, the eggs are laid singly, in clusters of two or three, or in huge batches. Some eggs are laid in impossible-to-find places, while others are dropped in full view. Always, however, the mother deposits the eggs in an environment where larvae will find a copious food supply.

4. Most larvae double and redouble their weight in short periods of time. Essentially eating machines, they frequently destroy things we value, such as wooden buildings, trees, cabbage plants, or woolen clothing. The job of the larva is to accumulate food and energy to carry it through the pupal transformation and into adulthood.

5. The larvae of grasshoppers, crickets, and cockroaches are called *nymphs*. Young dragonflies and mayflies are called *naiads*. The larvae of moths and butterflies are called *caterpillars*. Other names used for insect larvae are *maggots*, *grubs*, and *worms*.

6. For some species, the larval stage is the longest period of the insect's life. The mayfly, for example, spends three to five years as a naiad but lives only a few hours as an adult. Some cicadas spend 17 years underground as nymphs. As adults, they finally emerge from their subterranean holes for just a few brief weeks of summer. The grubs of wood-boring beetles may dwell over 20 years within a tree trunk.

7. The larvae of insects that undergo incomplete metamorphosis look somewhat similar to adults of the same species. Those larvae, however, never have wings like their adult counterparts. Such larvae also lack the thorax pads and reproductive organs of the adults. During incomplete metamorphosis, a larva changes into an adult during the course of a single, final molt. The last larval exoskeleton cracks open, the adult emerges, expands its wings, and flies away.

8. For most insects, the larva appears very different from the adult. A caterpillar, for example, looks nothing like a butterfly. A maggot has little in common with a fly. More often than not, larvae live in different environments and feed differently than their adult counterparts, too. After shedding their exoskeletons a number of times, the larvae are ready to enter the pupal stage. Those living underground or within a plant stay quietly where they are. Many larvae living in the open surround themselves during this critical stage with a protective case, or cocoon.

9. The process of shedding is controlled by hormones formed by the insect's endocrine glands. One set of glands causes loosening and

cracking of the old exoskeleton. Other glands produce a new, larger exoskeleton. Increases in size take place once the old shell is gone and before the new one forms. The growth of the insect then is a series of starts and stops, not the continuous growing process of mammals.

10. Once an insect enters the pupal stage, it is called a pupa. The entire body of the larva is not changed into an adult. Rather, the adult grows from a group of cells, called the *imaginal disk*, on the larval body. It is now that the food gathered as a larva is so essential for growth. This startling transformation can take a few days or an entire winter. Eventually, however, the adult insect breaks out of the pupal skin as well as any protective covering and dries its wings. The new adult, called an *imago*, will not change or increase in size again.

11. With more than a million species of insects, there are many exceptions to the stages of complete metamorphosis described here. In general, however, each stage of this process is adapted for the survival of the insect species. The egg is a small, easily transportable unit, a well-protected structure that allows early development to take place. The larval stage is a practical, food-eating stage in which the insect need not concern itself with moving around or reproducing. The pupal stage, like the egg stage, is basically inactive, concerned with internal changes and development. Finally, for the adult, the focus is on reproduction. Living off what it ate as a larva, the adult finds a mate and locates suitable places to deposit eggs. Often this includes colonizing new areas.

Anatomy of a Grasshopper

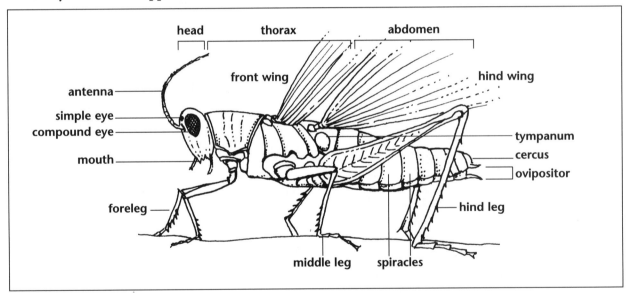

51. What is the unstated main idea of paragraph 2?
    a. Complete metamorphosis involves four different stages of development.
    b. Insects can undergo incomplete or no metamorphosis.
    c. There are three basic types of insect metamorphosis.
    d. About 87 percent of all insects undergo complete metamorphosis.

52. The main idea of paragraph 4 is
    a. stated in sentence 1.
    b. stated in sentence 2.
    c. stated in sentence 3.
    d. unstated.

53. What is the unstated main idea of paragraph 5?
    a. Larvae of grasshoppers, crickets, and cockroaches are called *nymphs*.
    b. The names of insect larvae show that people consider them pests.
    c. Insect larvae have a great many different names.
    d. Young dragonflies and mayflies are called *naiads*.

54. Think about the unstated main idea of paragraph 3. Then choose the detail that supports this idea.
    a. Depositing eggs is the main role of an adult female insect.
    b. Insect eggs may be round, oval, flat, or oddly shaped.
    c. Insect eggs make up part of the diet of many birds and animals.
    d. Female insects have a difficult time finding a safe place to lay their eggs.

55. The growth of a larva is not continuous because
    a. it grows between molting an old exoskeleton and growing a new one.
    b. moving around makes larvae hungry.
    c. the quantity of its food varies according to place and time.
    d. of seasonal changes in the weather.

56. Insect larvae eat a great deal because
    a. they need to store up energy to carry them through the pupal stage.
    b. otherwise they will not experience complete metamorphosis.
    c. the process of molting requires large amounts of energy.
    d. they need to store food for periods of drought.

57. The boll weevil is an insect that undergoes complete metamorphosis. We can infer that
    a. it looks quite different as a larva than as an adult.
    b. it does not have wings.
    c. it will not destroy things we value.
    d. it will not have the thorax pads of an adult.

58. We can infer that a wood-boring beetle larva doesn't need a cocoon because
    a. it is already protected inside a tree.
    b. it does not need extra food during its pupal stage.
    c. its process of molting is controlled by hormones.
    d. it does not have any natural enemies.

59. Unlike its naiad stage, the adult mayfly
    a. focuses on eating and storing energy.
    b. stays quietly where it is.
    c. doesn't live very long.
    d. cannot reproduce.

60. Insects that undergo complete metamorphosis and those that undergo incomplete metamorphosis are alike in that
    a. they both have a pupal stage.
    b. both have larva and adult forms that are quite similar in appearance.
    c. they are both primitive forms of insects.
    d. they both undergo molting.

61. In any random group of insects, most would grow by
    a. ametabolic metamorphosis.
    b. incomplete metamorphosis.
    c. complete metamorphosis.
    d. both a and b.

62. You would be able to identify an insect that underwent ametabolic metamorphosis by
    a. its long pupal stage and short adult life span.
    b. its type of cocoon.
    c. its lack of wings.
    d. its change in color.

63. Insect eggs tend to be
    a. white or light-colored.
    b. deposited near the female's nest.
    c. flat and oval in shape.
    d. deposited near large food supplies.

64. A dragonfly, which undergoes incomplete metamorphosis,
    a. wouldn't have wings in its larval stage.
    b. would be among the most primitive insects on Earth.
    c. would not need to eat heavily as a naiad.
    d. would not double in size as a larvae.

65. What is the meaning of *striking* in paragraph 1?
    a. hitting
    b. unnoticeable
    c. attacking
    d. remarkable

66. What is the meaning of *critical* in paragraph 8?
    a. finding fault with
    b. important
    c. based on sound judgment
    d. urgent

67. What is the meaning of *copious* as used in paragraph 3?
    a. plentiful
    b. liquid
    c. stored
    d. single

68. What is the meaning of *subterranean* in paragraph 6?
    a. comfortable
    b. tiny
    c. hot
    d. underground

Use the diagram on page 104 to answer questions 69 through 71.

69. The thorax refers to the
    a. wings of the grasshopper.
    b. middle section of the grasshopper.
    c. legs of the grasshopper.
    d. hind section of the grasshopper.

70. Which of the following parts is *not* located in the head of the grasshopper?
    a. antenna
    b. mouth
    c. spiracles
    d. simple eye

71. Which of the following parts is *not* located in the abdomen of the grasshopper?
    a. cercus
    b. spiracles
    c. thorax
    d. ovipositor

Questions 72 through 75 are word problems. Use a separate sheet of paper for your calculations.

72. A pine forest in Wisconsin was infested with a tiny insect called a crawler. Each square inch of the forest had 175 of the crawlers. How many crawlers would be found in one acre (43,560 square feet)?
    a. about 100,000
    b. about 100 million
    c. about 1 billion
    d. about 10 billion

73. A queen termite lays one egg every 20 seconds. How many eggs does she lay each week?
    a. 4,000
    b. 15,000
    c. 30,240
    d. 35,750

74. Over a lifetime, the queen termite lays 9 million eggs. High temperatures prevent 17% of them from hatching. Predators destroy another 29%. Disease also destroys many of the eggs. If 1.7 million of the eggs eventually hatch, what percentage was lost to disease?
    a. about 20%
    b. about 30%
    c. about 40%
    d. about 50%

75. A cicada spends 17 years as a larva and 2 weeks as an adult. How many days does he spend as a larva for each day as an adult?
    a. about 337 days
    b. about 403 days
    c. about 443 days
    d. about 479 days

A. Use the following dictionary entry to answer questions 76 through 80.

ques tion (kwes´ chǝn) *n.* **1.** something that is asked in order to learn or know **2.** doubt [There is some *question* about his honesty.] **3.** a matter to be considered; problem [It's not a *question* of money.] **4.** a matter that is being talked over by a group *v.* **1.** to ask questions of **2.** to object to; to have doubts about [to *question* the ref's call] **— beside the question,** not having anything to do with the subject being talked about **— beyond question,** without any doubt **— in question,** being considered or talked about **— out of the question,** impossible **— ques tion´ er** *n.*

76. How many verb meanings of the entry word are given?
    a. two   c. four
    b. three   d. none

77. Which noun definition of *question* is used in the following sentence? *The question of privacy prevented me from agreeing to an interview.*
    a. definition 1   c. definition 3
    b. definition 2   d. definition 4

78. How many idioms containing *question* are included in the entry?
    a. two   c. four
    b. three   d. five

79. The idiom *beyond question* means
    a. not having anything to do with the subject.
    b. without any doubt.
    c. impossible.
    d. being considered or talked about.

80. The word *questioner* in the entry is
    a. a verb.
    b. an idiom.
    c. an adjective.
    d. none of the above

B. Think about word parts to answer questions 81 through 100.

81. The prefix in the word *transcontinental* means
    a. across.
    b. before.
    c. under.
    d. without.

82. The prefix in the word *disestablish* means
    a. together.
    b. apart.
    c. wrong.
    d. undo.

83. The prefix in the word *misconceived* means
    a. middle.
    b. badly.
    c. not.
    d. well.

84. The prefix in *depopulate* means
    a. undo.
    b. before.
    c. over again.
    d. in part.

85. The suffix in *comparable* means
    a. that can be.
    b. the process of.
    c. like in manner.
    d. different from.

86. The suffix in *pompous* means
    a. the act of.
    b. characterized by.
    c. lacking in.
    d. in effect.

87. Which suffix would you add to change the meaning of *sober* to "in a sober manner"?
    a. *-ness*
    b. *-ful*
    c. *-ous*
    d. *-ly*

88. Choose the correct way to divide the word *mistake* into syllables.
    a. mi stake
    b. mis take
    c. mist ake
    d. mis ta ke

89. Choose the correct way to divide the word *favorite* into syllables.
    a. fa vor ite
    b. favor ite
    c. fa vo rite
    d. fav or ite

90. Choose the correct way to divide the word *performance* into syllables.
    a. per form ance
    b. per for mance
    c. perf or mance
    d. perf orm ance

91. Choose the correct way to divide the word *transparent* into syllables.
    a. tran spar ent
    b. trans pa rent
    c. trans par ent
    d. tran spa rent

92. Choose the correct way to divide the word *belligerence* into syllables.
    a. bel lig er ence
    b. bell i ger ence
    c. bel li ge rence
    d. be lli ger ence

93. The words *recede* and *cession* have a root that means
    a. carry.
    b. shape, form.
    c. to go, yield.
    d. stationary.

94. The words *deport* and *transport* have a root that means
    a. stationary.
    b. shape, form.
    c. to go, yield.
    d. carry.

95. Which word has its accent on the first syllable?
    a. conclusion
    b. describing
    c. several
    d. maintain

96. Which word has its accent on the second syllable?
    a. dozen
    b. justice
    c. bookcase
    d. surprise

97. Which syllable of *manufacture* has the most stress?
    a. first
    b. second
    c. third
    d. fourth

98. Which syllable of *rehabilitate* has the most stress?
    a. first
    b. second
    c. third
    d. fifth

99. The schwa sound in *sanitary* can be heard in the
    a. first syllable.
    b. second syllable.
    c. third syllable.
    d. fourth syllable.

100. The schwa sound in *matrimony* can be heard in the
    a. first syllable.
    b. second syllable.
    c. third syllable.
    d. fourth syllable.

Read the following selection. Then choose the best answer for each question. Mark your answers on the answer sheet.

The Open Window
(Adapted from the short story by H. H. Munro)

1. "My aunt will be down in a minute, Mr. Nuttel," said the young woman who had let him in a few minutes earlier. "In the meantime, you will have to put up with me. I'm Mrs. Sappleton's niece, Vera."

2. Framton Nuttel listened nervously and answered her questions as best as he could. He couldn't imagine how someone of 15 could speak to a stranger so boldly and act with such poise. He, at 55, was not half that confident. He remembered that at 15 he had barely spoken to anyone. "Do you know many of the people around here?" asked the niece.

3. "Hardly a soul," Framton said, looking at the stairway, where he hoped Mrs. Sappleton would appear soon. "My sister lived here during the summer a few years ago. She liked it very much. When she knew I was coming to stay here for a while, she gave me some letters of introduction to a few people in the community."

4. Framton wondered now why he ever promised his sister that he'd meet these people. He felt uneasy about it, but he remembered how his sister had pleaded. "Framton, please meet some of the lovely neighbors. It will do you good! On the other hand, it will do you no good at all to go to a rural retreat for a nerve cure if you just sit in the cottage."

5. "So, then," Vera went on, "you know almost nothing about my aunt?"

6. "Only her name and address," admitted the caller. "I have never met her." Briefly he wondered whether Mrs. Sappleton was, perhaps, a widow. Somehow, though, the room suggested that a man was living here, too. But he thought little more about it.

7. "Then you know nothing about my aunt's tragedy, Mr. Nuttel?" asked Vera, lowering her voice.

8. "Tragedy? No. My sister didn't mention anything about a tragedy."

9. "When was your sister here last?"

10. "Four or five years ago," he said.

11. "Well," the young woman continued, just above a whisper, "the tragedy occurred three years ago—in fact, just three years ago *today*."

12. To a man like Framton Nuttel, it seemed as if all tribulations occurred in big cities. Somehow, big problems seemed out of place in this restful country spot. But he listened to the young woman as she went on in a soft voice. "You may wonder why we keep that window open on an October afternoon," she said, pointing to a large French window, or door, that opened to the lawn.

13. "It's quite warm for this time of year," remarked Framton. "But does the window have something to do with the tragedy?"

14. "Out of that window," Vera whispered, "three years ago today, my aunt's husband and her two younger brothers went for a day's shooting. They never came back."

15. Framton listened with interest at the building mystery as the young woman went on, leaning toward him in her chair. "They were crossing a footbridge over a rushing stream. It broke while all three of them were on it." Her voice cracked a little with emotion as she continued. "They never had a chance in a torrent like that. A rescue team went out but never recovered the bodies. The mouth of the stream is not far from the open ocean, and the men must have been washed out to sea," explained Vera.

16. Noticing that her listener had tears in his eyes, Vera sat up and seemed to regain her poise. "My poor, dear aunt," she explained, "thinks that someday, probably on an anniversary of their death—like today—they will return. I have heard her say many times that she is sure that her husband, her two brothers, and the brown spaniel that was lost with them will return through that window—the way they went out."

17. Framton Nuttel didn't know what to think and certainly didn't know what to say. The young woman noticed that the guest was getting more nervous by the minute. She looked around and, seeing that her aunt was still not coming down, went on. "My aunt actually believes that all three of them will come across the lawn one day toward this window with their guns in their hands. She even thinks that the dog will be running on ahead of them. Maybe you can't believe that, Mr. Nuttel. But if you heard my aunt talk about it, you'd get a feeling that it's really going to happen. It gives me a creepy feeling to talk about it." She broke off with a shudder.

18. It was a relief when the aunt finally came down the stairs and apologized for being late. "I hope Vera has been amusing you," she said, as her niece left the room.

19. "Oh—oh, she has," replied Framton.

20. Mrs. Sappleton looked toward the open window. "I hope you don't mind the window open. I expect my husband and brothers anytime. They've been out shooting and they always come in this way." Then with one eye on the window, she tried to talk with Framton.

21. "How strange! She really does expect the men to come," he thought. Framton became so nervous he didn't know what to do. What an unfortunate coincidence—that he should make this visit on the anniversary of such an appalling tragedy! And the woman had to make it worse, acting as if the men had only been gone since the morning.

22. Finally, Mrs. Sappleton turned from the window and gave Framton a moment of her attention. "And what brings you to our community?" she asked.

23. Imagining that it might be good for her to listen to someone else's problems for a minute, he began, "My doctors ordered a complete rest for me for at least three months without any mental excitement or strenuous physical exercise." Since she actually seemed interested in his problems, he continued. "As for my nerves, I must never get excited or . . ."

24. "Here they are at last!" cried Mrs. Sappleton, leaping from her chair and moving toward the window. "Just in time for tea."

25. Framton staggered to his feet, not believing his eyes. In the deepening twilight, he saw three figures and a dog walking across the lawn toward the window. The men carried guns, and one had a raincoat over his shoulder. Nuttel grabbed wildly for his hat and cane, then dashed out the door and across the driveway to his car. Stones in the road went flying as he sped away.

26. "Well, here we are, my dear," said the man with the raincoat as he came through the window. "But who was that who bolted out as we came up?"

27. "A most extraordinary man—a Mr. Nuttel," said Mrs. Sappleton. "He could only talk about his nerves, and he dashed off without saying good-bye when you arrived. One would think he had seen an apparition!"

28. "I think maybe it was the dog, Auntie," said Vera, who had suddenly appeared again. "He told me he had a horror of dogs. In my conversation with him, he said a pack of mad dogs had chased him one time on the banks of the Ganges River. He said he had spent the night in a newly dug grave with the dogs snarling and foaming above him. . . ." Making up tall stories on short notice was Vera's specialty.

1. Choose the words that best describe Framton Nuttel.
   a. intelligent and bold
   b. positive and confident
   c. rebellious and overbearing
   d. anxious and shy

2. How would you describe Mrs. Sappleton's niece, Vera?
   a. playful and quick-witted
   b. serious and good-natured
   c. bored and angry
   d. sad and lonely

3. Choose the word that best describes Mrs. Sappleton's attitude toward Mr. Nuttel at the end of the story.
   a. warm
   b. bewildered
   c. annoyed
   d. satisfied

4. Knowing why Mr. Nuttel is in this new community, the reader knows that
   a. one cannot really believe what he says.
   b. he might act in dangerous ways.
   c. he is in a delicate emotional state.
   d. he needs someone to look after him.

5. Framton Nuttel's basic conflict is with
   a. his own feelings.
   b. another character.
   c. society as a whole.
   d. the forces of nature.

6. Framton has a conflict with Mrs. Sappleton because
   a. he never really wanted to visit his sister's friends.
   b. what he thinks is her belief makes him very uneasy.
   c. she is really paying no attention to his conversation.
   d. she was not expecting him to visit her.

7. Framton attempts to resolve his final conflict by
   a. rushing from the house.
   b. talking to Mrs. Sappleton about his health.
   c. waiting for Mrs. Sappleton's husband and brothers to return.
   d. questioning the validity of Vera's story.

8. The first important event in the story occurs when
   a. Mrs. Sappleton's husband and brothers are drowned.
   b. Vera tells Nuttel about what her aunt expects to happen.
   c. Framton's sister tells him to visit her friends in the country.
   d. Framton explains that his sister once lived at the house.

9. When Mrs. Sappleton finally appears, the action continues to rise because
   a. she denies her niece's story.
   b. she tells Framton that she is indeed expecting her husband and brothers.
   c. Framton realizes that Mrs. Sappleton knows nothing about him.
   d. she is not the woman Framton expected to see.

10. The climax of the story occurs when
    a. Mrs. Sappleton explains to her husband who Framton is.
    b. someone bolts the window shut.
    c. the niece describes Framton's experience with the wild dogs.
    d. Framton sees the three men approach.

11. The conclusion of the story is important because we learn
    a. what happens to Framton after he leaves the Sappletons.
    b. more about Mrs. Sappleton's niece.
    c. what happened to Framton in India that caused his emotional problems.
    d. why the three men went hunting.

12. What is one of the themes of this story?
    a. Some real-life situations are too strange to explain logically.
    b. Things aren't always what people claim they are.
    c. Playing tricks on people is a good way to make them relax.
    d. Life is stranger than fiction.

13. Which might be the best alternate title for this story?
    a. "A Country Tragedy"
    b. "The Extraordinary Visitor"
    c. "Mrs. Sappleton's Secret"
    d. "No Cure for Nerves"

14. What is another theme of the story?
    a. Everyone has to find his or her own way to relax.
    b. The country really is a restful place.
    c. Pranks and practical jokes can have unexpected results.
    d. Prepare for the unexpected.

15. We can infer that the reason Vera asked Framton if he knew her aunt was that Vera
    a. didn't trust anyone from the city.
    b. wanted to find out whether he knew that her uncle was still alive.
    c. was embarrassed that her aunt had such a strange belief.
    d. wanted to find out why Framton had come to visit.

16. We can infer that the niece might look over to the stairs for her aunt while talking to Framton because she wouldn't want her aunt to
    a. know that Mr. Sappleton is really dead.
    b. interrupt her story.
    c. make Framton more nervous.
    d. hear her made-up story.

17. We can infer that the niece knows that
    a. her uncles will return shortly.
    b. her aunt does not really like Framton.
    c. Framton is in desperate need of rest and quiet.
    d. Mrs. Sappleton cannot discipline her niece.

18. What is the unstated main idea of paragraph 2?
    a. Framton doesn't know very many people in his new neighborhood.
    b. Mrs. Sappleton's niece is a kind and outgoing young woman.
    c. Framton is painfully shy and lacks social skills.
    d. Vera tries to make Framton feel unwelcome.

19. What is the unstated main idea of paragraph 28?
    a. Framton's emotional problems result from his experiences in India.
    b. The niece made up the entire story she told Framton.
    c. The niece is understanding and creative.
    d. Mrs. Sappleton should have never invited Framton to her home.

20. In this story, the narrator is
    a. a story character who takes an active role in the events.
    b. an outsider who sees into the minds of some of the characters.
    c. an outsider who merely observes events.
    d. a story character who takes a passive role in the story's events.

21. Why is this point of view a good one from which to tell this story?
    a. The narrator was a character in the story.
    b. The narrator liked Framton better than Vera.
    c. The narrator can describe everything that happens.
    d. The narrator can include his or her own feelings about the characters.

22. What is the meaning of the word *bolted* in paragraph 26?
    a. locked a door
    b. gulped food hastily
    c. darted away
    d. blocked

23. What is the meaning of the word *retreat* in paragraph 4?
    a. an act of going back or of withdrawing from a battle
    b. a period of retirement by a group of people for religious purposes
    c. a safe, quiet place
    d. an act of taking flight

24. What is the meaning of *apparition* in paragraph 27?
    a. a ghost
    b. an old friend
    c. a large sum of money
    d. a shadow

25. What is the meaning of *tribulations* as used in paragraph 12?
    a. unexpected events
    b. small annoyances
    c. unusual circumstances
    d. serious difficulties

Read the following selection. Then choose the best answer for each question.
Mark your answers on the answer sheet.

The Berlin Airlift and the Berlin Wall

1. At the end of World War II, the victorious countries divided Germany into four zones. Each zone was to be governed by one of the four major powers—the United States, France, Great Britain, and the Soviet Union. Berlin, the former German capital, also was divided into four similar zones. Because Berlin lay deep within the Soviet zone of Germany, in order for the Americans, British, or French to get to their zones within Berlin, they had to cross areas controlled by the Soviet Union.

2. The Western Allies and the Soviet Union were supposed to work together in the running of Germany and Berlin, but basic differences in ideas and political beliefs prevented this cooperation. For example, the Americans, British, and French introduced a Western political system in their zones of Berlin, while the Soviet Union created a Communist economy and government in its zone. Thus, Berlin had two competing systems, which the sponsoring countries used to show off their ideals.

3. Almost immediately, the Western-occupied zone of Berlin became an escape route. As if drawn to a magnet, hundreds of thousands of Eastern Europeans fleeing oppression crossed the open border into West Berlin. From there, they secured passage to Western Europe, the United States, and other nations around the world. That these refugees were so anxious to leave was an embarrassment to the Soviets, as well as an economic drain, for most of them were young and well-educated.

4. To plug the escape route, the Soviets wanted the Americans, British, and French to leave Berlin. The Western powers, however, were determined to stay. For one thing, the Soviets and the world would have seen the withdrawal as a defeat. This was politically impossible for the Western governments. Berlin was also an important "listening post," a place where Western intelligence agents gathered information about the emerging Communist powers. Furthermore, relations between the United States and the Soviet Union were rapidly breaking down. If war were to break out, the Western powers would need to use their 10,000 troops in Berlin as a valuable first line of defense.

5. By 1948, the Western powers were convinced that the Soviet Union was not going to cooperate with them in setting up new economic and political structures in Germany. So the United States, France, and Great Britain went ahead and laid the foundations of what would become West Germany. Part of the Western plan was a common currency for the three sectors, a plan to which the Soviet Union strongly objected. When the Western powers introduced the currency despite these objections, the Soviets blockaded West Berlin.

6. In negotiating their presence in Berlin right after the war, the West had made a major error. The agreement they signed did not give them official access to Berlin through East Germany. So the Soviets actually broke no treaties when, on June 24, 1948, they closed all land routes into West Berlin from the Western-occupied sections of Germany. This effort to force Western powers out of Berlin soon came to be called the Berlin Blockade.

7. In practical terms, the blockade meant that more than 2 million people in West Berlin would have almost no way to get necessary supplies from the West. At the start of the blockade, for example, West Berlin had only enough food and coal to last 40 days. To maintain the civilian population and troops, American and British transport planes would have to fly in 4,500 tons of supplies to West Berlin every day.

8. In a news story for July 4, 1948, the Associated Press described the situation this way: "The dentist works his drill with a foot pedal, and the barber has replaced his electric clippers with hand shears. That's life these days for the Germans in West Berlin since the

Russians cut off electric-current supplies. Without these supplies, the Western sectors can produce only about half of their power needs. And even this can't last if some way is not found to bring in coal over the Russian blockade, which has stopped all railroad freight between Berlin and West Germany."

9. To maintain their presence in Berlin, the Americans and British began an airlift named "Operation Vittles." At first, the planes were able to bring in only 4,000 tons of food a day. That was enough to keep the West Berliners alive, but only barely. Later, larger aircraft and more receiving airports were put into service. By the height of the airlift, nearly 13,000 tons of food, fuel, and other goods were ferried by air into West Berlin every day. In all, over 200,000 flights were made by British and American planes during the 15-month blockade.

10. The Soviets had not thought the West would be able to supply West Berlin by air. When it became clear that the airlift was successful and would continue indefinitely, the Soviets lifted the blockade, on May 12, 1949. Meanwhile, the troubled citizens of West Berlin had captured the hearts of people everywhere. Additionally, the West had won an important victory in the minds of all by not capitulating to the Soviets.

11. After the lifting of the blockade, the Western zones of Germany were united into the German Federal Republic (West Germany), while the Soviets established the German Democratic Republic (East Germany). The new German governments quickly began taking over the tasks of the powers that had occupied them. But the Soviet and Western militaries continued to maintain their presence in the divided land. Dissatisfaction among the East German people with Soviet rule led to strikes and uprisings in East Berlin in the early 1950s. These were suppressed by Soviet tanks.

12. The East Germans used barbed wire and machine-gun nests to close their border with West Germany. But the border between West Berlin and East Berlin remained open. The original 1949 agreement between the four Allies had stated that there would be free

movement for the French, British, Americans, and Soviets anywhere within the city. As a result, between 1954 and 1961, some 2,750,000 Eastern Europeans traveled to East Berlin, crossed into West Berlin, and found a way to relocate in the West. East German authorities tried to stop the flow with stiff passport requirements. They also threatened to confiscate the property of those who left. These measures, however, were largely not effective.

13. In August 1961, the East Germans and their Soviet advisors decided to block the fleeing refugees. Occupying all crossing points on the Eastern side of the border between the two parts of Berlin, they tore up the roads and built barricades. The action, a violation of the 1949 agreement, caught the newly elected U.S. President, John F. Kennedy, and his administration by surprise. At first, the Soviets assured the Americans that the barriers were a temporary measure to provide for more

Post–World War II Germany, 1948

orderly movement. However, the building of a permanent barrier, the Berlin Wall, began a few days later. For a while, the West considered pulling down the wall, but they feared that such an action would prompt the Soviets to fight back with nuclear weapons.

14. The Berlin Wall stood until November 9, 1989. By the late 1980s, the Soviet Union was beginning to disband. This allowed the Berlin Wall to fall and for Germany to be unified.

26. What is the unstated main idea of paragraph 2?
- **a.** The Western powers created their own style of government and economic system in Berlin.
- **b.** The Soviet Union and the West competed with each other in Berlin.
- **c.** East Berlin had a Communist-style government and economy.
- **d.** The Western powers wanted total control over Germany and Berlin.

27. The main idea of paragraph 6 is stated in the
- **a.** first sentence.
- **c.** third sentence.
- **b.** second sentence.
- **d.** last sentence.

28. What is the unstated main idea of paragraph 9?
- **a.** The Berlin Airlift was named "Operation Vittles."
- **b.** The Berlin Airlift was designed to maintain a Western presence in Berlin.
- **c.** A 15-month Western airlift brought in enough supplies to West Berlin.
- **d.** Larger aircraft were needed to keep the Berlin Airlift going.

29. Choose the detail that would support the main idea of paragraph 9.
- **a.** Airlift planes flew around the clock, in good weather and bad.
- **b.** A canal leading to West Berlin was also blockaded by the Russians.
- **c.** Over the years, the two halves of Berlin served as a "barometer" for relations between East and West.
- **d.** The Soviets didn't think the operation would be successful.

30. The main idea of paragraph 4 is that West Berlin had strategic importance for the Western nations. Which detail supports this main idea?
- **a.** The Soviets wanted to plug the escape route through West Berlin.
- **b.** The Western powers had over 10,000 troops in West Berlin.
- **c.** The West had no official access to West Berlin by land.
- **d.** People living in East Berlin fled to West Berlin to live.

31. The Soviets broke no treaties when they blockaded land routes into West Berlin because
- **a.** the West and the Soviet Union were not cooperating in Berlin.
- **b.** the West knew the blockades were only temporary.
- **c.** the West had enough airplanes to provide supplies to West Berlin.
- **d.** the West never had official access to West Berlin.

32. The Soviets eventually lifted the Berlin Blockade because
- **a.** they did not want to cause further suffering in West Berlin.
- **b.** the Western powers agreed to leave the city.
- **c.** the blockade was not achieving its goals.
- **d.** they had lost interest in controlling Berlin.

33. The West decided not to pull down the Berlin Wall in 1961 because
- **a.** such an action might bring about a war with the Soviet Union.
- **b.** far too many refugees had been coming to the West through Berlin.
- **c.** the agreement that guaranteed free movement in the city had expired.
- **d.** the barricade was successful.

34. Unlike the border between East and West Germany during the 1950s, the border between East and West Berlin
    a. was closed.
    b. was guarded.
    c. was blockaded.
    d. was open.

35. Compared to shipments at the beginning of the blockade, daily shipments to West Berlin by the end of the blockade had
    a. almost doubled.
    b. more than tripled.
    c. decreased only slightly.
    d. decreased by almost half.

36. Unlike East Berlin, West Berlin
    a. had a Communist economic system.
    b. had a Western-style democratic government.
    c. was not occupied by the troops of the former Allies.
    d. did not have a formal government structure in place.

37. From the details in paragraph 10, we can infer that
    a. the Soviets really did not care that much if the West left Berlin.
    b. the Soviets outwitted the West.
    c. the airlift greatly strengthened the air forces of the Western nations.
    d. blockading West Berlin had not projected to the world a positive image of Soviet power.

38. From the details in paragraph 11, we can infer that
    a. the Soviets and the West became bitter rivals in Berlin.
    b. the West had a great number of spies in Berlin.
    c. the Americans, French, and British were tired of refugees flooding into West Berlin.
    d. The Soviets and the West had to supply Berlin by air.

39. We can infer from paragraph 12 that
    a. life in Eastern Europe improved steadily during the 1950s.
    b. the West did everything it could to encourage Eastern Europeans to become refugees.
    c. conditions in Eastern Europe were quite grim during the 1950s.
    d. East Germans lived more comfortably than their West German neighbors.

40. *The blockade meant that more than 2 million people in West Berlin would have almost no way to get necessary supplies.* This statement is
    a. a fact.
    b. an opinion.
    c. neither a fact nor an opinion.
    d. both a fact and an opinion.

41. *The blockade was a harsh and ill-planned attempt to manipulate the West.* This statement is
    a. a fact.
    b. an opinion.
    c. neither a fact nor an opinion.
    d. both a fact and an opinion.

42. The primary-source information referred to in this reading selection is
    a. a speech.
    b. a news story.
    c. an eyewitness interview.
    d. a diary.

43. How long had the Berlin Blockade been in effect when this primary source was released?
    a. less than two weeks
    b. about three months
    c. a little less than a year
    d. more than a year

44. From the facts in this primary source, you learned that
    a. the Russians blocked electricity to West Berlin.
    b. the Americans knew about the blockade months before it began.
    c. West Berliners had stockpiled food and coal in case of a blockade.
    d. the Soviets wanted the Western Allies to stay in Berlin.

45. Based on the facts in this reading selection, which of these generalizations seems most valid?
    a. The Western Allies and the Soviet Union worked together to solve the Berlin problem.
    b. Without Berlin, the United States and the Soviet Union would not have cooperated so closely.
    c. Many different countries enforced the blockade of Berlin and the building of the Berlin Wall.
    d. Berlin was a pawn in the conflict between the United States and the Soviet Union.

46. Based on the facts in this reading selection, which of these other generalizations seem most valid?
    a. The Berlin Blockade showed the Western Allies how powerful the Soviet Union could be.
    b. The Berlin Blockade caused a division between the Western powers over how to manage West Berlin.
    c. The Berlin Blockade effectively stopped the outflow of refugees to the West for many years.
    d. The Berlin Blockade proved to be a major defeat for the Soviet Union in East Germany.

47. What is the meaning of the word *capitulating* in paragraph 10?
    a. cooperating
    b. disagreeing
    c. giving in
    d. winning over

Use the map on page 114 to answer questions 48 through 50.

48. According to the map, how many railroad links must have been blockaded by the Soviets?
    a. two
    b. three
    c. four
    d. none

49. According to the map, the flight distance from Frankfurt to Berlin was about
    a. 50 miles.
    b. 100 miles.
    c. 200 miles.
    d. 500 miles.

50. According to the map, Berlin is located in Germany's
    a. northwest region.
    b. south central region.
    c. northeast region.
    d. southwest region.

Read the following selection. Then choose the best answer for each question. Mark your answers on the answer sheet.

Surgical Advances

1. Surgery is a field of medicine in which great advances are continually being made. Organ transplants, reattaching severed limbs, and other remarkable procedures occur more and more frequently now than they have in the past. New equipment enables surgeons to diagnose and treat patients efficiently. Many people who would have had little hope of treatment in the recent past can now benefit from surgery.

2. One of the most important surgical instruments is the endoscope. Basically, the endoscope is a long, flexible tube used to look inside a patient's body. An endoscope makes use of a process called fiber optics, in which light is carried by a filament to the site the surgeon wants to examine. The endoscope can also be a surgical tool. Fitted with a loop or blade, it can cut tissue. Stones in the bladder, for example, can now be cut and washed out with an endoscope. This eliminates the need for more invasive and painful abdominal surgery.

3. Microsurgery deals with the tiniest and most sensitive parts of the body. Generally, the microsurgeon works with a microscope attached to a visual display unit, a TV screen. Magnifying nerve endings and blood vessels helps the surgeon to reattach limbs. Microsurgery also plays a key role in surgery on the tiny bones in the ear and the larynx, or voice box.

4. Another relatively new surgical technique uses extreme cold (–4°F, or –20°C) to destroy tissue. Called cryosurgery, this process is used occasionally in operations on the brain and the eye. Cryosurgery is also effective in treating some skin disorders, for example, the removal of warts.

5. In many operating rooms, intense beams of energy, called lasers, are now being used to "weld" back a detached part of an eye's retina. Lasers can also remove unhealthy tissue in some precancerous conditions. Lasers have a great many applications and advantages in modern surgery. One advantage is that a laser is totally aseptic, free of bacteria. The heat from the laser also cauterizes, or seals, small blood vessels immediately. This minimizes blood loss and the shock that can result. Often lasers are used in combination with an endoscope.

6. Nearly all parts of the body can be treated surgically. Until quite recently, general surgeons performed most operations. Today, general surgeons are still likely to deal with operations on the appendix, gall bladder, stomach, and intestines. But for operations involving the brain, heart, and bones, surgery specialists are in charge.

7. Brain tumors and accidental injuries to the brain and spine often require specialized surgery, called neurosurgery. Congenital defects, that is, those a person is born with, also require neurosurgery. For example, hydrocephalus, a condition in which a person has excess fluid around the brain, is one defect neurosurgery can treat. Neurosurgeons are likely to use lasers as well as cryosurgery in brain operations.

8. An orthopedic surgeon deals with disorders of the bones and joints. Common operations include the correction of congenital defects, such as clubfoot or a curving spine, called scoliosis. Orthopedic surgeons also replace damaged or diseased joints, such as hips and knees, with artificial inserts. Other orthopedic operations can treat fractured bones, slipped disks in the backbone, or bone cancer.

9. Technological advances have also benefited the cardiac, or heart, surgeon. One notable development is the heart-lung machine, which takes over the functions of a patient's heart and lungs during surgery. Essentially, this machine allows the surgeon to stop a patient's heart to work on it. The heart-lung machine also monitors the patient's progress and cools the patient's blood to slow the body's chemical processes during an operation. Although heart transplant operations are still relatively rare, cardiac surgeons can replace damaged heart valves and blood vessels with artificial parts.

10. Other surgical specialties focus on specific body organs or systems. Ophthalmic surgeons work on the eyes. Microsurgery and lasers benefit these specialists in such operations as the removal of cataracts (nontransparent patches in the lens) or the replacement of diseased corneas, which cover the eye. Plastic surgeons specialize in the reconstruction of tissue after damage caused by burns or injuries. ENT (ear, nose, and throat) specialists remove tonsils, treat inner-ear problems, and remove tumors from the mouth and throat areas.

Heart-Lung Machine

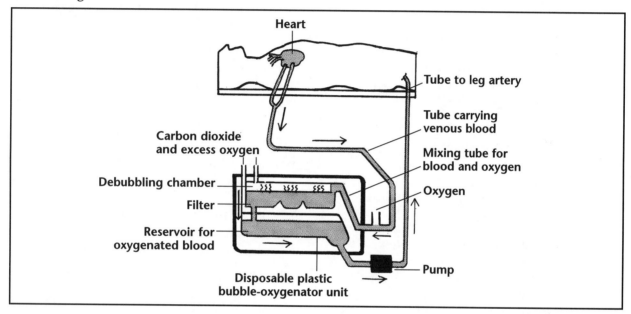

51. The main idea of paragraph 5 is stated in the
   a. first sentence.
   b. second sentence.
   c. third sentence.
   d. last sentence.

52. What is the unstated main idea of paragraph 6?
   a. Nearly all parts of the body can be treated surgically.
   b. General surgeons performed most operations until quite recently.
   c. Operations have not been performed until recently.
   d. General surgeons still perform many operations, but specialists are playing a larger role today.

53. What is the unstated main idea of paragraph 7?
   a. Neurosurgeons are concerned with operations on the brain and spine.
   b. Neurosurgery requires extraordinary skill.
   c. Neurosurgeons perform operations only on the nerves.
   d. Lasers have made the neurosurgeon's job easier.

54. Which detail below would best support the main idea of paragraph 10?
   a. Urological surgeons deal with disorders of the body's urinary, or liquid-waste, tract.
   b. Some patients require plastic surgery for mental-health reasons.
   c. After serious operations, most patients require intensive care.
   d. The removal of cataracts requires careful surgery.

55. Laser surgery reduces blood loss because
    a. it can make such fine cuts.
    b. it cauterizes, or seals, blood vessels.
    c. it is used in combination with an endoscope.
    d. it can remove unhealthy tissues.

56. The heart-lung machine is of benefit to a cardiac surgeon because it
    a. allows the surgeon to work on a stopped heart.
    b. replaces damaged heart valves and blood vessels.
    c. reduces blood loss and shock.
    d. magnifies the heart so a surgeon can see it better.

57. Like the reattachment of a severed limb, the operation for cataracts
    a. is a new surgical procedure.
    b. requires an endoscope.
    c. includes the use of cryosurgery.
    d. is aided by microsurgery.

58. Both cryosurgery and microsurgery
    a. are used to treat skin disorders.
    b. are two new advances in the field of medicine.
    c. have been used for hundreds of years.
    d. are still in the experimental stage.

59. We can infer that heart surgery would be more difficult without the heart-lung machine because
    a. the patient's heart would be beating.
    b. the heart's valves would be damaged.
    c. the patient would go into shock from loss of blood.
    d. the doctor would not be able to see what he or she was doing.

60. We can infer that microsurgery on nerves when reattaching a limb is necessary
    a. in order for the patient to have movement and feeling in the limb.
    b. to avoid unnecessary and invasive surgery.
    c. to correct any congenital defects.
    d. in order for the patient to be more comfortable.

61. We can infer that surgical specialties are becoming more common because
    a. people are living longer and need more medical care in their last years.
    b. many new, high-tech surgical techniques are now available.
    c. modern medicine has eliminated the need for most routine, general operations.
    d. people are more willing to pay for a specialist to treat them.

62. The condition called cataracts would normally be treated by
    a. a plastic surgeon.
    b. an orthopedic surgeon.
    c. a cardiac surgeon.
    d. an ophthalmic surgeon.

63. An orthopedic surgeon would be needed to
    a. replace the valves of the heart.
    b. reattach the retina of the eye.
    c. insert an artificial hip.
    d. remove tonsils.

64. The removal of an appendix would be considered
    a. cryosurgery.
    b. general surgery.
    c. transplant surgery.
    d. microsurgery.

65. What is the meaning of *congenital* in paragraph 7?
    a. present from birth
    b. unexpected
    c. difficult to describe
    d. unpleasant

66. What is the meaning of *invasive,* as used in paragraph 2?
    a. involving high-tech equipment
    b. unlikely to be successful
    c. involving entry into the body
    d. with the intent of taking over

67. What is the meaning of *systems* in paragraph 10?
    a. orderly ways of doing things
    b. groups of parts working together to form a whole
    c. the body as a whole
    d. plans

68. What is the meaning of *applications* in paragraph 5?
    a. written requests for employment or admission
    b. advancements
    c. close efforts or attention
    d. specific uses

Use the diagram on page 119 to answer questions 69 through 71.

69. Oxygenated blood returns to the patient's
    a. heart.
    b. lungs.
    c. leg artery.
    d. head.

70. After leaving the heart, what happens first to a patient's blood?
    a. It enters the debubbling chamber.
    b. It enters the tube carrying venous blood.
    c. It is filtered.
    d. It releases excess oxygen.

71. According to the diagram, a patient's blood is pumped
    a. from his or her heart directly to the debubbling chamber.
    b. from his or her heart, through the heart-lung machine, and back to his or her heart.
    c. back to his or her leg artery.
    d. into a reservoir for oxygenated blood.

Questions 72 through 75 are word problems. Use a separate sheet of paper for your calculations.

72. A capillary, or tiny blood vessel, has a diameter of 1.5 microns. A micron is about 0.0000039 of an inch long. How long would the diameter of the capillary appear if it were magnified 1 million times?
    a. 5.8 inches
    b. 6.4 inches
    c. 7.2 inches
    d. 7.9 inches

73. Each microliter (0.00003 ounce) of blood contains about 5 million red blood cells. How many red cells are found in 3 ounces of blood?
    a. 1 billion
    b. 5 billion
    c. 50 billion
    d. 500 billion

74. In a recent year, the population of the United States was 220 million. Each day during that year, 1,800 people died from heart attacks. What percentage of the population died from heart attacks that year?
    a. 0.3%
    b. 0.03%
    c. 0.003%
    d. 0.0003%

75. The human brain uses about 20% of the body's oxygen. If 85% of that oxygen is used by the part of the brain called the *cerebrum,* what percentage of the body's oxygen is used by the cerebrum?
    a. 4.75%
    b. 5.25%
    c. 10%
    d. 17%

A. Use the following dictionary entry to answer questions 76 through 80.

> **ad vance** (ad vans´), **v. ad vanced´, ad vanc´ ing.**
> **n. 1.** a moving forward; progress **2.** a rise in value or cost **3.** a payment made before it is due, as of wages **4. advances,** *pl.,* attempts to gain favor or become friendly **v. 1.** to go or bring forward; move ahead **2.** to suggest; offer **3.** to help to grow or develop; promote **4.** to cause to happen earlier **5.** to make or become higher; increase **6.** to lend **7.** to get a higher or better position **adj. 1.** in front [*advance* troops] **2.** ahead of time [*advance* information] **— in advance 1.** in front **2.** before due; ahead of time

76. How many adjective meanings of the entry word are given?
   a. one   **c.** four
   b. two   **d.** seven

77. Which noun definition of *advance* is used in the following sentence? *The new advance in data storage made desktop computers much more powerful.*
   a. definition 1
   b. definition 2
   c. definition 3
   d. definition 4

78. How many idioms, or expressions, containing *advance* are included in the entry?
   a. none   **c.** two
   b. one   **d.** three

79. What part of speech is *advance*, as used in the following sentence? *Some teachers advance into school administration.*
   a. verb   **c.** adjective
   b. noun   **d.** adverb

80. Which verb definition of *advance* is used in the following sentence? *We can advance the date of our trip from August to July.*
   a. definition 2
   b. definition 4
   c. definition 5
   d. definition 7

B. Use the following part of a book index to answer questions 81 through 85.

> Toad, 26, 33, 79–80, 125; *see also Frog*
> Tracks, animal, 132, 212–213; *see also Signs*
> Transpiration, 96, 148
> Tree, anatomy of, 94
>   defined, 13
>   flowering, 14–15
>   predominant, 18
>   and soil, 36–37, 147, 159 *chart*
>   world's tallest, 157
> Trillium, 77, 78
> Tundra, 184–186, 211

81. How many pages in the book have information about transpiration?
   a. none
   b. two
   c. three
   d. four

82. For more information about animal tracks, you would look under
   a. animals.
   b. tundra.
   c. footprints.
   d. signs.

83. On which page(s) would you look for a chart about trees and soils?
   a. 36–37
   b. 147
   c. 157
   d. 159

84. In how many different sections does the book discuss tundra?
   a. two
   b. three
   c. four
   d. none

85. On which page(s) would information about flowering trees be found?
   a. 13
   b. 14–15
   c. 18
   d. 77, 78

C. **Think about word parts to answer questions 86 through 100.**

86. The prefix in the word *misperception* means
    a. changed.
    b. earlier.
    c. repeated.
    d. wrong.

87. The prefix in *declassify* means
    a. not.
    b. before.
    c. over again.
    d. undo.

88. A *biennial* election takes place
    a. every two years.
    b. every three years.
    c. every four years.
    d. every five years.

89. Which suffix will change the meaning of *disinfect* to "a thing that disinfects"?
    a. -ment
    b. -ness
    c. -ation
    d. -ant

90. Which suffix will change the meaning of *polite* to "the quality of being polite"?
    a. -ous
    b. -ance
    c. -ness
    d. -tion

91. Which word properly completes the following sentence? *Jay still writes quite _____.*
    a. sloppyily
    b. sloppyly
    c. sloppily
    d. slopply

92. The words *rejection* and *interjection* both come from a root meaning
    a. to take.
    b. to write.
    c. to come.
    d. to throw.

93. The words *transcription* and *inscribe* both come from a root meaning
    a. to hold.
    b. to write.
    c. to come.
    d. to feel.

94. Choose the correct way to divide the word *transmission* into syllables.
    a. tran smiss ion
    b. trans miss ion
    c. trans mis sion
    d. tr ans mi ssion

95. Choose the correct way to divide the word *acceptance* into syllables.
    a. ac cep tance
    b. acc ept ance
    c. ac cept ance
    d. accept ance

96. Which word has its accent on the second syllable?
    a. rotate
    b. nucleus
    c. imitate
    d. attend

97. Which syllable of *electrifying* has the most stress?
    a. second
    b. third
    c. fourth
    d. fifth

98. The schwa sound in *atmosphere* can be heard in the
    a. first syllable.
    b. second syllable.
    c. third syllable.
    d. first and second syllables.

99. An antonym of *valiant* is
    a. cowardly.
    b. fearlessly.
    c. exceptional.
    d. adventurous.

100. A synonym of *spontaneous* is
    a. clean.
    b. powerless.
    c. unplanned.
    d. forced.

Read the following selection. Then choose the best answer for each question.
Mark your answers on the answer sheet.

The Judge's Prophecy

1. In all of feudal Japan, no judge was so perceptive and so humane as the great Ooka. In a world dark with lies, theft, and injustice, Judge Ooka was a bright flame. To be in his court was to come face to face with wisdom, and people of both high and low estate would discuss his rulings eagerly. None so much so as the case of the baby with two mothers, in which Judge Ooka revealed another extraordinary facet of his character.

2. The baby was a boy, less than a year old, and two women, we'll call them X and Y, claimed to be his mother. Official investigations proved fruitless, for both women had recently migrated from the distant countryside to Yedo, as Old Tokyo was then called, and nothing could be learned of their backgrounds or families. In short, there were no witnesses and no depositions; so the noble judge would have little to guide him in the disposition of the case.

3. The judge's first attempts at meting out justice brought little result. "Place the infant on the floor," he commanded, "for surely it will crawl to its mother." Alas, the baby did no such thing, preferring to toddle up to the judge himself, provoking some merriment in the court. His ears turning pink, Judge Ooka then commanded each woman to take hold of one of the baby's arms and pull as hard as possible. "The real mother will be given the strength to win the struggle!" he explained. What he really expected, of course, was the real mother to stop pulling, lest she hurt her baby. X and Y, however, quickly saw through the judge's stratagem and told the court they wanted justice, not a trick.

4. The difficulty of dispensing justice made Judge Ooka sigh. Then, calling to the court attendant, he commanded, "Go and purchase a bowl of goldfish, a handful of bamboo sticks, three pieces of wood, and a magnifying glass. Bring them here to me along with the best book on fortune-telling you can find!" What odd requests! Loud laughter echoed through the court but was quickly stifled by Judge Ooka's fierce frown.

5. In time, the attendant returned with the requested articles, and Judge Ooka spread them out on the table in front of him. "It should be obvious to all that I cannot solve this case by normal jurisprudence," he admitted, a note of shame creeping into his voice. "Thus, I must resort to the questionable device of fortune-telling. Please excuse me as I use these objects to peer briefly into the future and so determine what my decision will be."

6. To say the spectators were astonished would be an understatement. Could it be that Judge Ooka, a name synonymous with logic and reason, might rely on superstition? True enough, fortune-telling was more common then than now, and held much weight among the common folk, but in the courtroom? Never!

7. Nevertheless, there was the judge, gravely examining each object from all angles and making the occasional consultation of the fortune-teller's manual. Judge Ooka held the pieces of wood next to his ears, listening for their echoes. He counted the bubbles in the goldfish bowl and divided by seven. He spoke with the bamboo sticks to learn their secrets, and he even studied the women's palms. An hour or more crept by, as Judge Ooka sought the wisdom of the unusual oracles, and the courtroom was relieved when at last the judge looked up and spoke. "The truth has been revealed to me. I see it clearly now. I have used all the best methods of prophecy, and they all concur. Therefore, what I see must be true." How anxiously the courtroom waited to hear what the judge had learned.

8. Judge Ooka continued, "In chilling detail, I have seen how the true mother and her son will be in 20 years. I have witnessed the tragic accident that befalls him and how he becomes an invalid. I have even seen the mother, haggard and worn, toiling in the rice fields to support her son."

9. Both women gasped in horror. This surely was not the future they had envisioned. Watching them carefully, the judge continued,

"But that is not all that I have seen. For this mother will also have—"

10. "Stop!" screamed Y. "This prophecy does not speak to me! Children are supposed to take care of their aged parents. It has always been so and so should always be!"

11. "Always?" wondered the judge, allowing himself a tiny smile. Then turning to X, he asked, "And how do you feel about the prophecy?"

12. "It makes no difference, Honorable Honor," the woman sighed. "I will work for my child while there is breath in my body, and then I will die, happy, knowing that I have served him well."

13. "Then this is your own true son," declared the judge. "The other mother wants him only to have someone to care for her in old age. Take the child with the court's good wishes."

14. So the happy mother took the child in her arms, and the impostor was led away. "But I have not finished the prophecy," Judge Ooka remarked casually, as the onlookers began to drift away. "You see, this child recovers from the injury he received in the accident. Indeed, he becomes rich and even famous. Yes, his mother, his wife, and his 13 healthy children all live happily and well together for many, many years. So it was revealed."

15. At first, of course, those in the courtroom assumed that there was no prophecy. The activities in the courtroom that day were like a game; the entire story had been fabricated by the judge in the interest of justice. How strange then were the events that occurred as the years passed. For the boy did have an accident, but recovered and soon grew rich. Yes, he married, too, and had more than a dozen children, and they all lived happily and well. Yes, the events surprised everyone, none more so than Judge Ooka. Doubtlessly, this explains the judge's curious remark when he finally stepped down from the bench at the age of 90. On that occasion many wondered what Judge Ooka meant when he was heard to say, "If I had not been called to the law, I might have become an excellent fortune-teller."

1. Choose the words that best describe Judge Ooka.
   a. devious and malicious
   b. stiff and authoritarian
   c. outgoing and good-natured
   d. intelligent and shrewd

2. How would you describe the woman known as Y?
   a. genuine
   b. confused
   c. dishonest
   d. ambiguous

3. To the spectators, Judge Ooka's approach to this case was surprising because he was usually quite
   a. logical.
   b. compassionate.
   c. dramatic.
   d. indecisive.

4. The basic conflict in the story centers on
   a. attitudes toward fortune-telling.
   b. the responsibilities of children toward their parents.
   c. the identity of the rightful mother.
   d. Judge Ooka's ability to dispense justice.

5. The case presents Judge Ooka with a conflict because
   a. he is only pretending to know how to tell fortunes.
   b. he doesn't want people to know that he decides cases by fortune-telling.
   c. he knows all along that X is the mother, although he has no proof.
   d. there is no evidence or witnesses.

6. Judge Ooka's prophecy causes conflict for Y because
   a. she loves the child so much and does not want to see him hurt.
   b. she doesn't believe fortune-tellers.
   c. she had wanted the child to take care of her in her old age.
   d. she is the child's real mother.

7. The first important event in the story occurs when
   a. the judge orders his attendant to bring him fortune-telling supplies.
   b. the judge orders the baby to be placed on the floor.
   c. the people in the court eagerly await the judge's prediction.
   d. Judge Ooka reveals that he has another extraordinary talent.

8. The climax of the story comes when
   a. Judge Ooka attempts to tell the future, using a fortune-telling book.
   b. Judge Ooka shares the last part of his prediction.
   c. the mothers identify themselves by their reactions.
   d. both mothers gasped in horror.

9. The conclusion of the story is most important because we learn
   a. the false mother will be punished.
   b. that the true mother will actually have a happy life.
   c. that Judge Ooka might become a fortune-teller after all.
   d. that the boy will be involved in an accident.

10. This story is set in Japan
    a. hundreds of years ago.
    b. early in this century.
    c. shortly after World War II.
    d. some time in the future.

11. This setting in Yedo is important because
    a. the courts there were the most advanced in the land.
    b. X and Y were strangers in the city.
    c. few people in Yedo took fortune-telling seriously.
    d. it tells what feudal Japan was like.

12. What is one theme of this story?
    a. Entertainment and creativity can serve the needs of justice.
    b. Judges shouldn't resort to tricks.
    c. The ways of the fortune-teller are difficult to understand.
    d. Fate overcomes justice.

13. Which might be the best alternate title for this story?
    a. "The Fortune-Teller"
    b. "The Selfish Mother"
    c. "The Courts of Old Japan"
    d. "Judge Ooka's Wisdom"

14. Which value does the story seem to encourage among people?
    a. caring for one's children
    b. respect for one's parents
    c. concern for the poor
    d. admiration of the legal system

15. We can infer that when Judge Ooka ordered the articles for fortune-telling,
    a. he knew the articles would help him rule justly.
    b. he routinely used fortune-telling as a way to solve difficult cases.
    c. he already knew which woman was the real mother of the baby.
    d. he only intended to trick the women into thinking he could see the future.

16. From paragraphs 10 and 13, we can infer that
    a. older Japanese were used to working hard in their old age.
    b. older Japanese once expected their adult children to support them.
    c. the woman named Y would have been an excellent mother.
    d. the woman named Y did not respect Judge Ooka.

17. Which word describes the tone of the story?
    a. formal
    b. playful
    c. satirical
    d. comic

18. In general, the mood of the story is
    a. matter of fact.
    b. grim.
    c. upbeat.
    d. lighthearted.

19. What is the unstated main idea of paragraph 6?
    a. Judge Ooka didn't like to admit to relying on fortune-telling.
    b. Fortune-telling was shunned in feudal Japan.
    c. The wealthy and educated look down on the superstitions of the common people.
    d. For a judge to believe in superstition was quite shocking.

20. What is the unstated main idea of paragraph 15?
    a. Ooka wasn't happy as a judge.
    b. Ironically, Judge Ooka's "prophecy" actually came true.
    c. Judge Ooka made up the prophecy.
    d. Judge Ooka has given a false reading.

21. What figure of speech in paragraph 1 compares Judge Ooka to a flame?
    a. a simile
    b. a metaphor
    c. personification
    d. exaggeration

22. What figure of speech in paragraph 15 is used to describe the activities in the court?
    a. a simile
    b. a metaphor
    c. personification
    d. exaggeration

23. What is the meaning of the word *prophecy* in paragraph 7?
    a. justice
    b. consultation
    c. fortune-telling
    d. divine ruling

24. What is the meaning of *depositions* used in paragraph 2?
    a. official statements
    b. witnesses in a law case
    c. newcomers to a city
    d. situations

25. What meaning of *reason* is used in paragraph 6?
    a. a statement offered as an explanation or justification
    b. an excuse
    c. the cause for why something happens
    d. thinking in an orderly way

Read the following selection. Then choose the best answer for each question.
Mark your answers on the answer sheet.

The Great Dust Bowl

1. A combination of natural and man-made circumstances brought on the famous "Dust Bowl" drought of the 1930s. More than 25,000 square miles of the midwestern United States became a wasteland of unproductive soil. The natural disaster, along with the economic problems of the Great Depression, forced over 300,000 farmers and their families off their land. One of every four farmsteads in the region was eventually abandoned, and an army of more than half a million homeless people moved westward in a desperate search for survival.

2. The area hardest hit by the disaster—called the Dust Bowl proper—encompassed southeastern Colorado, western Kansas, and the panhandles of Texas and Oklahoma. This area, once called "the Great American desert" was originally considered too dry for agriculture. Nevertheless, generations of farmers and ranchers had weathered the cycles of rainfall and drought that are typical in the region. In addition, since 1914, farmers there had been enjoying an unusually moist period.

3. At about the same time—1914—World War I began, and the high price of wheat to feed soldiers in Europe encouraged farmers to turn pasture land into wheat fields. By plowing under all their available land and planting wheat, the farmers did well during the war years. Later, when the demand for wheat dropped, the farmers returned the plowed land to grazing land for livestock without properly seeding it. Cattle hooves pulverized the unprotected soil, and when strong winds blew in from the northwest, the topsoil was borne eastward.

4. The region's first dust storms blew up in early 1932, and for the next five years or so they were an all-too-common fact of life. Billows of wind-driven dirt, hundreds of feet high, rolled over the fields, piling like snowdrifts against houses and barns. The storms clogged traffic, derailed trains, buried fences, and either ruined fields or smothered crops. Countless cattle were smothered in the "dusters." Although few people actually perished, the constant inhalation of dust did bring on an epidemic of bronchitis, emphysema, and other respiratory illnesses. The problem was serious enough for the Red Cross to open a dozen field hospitals and to distribute thousands of dust masks, similar in appearance to gas masks.

5. Describing a dust storm in a magazine article of the 1930s, Lawrence Svobida wrote, "I've known dust storms to last 12 hours. Dirt clicked like sleet against the window glass. You'd hear almost continuous thunder, and the crackle of lightning—the friction of dust particles throws off a lot of static electricity. Streaks of electricity ran back and forth around metal structures. . . . Static electricity made the ignition systems of cars fail. That could be fatal if you got caught on the road in a storm. . . ."

6. If rain had fallen, loose dirt and dust would have settled, but the region was in the grip of the worst drought on record. Beginning in 1934, little or no rain fell on most of the Dust Bowl for over three years. In the winter and spring of each year, northwest winds blew relentlessly, driving the dust and traces of the wheat crop as far east as New York City and Washington, D.C. Then, in summer, hot winds rolled in from the Southwest, baking the region in record-breaking heat. Temperatures of 110°F for days on end were not uncommon.

7. By that time, the nation had skidded into the Great Depression, brought on by the 1929 stock market crash. As the dust and drought killed their crops, farmers were unable to meet loans they had taken out to expand their farms or buy equipment during the prosperous 1920s. Banks were forced to foreclose on mortgages, forcing farm families off their land. Grain stores, equipment dealerships, and other small businesses closed down, their services unneeded. Eventually, the banks had to close their doors, too.

8. Before long, a great western migration began. Some half a million people, disparagingly called "Okies" (even though most came from Kansas), set out for California, lured by dreams

of jobs and prosperity. Those who made it to California were often turned away at the borders. Others were exploited in low-paid agricultural work. In his powerful novel *The Grapes of Wrath*, John Steinbeck vividly chronicles the woes of this army of nomads.

9.   Meanwhile, back in the Dust Bowl, soil conservation specialists moved in to advise on grazing and planting practices. A new method of plowing at right angles to the prevailing winds helped trap windblown soil. The Civilian Conservation Corps planted thousands of trees to serve as windbreaks. In addition, federal agricultural subsidies and other so-called "New Deal" federal programs enabled farmers to hold onto their land. Thus, the diehards who

Normal Midwest Precipitation in the Central Plains, 1931–1960

January   **July**

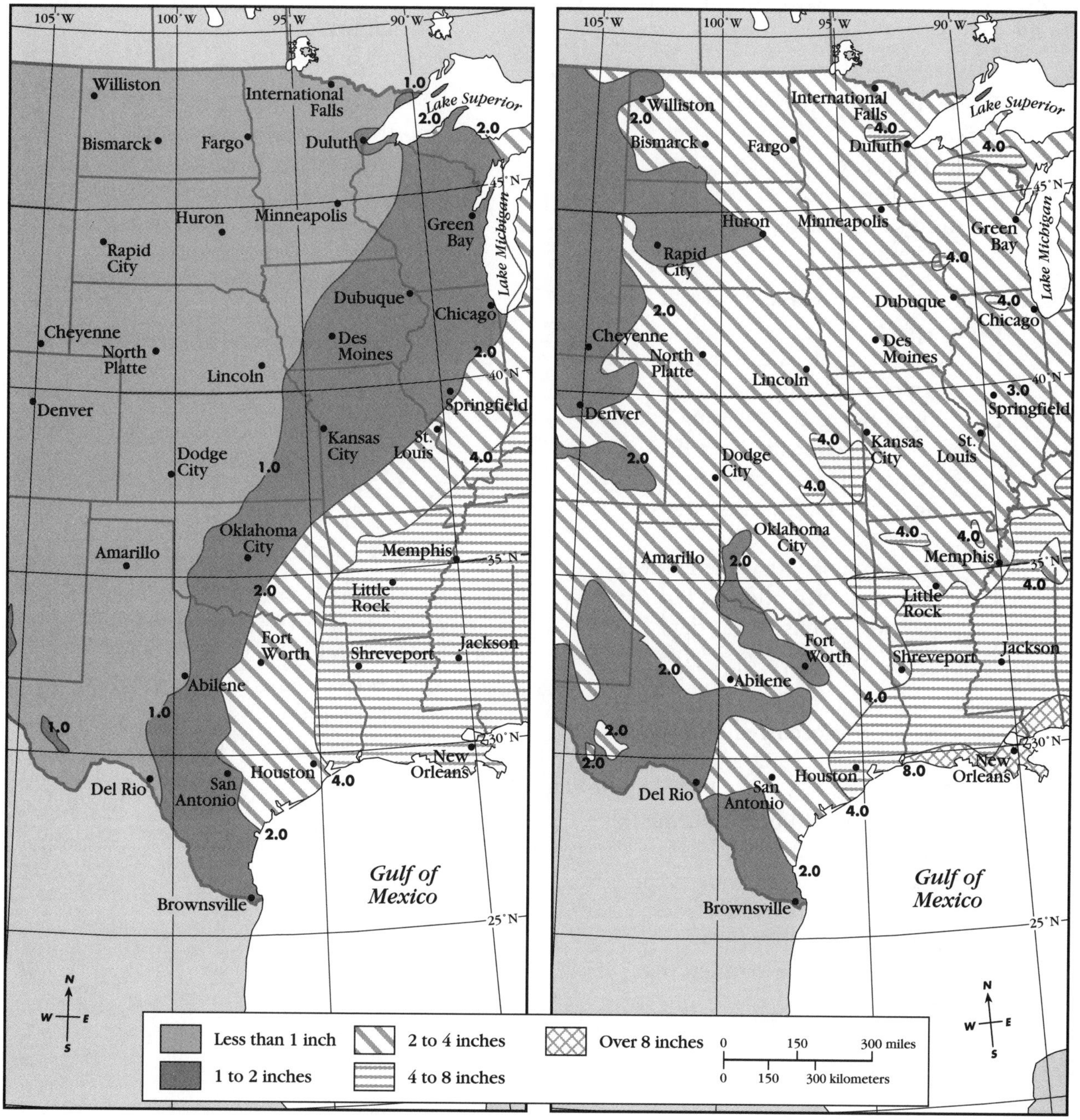

Legend:
- Less than 1 inch
- 1 to 2 inches
- 2 to 4 inches
- 4 to 8 inches
- Over 8 inches

0   150   300 miles
0   150   300 kilometers

stuck out the drought in the Dust Bowl often fared better than those who left.

10. The drought continued through 1936 and into 1937. Gradually though, in county after county, the rains returned. The 1938 harvest was the best in years, and by 1939, heavy rains had begun to fall. The rain, along with reseeding and erosion prevention techniques, revitalized the Central Plains region of the United States, restoring its reputation as the "Breadbasket of the Nation." Even so, it was too late for the Dust Bowl "refugees" who had lost their land and way of life forever.

26. The main idea of paragraph 9 is stated in the
  a. first sentence.
  b. second sentence.
  c. third sentence.
  d. last sentence.

27. What is the unstated main idea of paragraph 3?
  a. Farmers in the Midwest were quite prosperous during World War I.
  b. Poor plowing and planting practices set the stage for the Dust Bowl.
  c. Fluctuations in prices caused farmers to increase and decrease the size of their crops.
  d. The wet climate that the Midwest enjoyed in 1914 allowed farmers to grow prosperous wheat fields.

28. What is the unstated main idea of paragraph 4?
  a. Dust storms occurred in the Dust Bowl between 1932 and 1937.
  b. Dust storms proved to be a deadly hazard in the Midwest during the Depression.
  c. Dust storms caused widespread damage to property, livestock, and human health.
  d. Dust storms were so great that they resembled snowdrifts.

29. The main idea of paragraph 7 is that drought and dust destroyed the agriculture-based economy of the Central Plains. Which detail supports this main idea?
  a. Farmers had to develop new ways of cultivating the land.
  b. To meet the high demand for wheat after 1914, 17 million additional Dust Bowl acres were cultivated.
  c. Most people from the Dust Bowl worked as agricultural laborers in California.
  d. One in four farms in the Dust Bowl was abandoned.

30. Find the main idea of paragraph 10 and choose the detail that best supports it.
  a. Despite problems in the Dust Bowl, no shortages of wheat arose during the Great Depression.
  b. During the drought, government subsidies paid farmers not to grow wheat that wouldn't have grown anyway.
  c. The heavy rains of 1939, along with new farming techniques, led to very high grain production.
  d. After World War I ended, wheat production increased as men were able to return to their fields.

31. Between 1914 and 1932, wheat production in the Central Plains was high because
  a. farmers found ways of planting wheat in the hostile environment.
  b. the area experienced an unusually moist period.
  c. a great western migration had led more agricultural workers to settle there.
  d. the government paid high prices to farmers to grow more grain.

32. Many Dust Bowl farmers lost their land during the 1930s because
    a. they were unable to repay loans made in prosperous years.
    b. small businesses and banks that served farmers closed down after the stock market crash.
    c. the government was unable to provide special services to help the farmers.
    d. the country was in the throes of a world war.

33. A major factor that contributed to the severity of the dust storms was
    a. the practice of plowing at right angles to the wind.
    b. the failure to properly reseed cropland that was turned into pastures for cattle.
    c. the record-breaking heat on the Plains during the summer.
    d. the lack of proper farming equipment.

34. The amount of land planted in wheat in the Dust Bowl at the onset of the Depression was
    a. less than during the World War I years.
    b. more than the World War I years.
    c. about the same as twenty years earlier.
    d. about the same as twenty years later.

35. Compared to the farmers who left, those who stayed in the Dust Bowl
    a. fared a little better economically.
    b. fared a little worse economically.
    c. fared about the same economically.
    d. fared no better and no worse economically.

36. Government efforts to help the Dust Bowl farmers
    a. were greater in the early 1930s.
    b. were greater in the late 1930s.
    c. remained at the same level throughout the 1930s.
    d. stopped during the Great Depression.

37. From the details in the passage, we can infer that the dust storms
    a. occurred regularly between 1914 and 1940 on the Central Plains.
    b. were worse in the northern plains than the southern plains.
    c. were worst during the summer months.
    d. had pretty much ended by 1937.

38. From the details in paragraph 9, we can infer that
    a. expert help did little to lessen the problems of dust storms.
    b. the Civilian Conservation Corps encouraged farm families to return to their farms.
    c. those who stayed in the Dust Bowl profited at the expense of those who left.
    d. the Federal Government helped those who remained in the Dust Bowl.

39. We can infer from paragraph 7 that
    a. banks in the Dust Bowl charged farmers very high interest on loans.
    b. banks in the Dust Bowl region had adequate funds.
    c. agriculture was the mainstay of the economy in the Central Plains.
    d. bank executives uncaringly forced farm families off their land.

40. *More than 25,000 square miles of the midwestern United States became unproductive.* This statement is
    a. a fact.
    b. an opinion.
    c. both a fact and an opinion.
    d. neither a fact nor an opinion.

41. *In his powerful novel* The Grapes of Wrath, *John Steinbeck vividly chronicles the woes of this army of nomads.* This statement is
    a. a fact.
    b. an opinion.
    c. both a fact and an opinion.
    d. neither a fact nor an opinion.

42. What primary source is quoted in this selection?
    a. a novel
    b. a magazine article
    c. a newspaper story
    d. an eyewitness account

43. According to the source, a dust storm could last as long as
    a. 4 hours.
    b. 8 hours.
    c. 12 hours.
    d. 24 hours.

44. From the facts in this primary source, you learned that
    a. Dust Bowl residents often required dust masks.
    b. dust storms generated huge amounts of static electricity.
    c. billows of dust could derail trains and smother cattle.
    d. dust storms were generally not fatal to human life.

45. What is the meaning of *disparagingly* in paragraph 8?
    a. fondly
    b. negatively
    c. falsely
    d. contrastingly

46. What is the meaning of *pulverized* in paragraph 3?
    a. packed down
    b. ground up
    c. wore out
    d. grazed

47. Which meaning of *meet* is intended in paragraph 7?
    a. to unite
    b. to encounter
    c. to fulfill
    d. to gather

Use the maps on page 129 to answer questions 48 through 50.

48. According to the map, how much rain does the western portion of the Central Plains normally get in January?
    a. less than 1 inch
    b. 1 to 2 inches
    c. 2 to 4 inches
    d. 4 to 8 inches

49. A farmer near Oklahoma City could expect to receive about twice as much rain in July as a farmer in
    a. New Orleans.
    b. Kansas City.
    c. Abilene.
    d. Denver.

50. In general, the climate of the Central Plains
    a. is wetter in July than in January.
    b. is wetter in January than in July.
    c. has about the same rainfall in July and January.
    d. typically has 4–8 inches of rainfall in July.

Read the following selection. Then choose the best answer for each question. Mark your answers on the answer sheet.

Water Treatment

1. Before drinking water flows from your faucet, it has probably been screened, pumped, stirred, settled, filtered, refiltered, stored, and finally pumped through miles of pipes to your home. Those processes occur at your local water treatment plant. It's likely to be located near the river, lake, or reservoir that supplies your community with its raw water.

2. One step in the water-purifying process, algae removal, often occurs before water actually enters the plant. Algae are small, plantlike organisms found in water when it is stored in lakes or reservoirs. Although they don't represent a health risk, algae give an unpleasant taste to the water. Algae can be destroyed by dissolving the chemical copper sulfate in the reservoir water. Some small reservoirs have a cover over the water. Preventing sunlight from reaching the water halts the process of photosynthesis by which all green plants grow. Any remaining algae are removed inside the plant in a process called micro-straining.

Steps of the Treatment Process

3. Untreated water enters the plant through huge pipes fitted with screens to turn back fish and floating debris. The water is pumped into large storage containers, where solid matter gradually settles to the bottom. In most plants, the treatment begins with chlorination. Chlorine is a gas that combines easily with many different substances. Since the early 1900s, chlorine has been used to kill harmful bacteria. The taste that many people dislike in chlorinated water is not from the chlorine itself but from matter that has been altered by chlorine. In fact, taste-altering compounds can often be removed by raising the amount of chlorine in the water.

4. Although the steps in water treatment vary according to the set-up of the waterworks, aeration usually occurs soon after chlorination.

Aeration introduces oxygen into the water. It is done by spraying the water through fine nozzles or having it flow down a series of steps. The oxygen in air combines with various foul-smelling materials in the water. Aeration releases carbon dioxide and hydrogen sulfide gases and combines with iron, causing it to form into a rustlike solid that can be removed with filters.

5. The process of aeration is sometimes combined with filtration. The filters are actually large beds of charcoal and sand several feet deep. As the water passes over the filter, carbon in the beds attracts organic chemicals and removes them. The filters, of course, must be washed or replaced regularly.

Chemicals Remove Impurities

6. By the time it has passed through aeration and filtration, the once murky, raw water is quite clear. Water is further purified in a process called coagulation. Chemicals, called coagulants, the most common being aluminum sulfate, or alum, are added to the water to combine with impurities. Alum has an electrical charge that is opposite of the impurities and attracts them much as a magnet attracts steel filings. Eventually, the alum and impurities combine into a white, sticky substance, called flocculence, or floc.

7. For the coagulants to work effectively, they must be mixed well with the water. This is usually done by passing the water through a mixing basin. The basins are often fitted with large plates that force the water from one side of the tank to the other. In some systems, the basins have mechanical paddles or propellers to stir the mixture.

8. One common effect of the chemical treatment of water is the production of acid. Often water has enough natural alkalinity to neutralize the acid. If not, calcium carbonate, or lime, is added. This salt combines with acid

in the water and settles to the bottom of the tanks. Throughout the treatment process, the water's chemical quality is checked. Computers record the water's temperature, oxygen level, chlorine level, and acidity or alkalinity. Chemical adjustments are made as necessary to keep these readings acceptable as purification proceeds.

9. After the coagulation and mixing operation, the water is piped into settling basins where the floc and impurities settle to the bottom. The huge settling tanks hold the water for 90 minutes to six hours or longer.

Chlorine and Fluoride Added

10. By this time, almost all impure matter has been removed from the water. Most plants, however, pass the water through a final rapid-sand filtration. Those filters remove any remaining bacteria, iron, or other matter. The sand, or in some plants, ground-up coal, is quite coarse so the water passes through it quickly. From here, the water is drained off through pipes. As a final step in the purification process, chlorine is usually added until it equals 1 PPM (one part chlorine for every million parts of water). The new chlorine is mainly to guard against any contamination that might occur in the distribution system. The chlorine added at the beginning of the process is largely gone. Sometimes the chlorine is mixed with ammonia. That bacteria-killing combination is weaker than pure chlorine, but longer lasting.

11. In many places, the final stages of treatment include fluoridation. Fluoride is added to the water supply because it is helpful in reducing tooth decay. It produces harder teeth by combining with tooth enamel during the formation of a child's permanent teeth.

12. The entire water treatment process may take only three hours, although longer holding in settling basins is beneficial if time and space are available. The plants usually operate around the clock to ensure that a supply of water is always available. The purified water may take a few minutes or an entire day to travel through the distribution system from the water plant to your house, depending on where you live.

Water Filtration

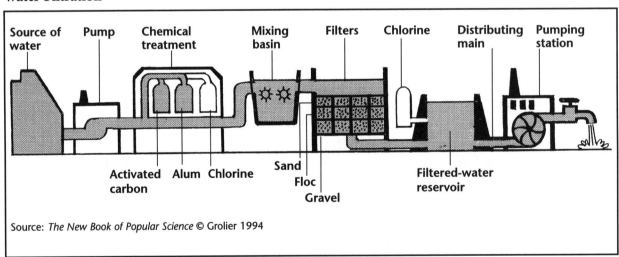

Source: *The New Book of Popular Science* © Grolier 1994

51. The main idea of paragraph 3 is stated in the
    a. first sentence.
    b. second sentence.
    c. third sentence.
    d. last sentence.

52. The main idea of paragraph 6 is stated in the
    a. first sentence.
    b. second sentence.
    c. third sentence.
    d. last sentence.

53. What is the main idea of paragraph 4?
   a. Aeration normally occurs after chlorination.
   b. Aeration oxidizes foul-smelling materials in water.
   c. Carbon dioxide and hydrogen sulfide are released during aeration.
   d. Aeration introduces oxygen into the water.

54. Which detail best supports the main idea of paragraph 6?
   a. Soda ash (sodium carbonate) is sometimes used instead of alum.
   b. Properly used, coagulants remove 99 percent of bacteria.
   c. If the raw water supply is pure enough, coagulation may be unnecessary.
   d. Coagulants must be mixed well in the water to be effective.

55. Calcium carbonate is often added after coagulation because
   a. the water has become acidic.
   b. the floc needs to settle.
   c. the charcoal filters must be cleaned.
   d. the purification process was unsuccessful.

56. Water is aerated in order to
   a. remove the odor of chlorine.
   b. oxidize foul-smelling matter.
   c. clear away remaining algae.
   d. eliminate all impurities.

57. Water is rechlorinated after being held in the settling tanks because
   a. many hard-to-kill bacteria remain in the water.
   b. the water may be contaminated in the distribution system.
   c. charcoal filtration has given the water a bad taste.
   d. algae may have grown back in holding tanks.

58. Both copper sulfate and reservoir covers are used to
   a. improve the effectiveness of the coagulation process.
   b. kill harmful bacteria.
   c. control algae.
   d. stop the water from overflowing.

59. We can infer that if readings showed the water in a treatment plant was too acidic, technicians would add
   a. chlorine.
   b. charcoal.
   c. alum.
   d. calcium carbonate.

60. If a water treatment plant was barely able to supply enough water to a community, we can assume that
   a. technicians would use more chlorine.
   b. the treatment process would have to be repeated.
   c. aeration would not occur.
   d. water would remain in settling basins for shorter periods.

61. We can assume that algae are more common in lakes and reservoirs than rivers because
   a. lakes and reservoirs aren't usually as deep as rivers.
   b. rivers are constantly flowing.
   c. rivers supply more drinking water than lakes and reservoirs.
   d. lakes and reservoirs are more likely to be polluted than rivers.

62. One process that does not serve to purify water is
   a. coagulation.
   b. aeration.
   c. fluoridation.
   d. chlorination.

63. During the water treatment process, the heaviest use of chlorine occurs
   a. at the beginning.
   b. in the middle.
   c. at the end.
   d. after fluoridation.

64. Carbon dioxide and hydrogen sulfide gases are normally released during
    a. chlorination. c. aeration.
    b. coagulation. d. fluoridation.

65. What is the meaning of *murky* in paragraph 6?
    a. treated c. clear
    b. cloudy   d. purified

66. What is the meaning of *organisms* as used in paragraph 2?
    a. instruments c. chemicals
    b. particles   d. living beings

67. What is the meaning of *distribution* in paragraph 12?
    a. delivering c. settling
    b. purifying   d. treating

68. What is the meaning of *altered* as used in paragraph 3?
    a. prevented c. changed
    b. attracted d. removed

Use the diagram on page 134 to answer questions 69 through 71.

69. Most of the mixing of water occurs
    a. before filtration.
    b. before chemical treatment.
    c. during storage in the filtered water reservoir.
    d. after the second chlorination.

70. During chemical treatment, which of the following is *not* added?
    a. alum
    b. activated carbon
    c. floc
    d. chlorine

71. According to the diagram, chlorine is added the second time
    a. during chemical treatment.
    b. in the mixing basin.
    c. after being filtered.
    d. after entering the distributing main.

Questions 72 through 75 are word problems. Use a separate sheet of paper for your calculations.

72. A water treatment facility supplies all the water to a city of 1.7 million people. Each person uses 64 gallons a day. In addition, the amount of water needed by factories, businesses, and other users amounts to 57 gallons per person per day. How much water must the plant be able to purify each day?
    a. 205,700,000 gallons
    b. 208,640,000 gallons
    c. 213,870,000 gallons
    d. 225,930,000 gallons

73. In one city, residents and businesses on average pay 45 cents per 1,000 gallons of water. If the water treatment plant supplies 1.8 billion gallons of water a day, about what are its daily revenues?
    a. under $600,000
    b. about $600,000
    c. over $800,000
    d. over $1,000,000

74. Coliform bacteria are frequently found in water. EPA standards allow 2.2 coliform bacteria per 100 milliliters of water. (100 milliliters is one-tenth of a liter.) If a town's water had 10 times the allowable limit, how many coliform bacteria would be found in a liter of its water?
    a. 220,000
    b. 22,000
    c. 2,200
    d. 220

75. Raw water entering a waterworks was found to contain 74 micrograms of aluminum per liter. Due to treatment with alum, the water leaving the plant contained 179 micrograms of aluminum per liter. What was the percentage increase of aluminum?
    a. about 240%
    b. about 180%
    c. about 140%
    d. about 120%

136

A. Use the following dictionary entries to answer questions 76 through 80.

flor in (flor´ in) *n.* **1.** a former coin of Great Britain, which was equal to 2 shillings **2.** a gold coin issued in Florence, Italy, in 1252 [<Old French <Italian *fiorino* Florentine coin marked with a lily <*fiore* flower <Latin *florem*]

flo til la (floh til´ ə) *n.* a fleet of small ships [<Spanish *flota* small fleet <Icelandic *floti*]

floun der (floun´ dər) *n.* any of several families of flatfish that are much used for food [<Middle French *flondre* <Scandinavian (Norwegian) *flundra*]

fluc tu ate (fluk´ choo ayt) *v.* **1.** rise and fall; change continually **2.** move in waves [<Latin *fluctuatum* moving as a wave <*fluctus* wave <*fluere* to flow]

flue (floo) *n.* tube or pipe used to convey smoke or hot air outside or to another part of a structure [origin unknown]

flum mer y (flum´ ər ee) *n.* **1.** a sweet pudding **2.** an empty compliment; nonsense [<Welsh *llymru*]

flur ry (flur´ ee) *n.* **1.** a sudden gust **2.** a light shower of snow [imitative of its sound]

76. The word *flounder* entered English from
   a. Latin.
   b. Middle French.
   c. Norwegian.
   d. Old French.

77. In Florence, a gold coin with a lily on it was called a
   a. fiorino.
   b. fiore.
   c. florem.
   d. florin.

78. Which word's etymology is unknown?
   a. flurry
   b. flue
   c. flummery
   d. fluctuate

79. The Latin word *fluctus* means
   a. rise and fall.
   b. to flow.
   c. moving as a wave.
   d. a wave.

80. Which word entered Icelandic from Spanish?
   a. florin
   b. flummery
   c. flotilla
   d. flounder

B. Think about word parts to answer questions 81 through 90.

81. The prefix in the word *misrepresentation* means
   a. not.
   b. middle.
   c. against.
   d. badly.

82. The prefix in *demagnetize* means
   a. within.
   b. before.
   c. over again.
   d. undo.

83. A *biweekly* newsletter is published
   a. twice a day.
   b. every two weeks.
   c. every three weeks.
   d. once a month.

84. Which suffix will change the meaning of *coagulate* to "a thing that coagulates"?
   a. *-ness*
   b. *-ation*
   c. *-ant*
   d. *-ment*

85. Which suffix will change the meaning of *prepared* to "the state of being prepared"?
   a. *-ly*
   b. *-ance*
   c. *-ous*
   d. *-ness*

86. Which word completes the following sentence? *I did the math too* ____
   a. hastyly.
   b. hastily.
   c. hastyily.
   d. hastly.

87. The words *projection* and *dejection* both come from a root meaning
    a. to carry.   c. to throw.
    b. to write.   d. to take.

88. The words *description* and *prescribe* both come from a root meaning
    a. to hold.   c. to come.
    b. to tell.   d. to write.

89. Choose the root in the word *dehydrated*.
    a. hydr   c. rated
    b. dehydr   d. dehyd

90. Choose the root in the word *infidelity*.
    a. infid   c. delity
    b. fid   d. infidel

C. **Think about word meanings to answer questions 91 through 100.**

91. Choose the words that best complete the following analogy. *Apparel is to person as*
    a. plumage is to bird.
    b. stage is to theater.
    c. water is to fish.
    d. leaf is to tree.

92. Choose the words that best complete the following analogy. *Height is to mountain as*
    a. shade is to tree.
    b. speed is to highway.
    c. depth is to trench.
    d. volume is to amount.

93. Choose the words that best complete the following analogy. *Famine is to starvation as*
    a. success is to achievement.
    b. war is to treaty.
    c. deluge is to flood.
    d. writing is to communication.

94. Choose the words that best complete the following analogy. *Physician is to medicine as*
    a. dentist is to teeth.
    b. judge is to courthouse.
    c. student is to grade.
    d. attorney is to law.

95. Choose the words that best complete the following analogy. *Water is to liquid as*
    a. rock is to hard.
    b. oxygen is to gas.
    c. metal is to shiny.
    d. glass is to opaque.

96. Choose the words that best complete the following analogy. *Ordinary is to commonplace as*
    a. forlorn is to upbeat.
    b. quiet is to jocular.
    c. exotic is to mysterious.
    d. decisive is to uncertain.

97. Which meaning of *discount* is used in the following sentence? *Don't discount what he has to say until he says it.*
    a. to sell for less
    b. to doubt or disregard
    c. to purchase or sell after deducting interest
    d. to make an allowance

98. Which meaning of *lobby* is used in the following sentence? *He met his friend in the lobby.*
    a. the waiting room at a building's entrance
    b. to influence a government to do favors for a special group
    c. a group that tries to influence legislatures
    d. to put pressure on a group or individual

99. Which meaning of *attends* is used in the following sentence? *Success often attends hard work.*
    a. cares for or serves
    b. gives attention to
    c. is a result of
    d. escorts

100. Which meaning of *arrested* is used in the following sentence? *The unusual bird and its strange song arrested us.*
    a. held back
    b. stopped the growth or development of
    c. seized by legal authority
    d. attracted the attention of

138

Name _____

Placement Test Student Answer Sheet

	a	b	c	d		a	b	c	d		a	b	c	d		a	b	c	d
1	○	○	○	○	17	○	○	○	○	33	○	○	○	○	49	○	○	○	○
2	○	○	○	○	18	○	○	○	○	34	○	○	○	○	50	○	○	○	○
3	○	○	○	○	19	○	○	○	○	35	○	○	○	○	51	○	○	○	○
4	○	○	○	○	20	○	○	○	○	36	○	○	○	○	52	○	○	○	○
5	○	○	○	○	21	○	○	○	○	37	○	○	○	○	53	○	○	○	○
6	○	○	○	○	22	○	○	○	○	38	○	○	○	○	54	○	○	○	○
7	○	○	○	○	23	○	○	○	○	39	○	○	○	○	55	○	○	○	○
8	○	○	○	○	24	○	○	○	○	40	○	○	○	○	56	○	○	○	○

_____   _____   _____   _____

	a	b	c	d		a	b	c	d		a	b	c	d
9	○	○	○	○	25	○	○	○	○	41	○	○	○	○
10	○	○	○	○	26	○	○	○	○	42	○	○	○	○
11	○	○	○	○	27	○	○	○	○	43	○	○	○	○
12	○	○	○	○	28	○	○	○	○	44	○	○	○	○
13	○	○	○	○	29	○	○	○	○	45	○	○	○	○
14	○	○	○	○	30	○	○	○	○	46	○	○	○	○
15	○	○	○	○	31	○	○	○	○	47	○	○	○	○
16	○	○	○	○	32	○	○	○	○	48	○	○	○	○

Placement Test

Teacher Answer Key

Level A

	a	b	c	d
1			●	
2				●
3			●	
4	●			
5	●			
6	●			
7		●		
8				●

Level B

	a	b	c	d
9	●			
10			●	
11		●		
12		●		
13				●
14		●		
15		●		
16				●

Level C

	a	b	c	d
17				●
18		●		
19			●	
20	●			
21				●
22		●		
23	●			
24			●	

Level D

	a	b	c	d
25	●			
26			●	
27	●			
28		●		
29			●	
30			●	
31	●			
32				●

Level E

	a	b	c	d
33	●			
34	●			
35		●		
36				●
37			●	
38	●			
39		●		
40		●		

Level F

	a	b	c	d
41	●			
42		●		
43			●	
44				●
45				●
46	●			
47	●			
48			●	

Level G

	a	b	c	d
49	●			
50		●		
51		●		
52			●	
53	●			
54	●			
55	●			
56	●			

Name _____

Diagnostic Test Student Answer Sheet

	Test 1		Test 2		Test 3		Test 4

Test 1 — a b c d

1 ○ ○ ○ ○
2 ○ ○ ○ ○
3 ○ ○ ○ ○
4 ○ ○ ○ ○
5 ○ ○ ○ ○
6 ○ ○ ○ ○
7 ○ ○ ○ ○
8 ○ ○ ○ ○
9 ○ ○ ○ ○
10 ○ ○ ○ ○
11 ○ ○ ○ ○
12 ○ ○ ○ ○
13 ○ ○ ○ ○
14 ○ ○ ○ ○
15 ○ ○ ○ ○
16 ○ ○ ○ ○
17 ○ ○ ○ ○
18 ○ ○ ○ ○
19 ○ ○ ○ ○
20 ○ ○ ○ ○
21 ○ ○ ○ ○
22 ○ ○ ○ ○
23 ○ ○ ○ ○
24 ○ ○ ○ ○
25 ○ ○ ○ ○

Test 2 — a b c d

26 ○ ○ ○ ○
27 ○ ○ ○ ○
28 ○ ○ ○ ○
29 ○ ○ ○ ○
30 ○ ○ ○ ○
31 ○ ○ ○ ○
32 ○ ○ ○ ○
33 ○ ○ ○ ○
34 ○ ○ ○ ○
35 ○ ○ ○ ○
36 ○ ○ ○ ○
37 ○ ○ ○ ○
38 ○ ○ ○ ○
39 ○ ○ ○ ○
40 ○ ○ ○ ○
41 ○ ○ ○ ○
42 ○ ○ ○ ○
43 ○ ○ ○ ○
44 ○ ○ ○ ○
45 ○ ○ ○ ○
46 ○ ○ ○ ○
47 ○ ○ ○ ○
48 ○ ○ ○ ○
49 ○ ○ ○ ○
50 ○ ○ ○ ○

Test 3 — a b c d

51 ○ ○ ○ ○
52 ○ ○ ○ ○
53 ○ ○ ○ ○
54 ○ ○ ○ ○
55 ○ ○ ○ ○
56 ○ ○ ○ ○
57 ○ ○ ○ ○
58 ○ ○ ○ ○
59 ○ ○ ○ ○
60 ○ ○ ○ ○
61 ○ ○ ○ ○
62 ○ ○ ○ ○
63 ○ ○ ○ ○
64 ○ ○ ○ ○
65 ○ ○ ○ ○
66 ○ ○ ○ ○
67 ○ ○ ○ ○
68 ○ ○ ○ ○
69 ○ ○ ○ ○
70 ○ ○ ○ ○
71 ○ ○ ○ ○
72 ○ ○ ○ ○
73 ○ ○ ○ ○
74 ○ ○ ○ ○
75 ○ ○ ○ ○

Test 4 — a b c d

76 ○ ○ ○ ○
77 ○ ○ ○ ○
78 ○ ○ ○ ○
79 ○ ○ ○ ○
80 ○ ○ ○ ○
81 ○ ○ ○ ○
82 ○ ○ ○ ○
83 ○ ○ ○ ○
84 ○ ○ ○ ○
85 ○ ○ ○ ○
86 ○ ○ ○ ○
87 ○ ○ ○ ○
88 ○ ○ ○ ○
89 ○ ○ ○ ○
90 ○ ○ ○ ○
91 ○ ○ ○ ○
92 ○ ○ ○ ○
93 ○ ○ ○ ○
94 ○ ○ ○ ○
95 ○ ○ ○ ○
96 ○ ○ ○ ○
97 ○ ○ ○ ○
98 ○ ○ ○ ○
99 ○ ○ ○ ○
100 ○ ○ ○ ○

	Test 1	Test 2	Test 3	Test 4		
Number Possible	25	25	25	25	Total	100
Number Incorrect	_____	_____	_____	_____	Total	_____
Score	_____	_____	_____	_____	Total	_____

Administering Starting Out Diagnostic Tests

The Diagnostic Tests for Starting Out are designed to measure students' level of achievement in each of the important comprehension and study skills that receive emphasis in *all* levels of *Be A Better Reader*. The tests may be used as pretests and/or posttests, depending on students' needs and your particular classroom management style. Combined with an overview of students performance on each lesson, the tests should enable you to refine your assessment of students' performance and determine students' readiness to advance to the next level.

The four tests in Starting Out can be administered separately or at one time, depending on time available. Because directions are provided for each test, students should be able to take the tests independently. However, enough time should be allowed for each student to complete the tests.

The skill for each test item is identified in the Answer Key below. Following the skill is the number of the lesson or the lessons in Starting Out where that skill is treated as a Skill Focus. To simplify the scoring process, you can use the Answer Key to make a scoring mask, which when placed over the answer sheet reveals only those items that are correct. The total score is equal to the number of correct items. Use the information on the Scoring Rubric located on page 11 to place students.

Answer Key and Skills Correlation

Starting Out

Test 1

1. b   Identifying the main idea (40)
2. b   Understanding character (1)
3. a   Understanding character (1)
4. c   Understanding setting (20)
5. d   Understanding setting (20)
6. d   Understanding plot (10)
7. a   Understanding plot (10)
8. a   Understanding conflict and resolution (39)
9. c   Understanding conflict and resolution (39)
10. a   Inferring theme (30)
11. c   Inferring theme (30)
12. d   Using context clues (all reading selection lessons)

Test 2

13. a   Identifying the main idea (2)
14. a   Identifying the main idea (2)
15. b   Identifying steps in a process (11)
16. b   Identifying cause and effect (22, 31)
17. d   Identifying cause and effect (22, 31)
18. b   Drawing conclusions (3)
19. d   Identifying fact and opinion (21)
20. c   Identifying fact and opinion (21)
21. a   Drawing conclusions (3)
22. c   Using context clues (all reading selection lessons)
23. b   Reading maps (8)
24. d   Reading maps (8)

Test 3

25. c Identifying the main idea (2)
26. d Identifying the main idea (2)
27. d Identifying cause and effect (22, 31)
28. c Identifying cause and effect (22, 31)
29. b Drawing conclusions (3)
30. a Identifying fact and opinion (21)
31. c Using context clues (all reading selection lessons)
32. a Reading diagrams (37)
33. d Reading diagrams (37)
34. d Reading diagrams (37)
35. b Solving word problems (4, 33)
36. d Solving word problems (4, 33)

Test 4

37. c Using a dictionary entry (46)
38. b Using a dictionary entry (46)
39. c Using a dictionary entry (46)
40. d Using parts of a book (36)
41. b Using parts of a book (36)
42. c Recognizing prefixes and suffixes (21, 22, 27)
43. b Recognizing prefixes and suffixes (21, 22, 27)
44. a Recognizing syllables (39, 40, 41, 45)
45. b Recognizing vowel digraphs (39, 40, 43)
46. c Recognizing hard and soft c and g (30, 31, 34)
47. a Recognizing r-controlled vowel sounds (20, 24)
48. c Recognizing possessive nouns (20, 26)
49. c Recognizing possessive nouns (20, 26)
50. d Recognizing diphthongs (41, 44)

Administering Level A Diagnostic Tests

The Diagnostic Tests for Level A are designed to measure students' level of achievement in each of the important comprehension and study skills that receive emphasis in *all* levels of *Be A Better Reader*. The tests may be used as pretests and/or posttests, depending on students' needs and your particular classroom management style. Combined with an overview of students performance on each lesson, the tests should enable you to refine your assessment of students' performance and determine students' readiness to advance to the next level.

The four tests in Level A can be administered separately or at one time, depending on time available. Because directions are provided for each test, students should be able to take the tests independently. However, enough time should be allowed for each student to complete the tests.

The skill for each test item is identified in the Answer Key below. Following the skill is the number of the lesson or the lessons in Level A where that skill is treated as a Skill Focus. To simplify the scoring process, you can use the Answer Key to make a scoring mask, which when placed over the answer sheet reveals only those items that are correct. The total score is equal to the number of correct items. Use the information on the Scoring Rubric located on page 11 to place students.

Answer Key and Skills Correlation

Level A

Test 1

1. a   Understanding character (43)
2. b   Understanding character (43)
3. c   Understanding character (43)
4. c   Understanding character (43)
5. d   Recognizing sequence of events (1)
6. c   Recognizing sequence of events (1)
7. a   Recognizing sequence of events (1)
8. b   Recognizing sequence of events (1)
9. b   Identifying setting (13)
10. a   Identifying setting (13)
11. c   Identifying setting (13)
12. b   Identifying setting (13)
13. c   Identifying conflict and resolution (24)
14. b   Identifying conflict and resolution (24)
15. d   Identifying conflict and resolution (24)
16. c   Identifying conflict and resolution (24)
17. a   Inferring theme (33)
18. b   Inferring theme (33)
19. a   Inferring theme (33)
20. d   Making inferences (49, 57)
21. b   Making inferences (49, 57)
22. a   Making inferences (49, 57)
23. b   Recognizing multiple meanings of words (59)
24. b   Making inferences (49, 57)
25. b   Making inferences (49, 57)

Test 2

26. c   Identifying cause and effect (2, 26)
27. a   Identifying cause and effect (2, 26)
28. b   Identifying cause and effect (2, 26)
29. d   Identifying cause and effect (2, 26)
30. b   Comparing and contrasting (25)
31. d   Comparing and contrasting (25)
32. c   Comparing and contrasting (25)
33. b   Distinguishing fact from opinion (39)
34. c   Distinguishing fact from opinion (39)
35. a   Distinguishing fact from opinion (39)
36. b   Distinguishing fact from opinion (39)
37. b   Making inferences (49, 57)
38. b   Making inferences (49, 57)
39. d   Making inferences (49, 57)
40. c   Identifying the main idea (6, 17, 18)
41. b   Identifying the main idea (6, 17, 18)
42. a   Identifying the main idea (6, 17, 18)
43. a   Identifying the main idea and supporting details (40, 45)
44. d   Identifying the main idea and supporting details (40, 45)
45. a   Using detail context clues (33, 44, 45)
46. c   Using detail context clues (33, 44, 45)
47. a   Using detail context clues (33, 44, 45)
48. b   Using a map (56)
49. b   Using a map (56)
50. b   Using a map (56)

Test 3

51. a   Identifying cause and effect (2, 26)
52. b   Identifying cause and effect (2, 26)
53. d   Identifying cause and effect (2, 26)
54. c   Classifying (3)
55. d   Classifying (3)
56. c   Classifying (3)
57. a   Using appositive context clues (15, 56)
58. a   Reading text with diagrams (15, 35)
59. c   Reading text with diagrams (15, 35)
60. c   Reading text with diagrams (15, 35)
61. d   Reading text with diagrams (15, 35)
62. a   Identifying the main idea (6, 17, 18)
63. d   Identifying the main idea (6, 17, 18)
64. a   Identifying the main idea (6, 17, 18)
65. b   Identifying the main idea and supporting details (40, 45)
66. b   Identifying the main idea and supporting details (40, 45)
67. b   Recognizing multiple meanings of words (59)
68. b   Recognizing multiple meanings of words (59)
69. a   Recognizing base words (29)
70. b   Using detail context clues (33, 44, 45)
71. c   Solving word problems (4)
72. d   Solving word problems (4)
73. c   Solving word problems (4)
74. c   Solving word problems (4)
75. b   Solving word problems (4)

Test 4

76. c   Using a dictionary entry (52)
77. d   Using a dictionary entry (52)
78. b   Using a dictionary entry (52)
79. a   Using a dictionary entry (52)
80. d   Using a dictionary entry (52)
81. a   Using an encyclopedia (62)
82. c   Using an encyclopedia (62)
83. d   Using an encyclopedia (62)
84. b   Using an encyclopedia (62)
85. a   Using an encyclopedia (62)
86. c   Recognizing base words (29)
87. a   Recognizing base words (29)
88. d   Recognizing base words (29)
89. b   Recognizing base words (29)
90. c   Adding suffixes to words (29, 61)
91. a   Adding suffixes to words (29, 61)
92. a   Adding suffixes to words (29, 61)
93. b   Adding prefixes to words (29, 60)
94. b   Adding prefixes to words (29, 60)
95. d   Adding prefixes to words (29, 60)
96. b   Adding prefixes to words (29, 60)
97. b   Adding prefixes to words (29, 60)
98. a   Dividing words into syllables (30, 31, 38, 47, 48)
99. d   Dividing words into syllables (30, 31, 38, 47, 48)
100. c   Dividing words into syllables (30, 31, 38, 47, 48)

Administering Level B Diagnostic Tests

The Diagnostic Tests for Level B are designed to measure students' level of achievement in each of the important comprehension and study skills that receive emphasis in *all* levels of *Be A Better Reader*. The tests may be used as pretests and/or posttests, depending on students' needs and your particular classroom management style. Combined with an overview of students performance on each lesson, the tests should enable you to refine your assessment of students' performance and determine students' readiness to advance to the next level.

The four tests in Level B can be administered separately or at one time, depending on time available. Because directions are provided for each test, students should be able to take the tests independently. However, enough time should be allowed for each student to complete the tests.

The skill for each test item is identified in the Answer Key below. Following the skill is the number of the lesson or the lessons in Level B where that skill is treated as a Skill Focus. To simplify the scoring process, you can use the Answer Key to make a scoring mask, which when placed over the answer sheet reveals only those items that are correct. The total score is equal to the number of correct items. Use the information on the Scoring Rubric located on page 11 to place students.

Answer Key and Skills Correlation

Level B

Test 1

1. a   Understanding character (20)
2. b   Understanding character (20)
3. a   Understanding character (20)
4. b   Understanding character (20)
5. a   Identifying conflict and resolution (11)
6. d   Identifying conflict and resolution (11)
7. c   Identifying conflict and resolution (11)
8. a   Identifying conflict and resolution (11)
9. c   Identifying plot (50)
10. b   Identifying plot (50)
11. b   Identifying plot (50)
12. a   Identifying setting (1)
13. a   Identifying setting (1)
14. d   Identifying setting (1)
15. b   Identifying setting (1)
16. b   Inferring theme (41)
17. c   Inferring theme (41)
18. d   Inferring theme (41)
19. c   Inferring theme (41)
20. c   Identifying point of view (30)
21. b   Identifying point of view (30)
22. a   Identifying point of view (30)
23. b   Using detail context clues (21, 30, 32, 41, 52)
24. b   Using synonym context clues (43)
25. b   Recognizing multiple meanings of words (59)

Test 2

26. d   Identifying the main idea (6)
27. b   Identifying the main idea (6)
28. a   Identifying the main idea (6)
29. a   Inferring the unstated main idea (18, 55)
30. b   Inferring the unstated main idea (18, 55)
31. d   Identifying the main idea and supporting details (45)
32. b   Identifying cause and effect (12, 22)
33. a   Identifying cause and effect (12, 22)
34. b   Identifying cause and effect (12, 22)
35. a   Identifying cause and effect (12, 22)
36. c   Comparing and contrasting (51)
37. b   Comparing and contrasting (51)
38. c   Comparing and contrasting (51)
39. d   Using appositive context clues (1, 13, 20, 22, 42)
40. d   Using synonym context clues (43)

41. c Distinguishing fact from opinion (17, 21, 35)
42. b Distinguishing fact from opinion (17, 21, 35)
43. a Distinguishing fact from opinion (17, 21, 35)
44. b Distinguishing fact from opinion (17, 21, 35)
45. c Making inferences (56)
46. b Using a map (42)
47. a Using a map (42)
48. b Using a map (42)
49. d Using a map (42)
50. b Using a map (42)

Test 3

51. b Identifying cause and effect (12, 22)
52. c Identifying cause and effect (12, 22)
53. b Identifying cause and effect (12, 22)
54. b Classifying (3, 32)
55. c Classifying (3, 32)
56. b Comparing and contrasting (51)
57. a Comparing and contrasting (51)
58. a Comparing and contrasting (51)
59. d Identifying the main idea (6)
60. a Identifying the main idea (6)
61. a Identifying the main idea and supporting details (45)
62. b Recognizing multiple meanings of words (59)
63. c Using appositive context clues (1, 13, 20, 22, 42)
64. a Reading text with diagrams (43)
65. b Reading text with diagrams (43)
66. a Reading text with diagrams (43)
67. c Making inferences (56)
68. a Making inferences (56)
69. b Making inferences (56)
70. c Skimming for information (58)
71. c Skimming for information (58)
72. d Solving word problems (23, 33)
73. b Solving word problems (23, 33)
74. c Solving word problems (23, 33)
75. a Solving word problems (23, 33)

Test 4

76. d Using a dictionary entry (48)
77. b Using a dictionary entry (48)
78. b Using a dictionary entry (48)
79. d Using a dictionary entry (48)
80. b Using a dictionary entry (48)
81. b Adding prefixes to words (9, 15, 16)
82. b Adding prefixes to words (9, 15, 16)
83. a Adding prefixes to words (9, 15, 16)
84. c Adding prefixes to words (9, 15, 16)
85. d Adding suffixes to words (9, 15, 16)
86. a Adding suffixes to words (9, 15, 16)
87. a Adding suffixes to words (9, 15, 16)
88. c Dividing words into syllables (24, 25, 26, 27, 34)
89. a Dividing words into syllables (24, 25, 26, 27, 34)
90. b Dividing words into syllables (24, 25, 26, 27, 34)
91. b Dividing words into syllables (24, 25, 26, 27, 34)
92. a Recognizing base words (9, 15, 16, 25)
93. b Recognizing base words (9, 15, 16, 25)
94. a Recognizing base words (9, 15, 16, 25)
95. b Recognizing base words (9, 15, 16, 25)
96. c Recognizing base words (9, 15, 16, 25)
97. b Recognizing base words (9, 15, 16, 25)
98. c Recognizing base words (9, 15, 16, 25)
99. a Recognizing base words (9, 15, 16, 25)
100. d Recognizing base words (9, 15, 16, 25)

Administering Level C Diagnostic Tests

The Diagnostic Tests for Level C are designed to measure students' level of achievement in each of the important comprehension and study skills that receive emphasis in *all* levels of *Be A Better Reader*. The tests may be used as pretests and/or posttests, depending on students' needs and your particular classroom management style. Combined with an overview of students performance on each lesson, the tests should enable you to refine your assessment of students' performance and determine students' readiness to advance to the next level.

The four tests in Level C can be administered separately or at one time, depending on time available. Because directions are provided for each test, students should be able to take the tests independently. However, enough time should be allowed for each student to complete the tests.

The skill for each test item is identified in the Answer Key below. Following the skill is the number of the lesson or the lessons in Level C where that skill is treated as a Skill Focus. To simplify the scoring process, you can use the Answer Key to make a scoring mask, which when placed over the answer sheet reveals only those items that are correct. The total score is equal to the number of correct items. Use the information on the Scoring Rubric located on page 11 to place students.

Answer Key and Skills Correlation

Level C

Test 1

1. c   Identifying conflict and resolution (41)
2. c   Identifying conflict and resolution (41)
3. b   Identifying conflict and resolution (41)
4. b   Identifying conflict and resolution (41)
5. b   Identifying plot (1)
6. b   Identifying plot (1)
7. c   Identifying plot (1)
8. c   Identifying plot (1)
9. a   Identifying setting (33)
10. d   Identifying setting (33)
11. b   Identifying setting (33)
12. c   Identifying theme (11)
13. b   Identifying theme (11)
14. b   Identifying theme (11)
15. d   Identifying theme (11)
16. c   Identifying theme (11)
17. b   Inferring the unstated main idea (8, 18)
18. b   Inferring the unstated main idea (8, 18)
19. a   Inferring the unstated main idea (8, 18)
20. c   Identifying point of view (48)
21. d   Identifying point of view (48)
22. c   Identifying point of view (48)
23. c   Recognizing multiple meanings of words (45)
24. d   Using detail context clues (2, 12, 34)
25. a   Using detail context clues (2, 12, 34)

Test 2

26. a   Identifying the main idea (8, 18, 27)
27. d   Identifying the main idea (8, 18, 27)
28. a   Identifying the main idea (8, 18, 27)
29. c   Inferring the unstated main idea (8, 18, 28, 50)
30. b   Inferring the unstated main idea (8, 18, 28, 50)
31. c   Identifying the main idea and supporting details (27)
32. a   Identifying cause and effect (12, 22, 35)
33. a   Identifying cause and effect (12, 22, 35)
34. b   Identifying cause and effect (12, 22, 35)
35. c   Identifying cause and effect (12, 22, 35)
36. d   Comparing and contrasting (2)
37. b   Comparing and contrasting (2)
38. c   Comparing and contrasting (2)

39. b   Using detail context clues (2, 12, 34)
40. b   Making inferences (28, 50)
41. a   Making inferences (28, 50)
42. d   Making inferences (28, 50)
43. a   Making inferences (28, 50)
44. b   Recognizing multiple meanings of words (45)
45. a   Using detail context clues (2, 12, 34)
46. d   Using a map (34)
47. c   Using a map (34)
48. a   Using a map (34)
49. d   Using a map (34)
50. a   Using a map (34)

Test 3

51. b   Identifying the main idea (8, 18, 27)
52. d   Identifying the main idea (8, 18, 27)
53. b   Identifying the main idea and supporting details (27)
54. b   Identifying the main idea and supporting details (27)
55. c   Identifying cause and effect (12, 22, 35)
56. a   Identifying cause and effect (12, 22, 35)
57. d   Identifying cause and effect (12, 22, 35)
58. b   Comparing and contrasting (2)
59. a   Comparing and contrasting (2)
60. d   Classifying (3)
61. a   Classifying (3)
62. a   Classifying (3)
63. b   Making inferences (28, 50)
64. b   Making inferences (28, 50)
65. a   Making inferences (28, 50)
66. b   Recognizing multiple meanings of words (45)
67. b   Using synonym context clues (3, 22)
68. c   Reading text with diagrams (13)

69. c   Reading text with diagrams (13)
70. c   Reading text with diagrams (13)
71. d   Reading text with diagrams (13)
72. b   Solving word problems (23)
73. b   Solving word problems (23)
74. b   Solving word problems (23)
75. d   Solving word problems (23)

Test 4

76. c   Using a dictionary (9)
77. b   Using a dictionary (9)
78. b   Using a dictionary (9)
79. a   Using a dictionary (9)
80. a   Using a dictionary (9)
81. b   Using an index (46)
82. b   Using an index (46)
83. c   Using an index (46)
84. d   Using an index (46)
85. b   Using an index (46)
86. c   Adding prefixes to words (17)
87. d   Adding prefixes to words (17)
88. b   Adding prefixes to words (17)
89. d   Adding suffixes to words (29)
90. b   Adding suffixes to words (29)
91. b   Adding suffixes to words (29)
92. a   Dividing words into syllables (7, 16, 24)
93. b   Dividing words into syllables (7, 16, 24)
94. c   Dividing words into syllables (7, 16, 24)
95. a   Dividing words into syllables (7, 16, 24)
96. a   Locating the accented syllable (25)
97. b   Locating the accented syllable (25)
98. a   Locating the accented syllable (25)
99. c   Locating the schwa sound (26)
100. b Locating the schwa sound (26)

Administering Level D Diagnostic Tests

The Diagnostic Tests for Level D are designed to measure students' level of achievement in each of the important comprehension and study skills that receive emphasis in *all* levels of *Be A Better Reader*. The tests may be used as pretests and/or posttests, depending on students' needs and your particular classroom management style. Combined with an overview of students' performance on each lesson, the tests should enable you to refine your assessment of students' performance and determine students' readiness to advance to the next level.

The four tests in Level D can be administered separately or at one time, depending on time available. Because directions are provided for each test, students should be able to take the tests independently. However, enough time should be allowed for each student to complete the tests.

The skill for each test item is identified in the Answer Key below. Following the skill is the number of the lesson or the lessons in Level D where that skill is treated as a Skill Focus. To simplify the scoring process, you can use the Answer Key to make a scoring mask, which when placed over the answer sheet reveals only those items that are correct. The total score is equal to the number of correct items. Use the information on the Scoring Rubric located on page 11 to place students.

Answer Key and Skills Correlation

Level D

Test 1

1. b Identifying setting (35)
2. d Identifying setting (35)
3. b Identifying setting (35)
4. d Understanding character (16)
5. a Understanding character (16)
6. b Understanding character (16)
7. b Identifying conflict and resolution (43)
8. b Identifying conflict and resolution (43)
9. c Identifying conflict and resolution (43)
10. a Identifying plot (9)
11. c Identifying plot (9)
12. b Identifying plot (9)
13. b Identifying plot (9)
14. a Making inferences (3, 40)
15. d Making inferences (3, 40)
16. c Making inferences (3, 40)
17. d Inferring the unstated main idea (6)
18. b Inferring the unstated main idea (6)
19. b Inferring the unstated main idea (6)
20. a Identifying point of view (1)
21. d Identifying point of view (1)
22. a Identifying point of view (1)
23. b Using synonym context clues (1, 28, 43)
24. b Using detail context clues (16, 27, 35)
25. d Using detail context clues (16, 27, 35)

Test 2

26. c Identifying the main idea (6, 14, 23, 28)
27. a Identifying the main idea (6, 14, 23, 28)
28. d Identifying the main idea (6, 14, 23, 28)
29. a Inferring the unstated main idea (6)
30. b Inferring the unstated main idea (6)
31. c Identifying the main idea and supporting details (14, 23, 28)
32. d Identifying cause and effect (10, 18, 37)
33. b Identifying cause and effect (10, 18, 37)
34. b Identifying cause and effect (10, 18, 37)
35. a Comparing and contrasting (27)
36. d Comparing and contrasting (27)
37. a Comparing and contrasting (27)
38. c Distinguishing fact from opinion (2, 39)
39. a Distinguishing fact from opinion (2, 39)

40. b   Distinguishing fact from opinion (2, 39)
41. d   Making inferences (3, 40)
42. c   Making inferences (3, 40)
43. b   Making inferences (3, 40)
44. c   Making inferences (3, 40)
45. b   Using detail context clues (16, 27, 35)
46. d   Using detail context clues (16, 27, 35)
47. a   Reading a map (36)
48. c   Reading a map (36)
49. b   Reading a map (36)
50. d   Reading a map (36)

Test 3

51. a   Identifying the main idea (6, 14, 23, 28)
52. b   Inferring the unstated main idea (6)
53. a   Infering the unstated main idea (6)
54. d   Identifying cause and effect (10, 18, 37)
55. b   Identifying cause and effect (10, 18, 37)
56. a   Identifying cause and effect (10, 18, 37)
57. b   Identifying cause and effect (10, 18, 37)
58. c   Comparing and contrasting (27)
59. b   Comparing and contrasting (27)
60. a   Comparing and contrasting (27)
61. a   Classifying (11)
62. a   Classifying (11)
63. d   Making inferences (3, 40)
64. d   Making inferences (3, 40)
65. b   Making inferences (3, 40)
66. a   Using synonym context clues (1, 28, 43)
67. d   Using detail context clues (16, 27, 35)
68. b   Using detail context clues (16, 27, 35)
69. a   Reading text with diagrams (45)
70. a   Reading text with diagrams (45)

71. b   Reading text with diagrams (45)
72. a   Reading and solving word problems (12, 19)
73. b   Reading and solving word problems (12, 19)
74. c   Reading and solving word problems (12, 19)
75. a   Reading and solving word problems (12, 19)

Test 4

76. b   Using a dictionary (24)
77. d   Using a dictionary (24)
78. a   Using a dictionary (24)
79. c   Using a dictionary (24)
80. a   Using a dictionary (24)
81. c   Using an index (41)
82. a   Using an index (41)
83. c   Using an index (41)
84. d   Using an index (41)
85. b   Using an index (41)
86. b   Recognizing prefixes (21)
87. c   Recognizing prefixes (21)
88. b   Recognizing prefixes (21)
89. c   Recognizing suffixes (22)
90. a   Recognizing suffixes (22)
91. d   Recognizing suffixes (22)
92. b   Recognizing syllables (5, 13)
93. c   Recognizing syllables (5, 13)
94. c   Recognizing syllables (5, 13)
95. c   Recognizing syllables (5, 13)
96. a   Locating accented syllables (20)
97. b   Locating accented syllables (20)
98. b   Locating the schwa sound (20)
99. c   Recognizing antonyms (30)
100. d Recognizing synonyms (30)

Administering Level E Diagnostic Tests

The Diagnostic Tests for Level E are designed to measure students' level of achievement in each of the important comprehension and study skills that receive emphasis in *all* levels of *Be A Better Reader*. The tests may be used as pretests and/or posttests, depending on students' needs and your particular classroom management style. Combined with an overview of students' performance on each lesson, the tests should enable you to refine your assessment of students' performance and determine students' readiness to advance to the next level.

The four tests in Level E can be administered separately or at one time, depending on time available. Because directions are provided for each test, students should be able to take the tests independently. However, enough time should be allowed for each student to complete the tests.

The skill for each test item is identified in the Answer Key below. Following the skill is the number of the lesson or the lessons in Level E where that skill is treated as a Skill Focus. To simplify the scoring process, you can use the Answer Key to make a scoring mask, which when placed over the answer sheet reveals only those items that are correct. The total score is equal to the number of correct items. Use the information on the Scoring Rubric located on page 11 to place students.

Answer Key and Skills Correlation

Level E

Test 1

1. c Identifying setting (1)
2. b Identifying setting (1)
3. b Understanding character (18)
4. c Understanding character (18)
5. c Understanding character (18)
6. c Identifying conflict and resolution (43)
7. d Identifying conflict and resolution (43)
8. c Identifying conflict and resolution (43)
9. b Identifying plot (1)
10. b Identifying plot (1)
11. b Identifying plot (1)
12. d Identifying theme (9)
13. b Identifying theme (9)
14. d Identifying theme (9)
15. a Identifying the unstated main idea (7)
16. a Identifying the unstated main idea (7)
17. c Identifying the unstated main idea (7)
18. d Identifying tone (27)
19. b Identifying figures of speech (36)
20. a Identifying figures of speech (36)
21. d Using detail context clues (2, 18, 20)
22. b Using detail context clues (2, 18, 20)
23. d Using detail context clues (2, 18, 20)
24. b Recognizing multiple meanings of words (33)
25. b Recognizing multiple meanings of words (33)

Test 2

26. a Identifying the main idea (7, 16, 23, 38)
27. d Identifying the main idea (7, 16, 23, 38)
28. c Identifying the unstated main idea (7)
29. a Identifying the unstated main idea (7)
30. b Identifying the unstated main idea (7)
31. d Identifying the main idea and supporting details (16, 23, 38)
32. b Identifying the main idea and supporting details (16, 23, 38)
33. c Identifying cause and effect (11, 28, 45)
34. b Identifying cause and effect (11, 28, 45)
35. b Distinguishing fact from opinion (6)
36. c Distinguishing fact from opinion (6)
37. b Making inferences (3, 15)
38. d Making inferences (3, 15)
39. d Making inferences (3, 15)
40. a Making inferences (3, 15)

41. b Recognizing multiple meanings of words (33)
42. a Using synonym context clues (1, 9, 11, 37)
43. a Using detail context clues (2, 18, 20)
44. c Using a primary source (44)
45. c Using a primary source (44)
46. b Making generalizations (37)
47. d Making generalizations (37)
48. b Comparing and contrasting (10)
49. c Comparing and contrasting (10)
50. b Comparing and contrasting (10)

Test 3

51. c Identifying the unstated main idea (7)
52. c Identifying the main idea (16, 23, 38)
53. c Identifying the unstated main idea (7)
54. b Identifying the main idea and supporting details (16, 23, 38)
55. a Identifying cause and effect (11, 28, 45)
56. a Identifying cause and effect (11, 28, 45)
57. a Making inferences (3, 15)
58. a Making inferences (3, 15)
59. c Comparing and contrasting (10)
60. d Comparing and contrasting (10)
61. c Comparing and contrasting (10)
62. c Making inferences (3, 15)
63. d Comparing and contrasting (10)
64. a Making inferences (3, 15)
65. d Recognizing multiple meanings of words (33)
66. b Recognizing multiple meanings of words (33)
67. a Using detail context clues (2, 18, 20)
68. d Using synonym context clues (1, 9, 11, 37)

69. b Reading text with diagrams (20)
70. c Reading text with diagrams (20)
71. c Reading text with diagrams (20)
72. c Reading and solving word problems (4, 12)
73. c Reading and solving word problems (4, 12)
74. b Reading and solving word problems (4, 12)
75. c Reading and solving word problems (4, 12)

Test 4

76. a Using a dictionary (41)
77. c Using a dictionary (41)
78. c Using a dictionary (41)
79. b Using a dictionary (41)
80. d Using a dictionary (41)
81. a Recognizing prefixes (14, 24)
82. d Recognizing prefixes (14, 24)
83. b Recognizing prefixes (14, 24)
84. a Recognizing prefixes (14, 24)
85. a Recognizing suffixes (22, 24)
86. b Recognizing suffixes (22, 24)
87. d Recognizing suffixes (22, 24)
88. b Recognizing syllables (5, 13, 31)
89. a Recognizing syllables (5, 13, 31)
90. a Recognizing syllables (5, 13, 31)
91. c Recognizing syllables (5, 13, 31)
92. a Recognizing syllables (5, 13, 31)
93. c Recognizing roots (24)
94. d Recognizing roots (24)
95. c Recognizing accented syllables (32)
96. d Recognizing accented syllables (32)
97. c Recognizing accented syllables (32)
98. c Recognizing accented syllables (32)
99. b Recognizing schwa sounds (32)
100. b Recognizing schwa sounds (32)

Administering Level F Diagnostic Tests

The Diagnostic Tests for Level F are designed to measure students' level of achievement in each of the important comprehension and study skills that receive emphasis in *all* levels of *Be A Better Reader*. The tests may be used as pretests and/or posttests, depending on students' needs and your particular classroom management style. Combined with an overview of students' performance on each lesson, the tests should enable you to refine your assessment of students' performance and determine students' readiness to advance to the next level.

The four tests in Level F can be administered separately or at one time, depending on time available. Because directions are provided for each test, students should be able to take the tests independently. However, enough time should be allowed for each student to complete the tests.

The skill for each test item is identified in the Answer Key below. Following the skill is the number of the lesson or the lessons in Level F where that skill is treated as a Skill Focus. To simplify the scoring process, you can use the Answer Key to make a scoring mask, which when placed over the answer sheet reveals only those items that are correct. The total score is equal to the number of correct items. Use the information on the Scoring Rubric located on page 11 to place students.

Answer Key and Skills Correlation

Level F

Test 1

1. d   Understanding character (1)
2. a   Understanding character (1)
3. b   Understanding character (1)
4. c   Understanding character (1)
5. a   Identifying conflict and resolution (16)
6. b   Identifying conflict and resolution (16)
7. a   Identifying conflict and resolution (16)
8. b   Identifying plot (10)
9. b   Identifying plot (10)
10. d   Identifying plot (10)
11. b   Identifying plot (10)
12. b   Identifying theme (23)
13. d   Identifying theme (23)
14. c   Identifying theme (23)
15. b   Making inferences (43)
16. d   Making inferences (43)
17. a   Making inferences (43)
18. c   Identifying the unstated main idea (8)
19. b   Identifying the unstated main idea (8)
20. b   Identifying omniscient point of view (31)
21. c   Identifying omniscient point of view (31)
22. c   Recognizing multiple meanings of words (20)
23. c   Recognizing multiple meanings of words (20)
24. a   Using detail context clues (2, 40)
25. d   Using synonym context clues (17, 41)

Test 2

26. b   Identifying the unstated main idea (8)
27. a   Identifying the main idea (7, 8, 18, 21)
28. c   Identifying the unstated main idea (8)
29. a   Identifying the main idea and supporting details (18, 21)
30. b   Identifying the main idea and supporting details (18, 21)
31. d   Identifying cause and effect (3, 11, 44)
32. c   Identifying cause and effect (3, 11, 44)
33. a   Identifying cause and effect (3, 11, 44)
34. d   Comparing and contrasting (24)
35. b   Comparing and contrasting (24)
36. b   Comparing and contrasting (24)
37. d   Making inferences (43)

38.	a	Making inferences (43)
39.	c	Making inferences (43)
40.	a	Distinguishing fact from opinion (36)
41.	b	Distinguishing fact from opinion (36)
42.	b	Using a primary source (2)
43.	a	Using a primary source (2)
44.	a	Using a primary source (2)
45.	d	Making generalizations (40)
46.	d	Making generalizations (40)
47.	c	Using detail context clues (2, 40)
48.	b	Reading a map (17)
49.	c	Reading a map (17)
50.	c	Reading a map (17)

Test 3

51.	c	Identifying the main idea (7, 8, 18, 21)
52.	d	Identifying the unstated main idea (8)
53.	a	Identifying the unstated main idea (8)
54.	a	Identifying the main idea and supporting details (18, 21)
55.	b	Identifying cause and effect (3, 11, 44)
56.	a	Identifying cause and effect (3, 11, 44)
57.	d	Comparing and contrasting (24)
58.	b	Comparing and contrasting (24)
59.	a	Making inferences (43)
60.	a	Making inferences (43)
61.	b	Making inferences (43)
62.	d	Classifying (25)
63.	c	Classifying (25)
64.	b	Classifying (25)
65.	a	Using synonym context clues (17, 41)
66.	c	Using detail context clues (2, 40)
67.	b	Recognizing multiple meanings of words (20)
68.	d	Recognizing multiple meanings of words (20)

69.	c	Reading text with diagrams (12)
70.	b	Reading text with diagrams (12)
71.	c	Reading text with diagrams (12)
72.	a	Reading and solving word problems (4, 13)
73.	d	Reading and solving word problems (4, 13)
74.	c	Reading and solving word problems (4, 13)
75.	d	Reading and solving word problems (4, 13)

Test 4

76.	b	Using a dictionary (37)
77.	a	Using a dictionary (37)
78.	b	Using a dictionary (37)
79.	a	Using a dictionary (37)
80.	b	Using a dictionary (37)
81.	b	Using an index (48)
82.	d	Using an index (48)
83.	d	Using an index (48)
84.	a	Using an index (48)
85.	b	Using an index (48)
86.	d	Recognizing prefixes (6)
87.	d	Recognizing prefixes (6)
88.	a	Recognizing prefixes (6)
89.	d	Recognizing suffixes (14)
90.	c	Recognizing suffixes (14)
91.	c	Recognizing suffixes (14)
92.	d	Recognizing roots (27)
93.	b	Recognizing roots (27)
94.	c	Recognizing syllables (5, 28)
95.	c	Recognizing syllables (5, 28)
96.	d	Recognizing accented syllables (35)
97.	a	Recognizing accented syllables (35)
98.	b	Recognizing schwa sounds (35)
99.	a	Recognizing antonyms (45)
100.	c	Recognizing synonyms (45)

Administering Level G Diagnostic Tests

The Diagnostic Tests for Level G are designed to measure students' level of achievement in each of the important comprehension and study skills that receive emphasis in *all* levels of *Be A Better Reader*. The tests may be used as pretests and/or posttests, depending on students' needs and your particular classroom management style. Combined with an overview of students' performance on each lesson, the tests should enable you to refine your assessment of students' performance and determine students' readiness to advance to the next level.

The four tests in Level G can be administered separately or at one time, depending on time available. Because directions are provided for each test, students should be able to take the tests independently. However, enough time should be allowed for each student to complete the tests.

The skill for each test item is identified in the Answer Key below. Following the skill is the number of the lesson or the lessons in Level G where that skill is treated as a Skill Focus. To simplify the scoring process, you can use the Answer Key to make a scoring mask, which when placed over the answer sheet reveals only those items that are correct. The total score is equal to the number of correct items. Use the information on the Scoring Rubric located on page 11 to place students.

Answer Key and Skills Correlation

Level G

Test 1

1. d Understanding character (1)
2. c Understanding character (1)
3. a Understanding character (1)
4. c Identifying plot (10)
5. d Identifying plot (10)
6. c Identifying plot (10)
7. a Identifying plot (10)
8. c Identifying plot (10)
9. b Identifying plot (10)
10. a Identifying setting (19)
11. b Identifying setting (19)
12. a Identifying theme (27)
13. d Identifying theme (27)
14. a Identifying theme (27)
15. d Making inferences (43)
16. b Making inferences (43)
17. b Identifying tone (42)
18. a Identifying mood (42)
19. d Identifying the unstated main idea (6, 21)
20. b Identifying the unstated main idea (6, 21)
21. b Identifying figurative language (35)
22. a Identifying figurative language (35)
23. c Using detail context clues (27, 42)
24. a Using detail context clues (27, 42)
25. d Recognizing multiple meanings of words (23)

Test 2

26. a Identifying the main idea (6, 21)
27. b Identifying the unstated main idea (6, 21)
28. c Identifying the unstated main idea (6, 21)
29. d Identifying the main idea and supporting details (6, 21)
30. c Identifying the main idea and supporting details (6, 21)
31. d Identifying cause and effect (36)
32. a Identifying cause and effect (36)
33. b Identifying cause and effect (36)
34. a Comparing and contrasting (46)
35. a Comparing and contrasting (46)
36. b Comparing and contrasting (46)
37. d Making inferences (43)
38. d Making inferences (43)
39. c Making inferences (43)
40. a Distinguishing fact from opinion (33)
41. c Distinguishing fact from opinion (33)
42. b Using a primary source (28)
43. c Using a primary source (28)
44. b Using a primary source (28)
45. b Using detail context clues (27, 42)
46. b Using detail context clues (27, 42)
47. c Recognizing multiple meanings of words (23)
48. a Reading a map (11)

49. d Reading a map (11)
50. a Reading a map (11)

Test 3

51. c Identifying the main idea (6, 21)
52. b Identifying the main idea (6, 21)
53. b Identifying the main idea (6, 21)
54. b Identifying the main idea and supporting details (6, 21)
55. a Identifying cause and effect (36)
56. b Identifying cause and effect (36)
57. b Identifying cause and effect (36)
58. c Comparing and contrasting (46)
59. d Making inferences (43)
60. d Making inferences (43)
61. b Making inferences (43)
62. c Classifying (44)
63. a Classifying (44)
64. c Classifying (44)
65. b Using antonym context clues (10)
66. d Using detail context clues (27, 42)
67. a Using detail context clues (27, 42)
68. c Using detail context clues (27, 42)
69. a Reading text with diagrams (29)
70. c Reading text with diagrams (29)
71. c Reading text with diagrams (29)
72. a Reading and solving word problems (30)
73. c Reading and solving word problems (30)
74. d Reading and solving word problems (30)
75. c Reading and solving word problems (30)

Test 4

76. b Etymologies (48)
77. a Etymologies (48)
78. b Etymologies (48)
79. d Etymologies (48)
80. c Etymologies (48)
81. d Recognizing prefixes (16)
82. d Recognizing prefixes (16)
83. b Recognizing prefixes (16)
84. c Recognizing suffixes (15)
85. d Recognizing suffixes (15)
86. b Recognizing suffixes (15)
87. c Recognizing word roots (17)
88. d Recognizing word roots (17)
89. a Recognizing word roots (17)
90. b Recognizing word roots (17)
91. a Completing analogies (8)
92. c Completing analogies (8)
93. c Completing analogies (8)
94. d Completing analogies (8)
95. b Completing analogies (8)
96. c Completing analogies (8)
97. b Recognizing multiple meanings of words (23)
98. a Recognizing multiple meanings of words (23)
99. c Recognizing multiple meanings of words (23)
100. d Recognizing multiple meanings of words (23)

Harbor City High School
East-#413G
2801 St. Lo Drive, Bldg D
Baltimore, MD 21213